To the Farmers

and their Families;

and to the Winemakers,

people crazy enough to mortgage

their future pursuing the

new version of Texas liquid gold.

Texas Wineries and Vineyards

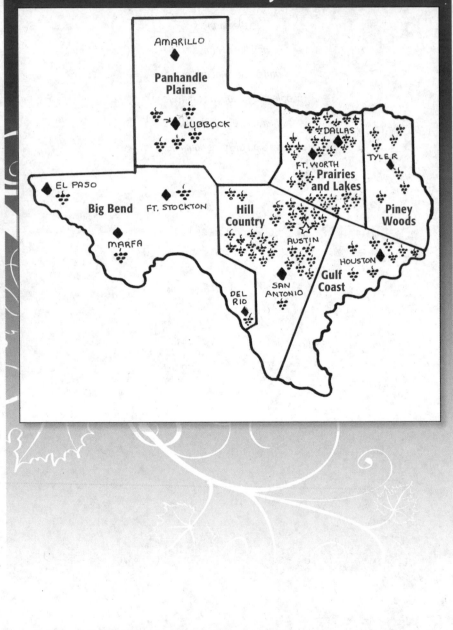

The Wine Roads of Texas

An Essential Guide to Texas Wines and Wineries

Wes Marshall

MAVERICK PUBLISHING COMPANY

About the Author

During the dot-com boom, Wes Marshall's hometown of Austin developed a thirst for fine wine. He wangled a job with a newspaper covering wine, and one day was asked to cover Texas wine. Under duress, he visited a few wineries and was shocked to discover good wines. In due course came the first edition of *The Wine Roads of Texas*, which won an award from the Texas Wine and Grape Growers Association and inspired Austin PBS affiliate KLRU-TV to create a three-part documentary with the same name. Wes was an executive producer for the series, distributed nationally by PBS. In addition to his column in the *Austin Chronicle*, he is a special contributor to the *Dallas Morning News* and writes regularly for the *San Francisco Chronicle*, *Wine Country International*, *Imbibe*, *Wines and Vines* and *Salud!*. He also writes about classic films, home theater equipment and opera for *Soundstage!*.

Maverick Publishing Company
P. O. Box 6355, San Antonio, Texas 78209

Library of Congress Cataloging-in-Publication Data

Marshall, Wes, 1953–
   The wine roads of Texas : an essential guide to Texas wines and wineries / Wes Marshall. – 2nd ed.
      p. cm.
   Includes index.
   ISBN 978-1-893271-43-2 (alk. paper)
   1. Wine and wine making–Texas–Guidebooks. 2. Wineries–Texas–Guidebooks.
   3. Texas–Guidebooks. I. Title.
   TP557.M34 2007
   641.2'209764–dc22

      2007013546

10 9 8 7 6 5 4 3 2 1

Cover, book design and electronic publishing — Nio Graphics, Inc. and Kell Designs.
Cover photo — Los Pinos Winery, Pittsburgh, TX by Jeff Snead; other photos by Wes Marshall.
Maps by Emily Marshall.

❧ Contents

🍁 Foreword to the Second Edition

BY FESS PARKER

Like many Texans, at a certain point in my life all I knew about wine was that it came in two colors, red and white. I never even contemplated the pink stuff.

My horizons were broadened when I moved to California in the 1950s to begin a career in the motion picture business. The people I worked and socialized with occasionally drank wine, and I did as well, although somewhat reluctantly. Nothing much appealed to me until my wife, Marcella, brought home a fortuitous purchase of several cases of 1961 Chateau Margaux and Chateau Lafite.

I had no way of knowing at the time that those particular wines would come to be regarded as some of the finest in the world. All I knew was that once I got over the whopping $6 per bottle price tag, I was enjoying wine for the first time. I kept drinking those wines even when their value worth increased to $1,500 per bottle. I was intrigued, to say the least.

When my son and I started our winery, we really were long on optimism and short on information. But why worry? My Texas roots include farmers and ranchers, so it came naturally that my family and I would begin a wine venture/adventure in Santa Barbara County in 1989. Along the way we had the good fortune of meeting and gaining insight from some of the industry giants like Robert Mondavi, the late Len Evans of the Hunter Valley in Australia, renowned winemaker Jed Steele and a grower by the name of Dale Hampton.

These gentlemen and others in the industry were supportive of our initial efforts and correctly advised us to plant the varietals that grew well in our soils and climates and to never scrimp when it came to quality. And I'm proud to say that after almost nineteen years, our family's pursuit of quality resulted in our son, Eli, being named the Andre Tchelistcheff Winemaker of the Year for 2006 at the San Francisco International Wine Competition.

I know that the character of my fellow Texans, the intensity of their persistence and vision for quality have already prevailed over those who said that it couldn't be done—that you can't make world-class wines from grapes grown in the soils of the Lone Star State. I have had the privilege of tasting several recent vintages of well-made Texas wines at the Buffalo Gap Food and Wine Summit. The wines were from a number of different producers whose vineyards are located throughout Texas. I applaud the results.

One last thing. Never underestimate a Texan .... in anything!

Enjoy!

Actor Fess Parker, a native Texan known to generations for his portrayal of frontiersmen Davy Crockett and Daniel Boone, remains active in the Fess Parker Winery & Vineyards in California's Santa Ynez Valley.

🍁 Foreword to the First Edition

BY ROBERT MONDAVI

I first saw the Texas wine scene in the 1950s, when I was traveling this country selling Charles Krug bulk and bottled wines. Not a vineyard was visible, and no one mentioned Texas wine.

A decade later, when we began the Robert Mondavi Winery and Tony La Barba represented us, Texas was one of the first states to recognize that we could make wines in the Napa Valley that ranked with the best wines in the world. And I met Bobby Smith, who said it could also be done in Texas.

I see distinct parallels between the Napa Valley in the middle of the last century and Texas as this century begins. First, both needed to pay attention to the grape varieties and the viticulture. Second was the need to adjust to the climate, then the need for committed pioneers and financial support to make growth happen. We realized all that then, and Texas is realizing it now.

From the beginning, we hoped that people would come to the winery. My wife, Margrit, started our summer concert series and we had a number of cultural activities to attract attention. Visitors would go away with some wine education and a sense of what we were accomplishing, and many of them became supporters.

This also applies to Texas. This book encourages you to visit Texas wineries and taste their wines. There really isn't a better wine education than going to the winery, learning firsthand how the wine is created and talking with the winemakers. Educational and, even better, enjoyable!

The informed consumer also helps the winemakers and the local wine industry. You can help shape the business by understanding wine quality and talking to the Texas vintners about what you want. I knew in the beginning that there were enough people who wanted quality wines so that we could build the business in Napa Valley. The same can be true in Texas.

Although I'm considered a pioneer in the fine wine industry, there were people who preceded me and made my path easier—Jacob Schram, Andre Tchelistcheff, and the professors at the University of California. This book mentions pioneers and mavericks; I assure you that the U.S. wine business wouldn't be where it is right now without their vision and persistence. I believe that some day, as the Texas wine industry grows and the wines get better and better, several of the young winemakers you meet will be respected names in the evolving Texas wine industry.

I would like to leave you with a couple of thoughts. First, I made a commitment to excel in my winemaking, and many winemakers make a similar commitment. Find them and support them.

Second, wine makes a great contribution to the quality of life. Medical researchers tell us that it can also make a contribution to your health, in most cases; but talk to your doctor about that.

Third, wine education is a continuing interest. Every new year brings new challenges and new solutions. Fortunately there are a number of writers and editors who follow the vintages. Wes Marshall's wine column in the Austin Chronicle is one of the best in the country and is a marvelous guide both to the Texas wine industry and to the available wines from all over the world.

So for immediate pleasure and long-lasting good memories, visit your area winemaker— and also come visit us in Napa Valley!

Robert Mondavi in 1966 founded the Robert Mondavi Winery, the first major winery built in California's Napa Valley since Prohibition. It became the foundation of California's modern-day wine industry.

❧ The New World of Texas Wines

Texas wine gets a lot of space in my column for the *Austin Chronicle* and articles in the *Dallas Morning News*. But despite my experience with wines, doing the research for this book surprised me again and again—especially in meeting the winemakers, a fascinating parade of pioneers, iconoclasts and mavericks. Talking with them and getting a chance to hear their true-life stories made me love Texas wine even more. It will for you, too. But to meet them, you have to go to the wineries.

While visiting with winemakers and grape growers, I found that the people sitting across from me had gripping stories to tell, full of comedy and tragedy and heroism. I'll never forget hearing Bobby Cox tell how he built his winery and the painful story of how he lost it to poor financial judgment. Or watching Richard Becker look at the fifty people in his tasting room with an expression of victorious delight. Or listening to Tommy Qualia tell of signing up for the Peace Corps and shipping off to Bolivia. Or seeing Ed Manigold, ankle-deep in mud, cleaning out after a flood. Or seeing Neal Newsom's resigned look after he lost eighty percent of his year's crop within two days. These weren't just winemakers, and their creations weren't just businesses.

I was surprised so often by the stories I heard that eventually I expected to be surprised. That's when I really started learning.

Texas is a big place. Driving from Brownsville to Dalhart takes longer than driving from Dallas to Chicago. When the first edition of this book appeared, Texas had 44 wineries. Gathering information for that book took sixteen months. I put 5,500 miles on my car, traveling from the Davis Mountains to the bayous of deep East Texas, from Dallas to Del Rio, from Galveston to Lubbock. I saw incredible sights, ate wonderful food and tasted more than four hundred wines. Collecting facts and doing interviews for this second edition took two years. I put 7,500 more miles on my car and this time tasted more than one thousand wines (tough work, but. . . .). When the first edition of this book appeared, Texas had 44 wineries. Now at least 130 licenses have been issued. Some authorities predict that there could be as many as 400 wineries in Texas in ten years.

Two things have driven the change. First, the laws changed. Ten years ago, a winery in a dry county couldn't sell wine from its own premises. Today, anyone can open a winery anywhere in Texas, despite the insane patchwork of wet and dry counties left over from Prohibition. Entrepreneurs and amateur winemakers alike have seized the opportunity to open wineries, tasting rooms and wine shops in once-dry communities like Tyler and Lubbock. It's also at last possible to ship Texas wine from the winery to your home, though if you want to ship wine out of the state or out of the country be sure to check first with appropriate authorities.

You are the second-biggest factor driving change in Texas wine. You, by virtue of holding this book in your hand, and many others like you like the idea of taking a day, a week or even a month to visit wineries. Agri-tourism is the technical term, but winery touring has become such a big business in Texas that staid communities otherwise priding themselves as the buckle in the Bible Belt are offering tax abatements for folks willing to open a winery. As competition for tourist dollars increases, winemakers will strive to make better wines so they can keep your business.

A side effect of changes in state laws has been a proliferation of wineries that mainly function as a wine bar and/or brew shop selling five-gallon car boys and grape must to aspiring winemakers. These are not covered in this book, but if you live in a town of over 50,000 people you can probably find one in the Yellow Pages. I did visit several such places, sometimes introducing myself and sometimes browsing anonymously. I can't speak about all of them, but I can tell you that the ones I visited all sell more wine by the glass and bottle than they do in winemaker kits. Now, I have nothing against learning how to make wine from a hobby shop. You can pick up a few valuable lessons about fermentation and balancing alcohol, sugar and acid, you have the opportunity to tell your friends you are a winemaker junior grade—and you might come out with something drinkable.

With the salutary changes in state laws and the proliferating numbers of Texas wines and wineries, I am more convinced than ever that Texas is on the road to becoming one of the top wine-growing areas of the United States. Yet there is some lag in this perception.

We were tasting Zinfandels at the monthly meeting of the Original Zinners when I mentioned that Bénédicte Rhyne had left Ravenswood Vineyards in California and moved to Texas. Someone asked, "Why would a California winemaker want to move to Texas?"

The question wasn't rhetorical, it was mocking, like Texas wine was a lost cause. I remained silent to hear the rest of the group's reaction. Most agreed. Only two argued, and that was half-heartedly. I felt disappointed and a little irritated. Here was a group of savvy wine drinkers, Texas people who knew every minuscule detail about California wines. Yet they didn't know about the great wines of Texas.

I came back with a laundry list of my favorites, sounding like Perry Mason: "Have you tried X? Have you tried Y? Have you tried Z?" A few admitted that X or Y or Z were okay, but they were still skeptical. I ended up feeling more like Hamilton Burger than Perry Mason.

But the conversation intrigued me. Why did those people think that Texas was an uninspiring place to make wine? Sure, there are some poor Texas wines, but there are dozens of wonderful Texas wines. The Italians, French, Germans, Spanish, Australians, Californians all make their fair share of poor wines, but no one says they can't make decent wine. Was this an example of wine not having honor in its own land? Didn't I once feel the same way?

After writing this book, my opinion had changed. I knew why a California winemaker would want to move to Texas.

One more thing. I have a limited number of pages for wine reviews and more than 1,000 wines to choose from. Almost every winery makes a wine that is either average or that I wouldn't recommend to my friends. Listing them would take up far too much space, so I have chosen to focus on the best wines each winery produces. But don't assume that you will consider the best wine from one winery to be competitive with the best wine from another; we each have our unique preferences. My goal is to guide you to what I believe to be the best wines at each winery so that you can have a starting point when you walk through the doors.

Drink Texas Wine—Save a Family Farm

When preparing the first edition of this book, I spent most of my time with winery owners and not so much with farmers, and thus missed the chance to learn about the grand traditions of the Texas farm. On this go-round, I had Bobby Cox take me to meet as many farmers as we could squeeze in. I respected the men and fell in love with their wives. I loved their laconically droll sense of humor and their honorable demeanor. One thing they kept asking me was what they could do to get the people of Texas to support their work. Bobby only took me to see good farmers, so the folks I met were growing exceptional fruit, and exceptional fruit leads to good wine. So why, they wondered, were so many fellow Texans buying so much foreign?

Most wineries in Texas purchase grapes, and as long as market forces aren't driving the price of Texas grapes too high, most wineries will choose to buy Texas grapes. Who's growing Texas grapes? Farmers still plowing even after suffering years of lousy cotton and sorghum and peanut prices. I had the opportunity to spend some time in the vineyards with West Texas farmers suddenly able to live a decent life because in most years they can sell grapes for up to $4,000 an acre. A twenty-acre vineyard can mean the difference between life as a farmer and having to get a job in town.

For Texas family farmers still daring to compete with giant agribusinesses and with foreign farmers growing subsidized crops, there are two lights at the end of the tunnel: small-crop organic produce and wine grapes. I want to see my fellow Texans have a go at it. If Texans convert 10 percent of their consumption of out-of-state wine to Texas wine, a whole lot of family farms will be able to stay out from under the auctioneer's gavel. Please think about it.

A Short History of Texas Wines

Grapes have grown wild in Texas for thousands of years. In fact, of the thirty-six species of genus Vitis, fifteen are native to Texas, a larger number than anywhere else in the world. Texas is the site of the first vineyard in North America, established in the seventeenth century by Spanish missionaries. When European settlers moved here in the nineteenth century, many brought grapevine cuttings and planted them.

During the 1840s, European winemakers were facing a devastating fungus called oidium, also known as powdery mildew. France alone lost 80 percent of its vines. In a rush to save their vineyards, the French brought in labrusca rootstock from the new world. For several years, the Europeans replanted and felt they had defeated the oidium. Unfortunately, they didn't realize the new rootstock carried an even worse parasite in the form of tiny aphid called phylloxera.

In the early 1860s, European vineyards, still recovering from powdery mildew, began to die again. It wasn't until 1868 that French winemakers identified phylloxera in their vineyards. They were too late. Europe lost almost all of its vineyards.

In April 1876, Thomas Volney Munson (1843–1913) moved to Denison, Texas. A nurseryman by trade, his hobby and obsession was grapes. It didn't take him long to discover the diversity of native Texas grapes. Like any curious plant lover, he started grafting experiments to see what he could create. Munson wrote several articles on his discoveries and became well known for his efforts, one of which was phylloxera-resistant rootstock. Eventually his work came to the attention of the French wine trade.

The French asked Munson for some of his hybrid rootstock and tested it by grafting on their grapes. It worked. European vineyard owners tore out all the remaining vines and replanted with Munson's hybrid. He had rescued the European wine industry from extinction, with the aid of fellow Texans Francois Guilbeau Jr. and Jules Poinsard, both horticulturists, and Matthew N. Knox, a nurseryman. In 1888, the French government sent a delegation to Denison to award Munson the French Legion of Honor Chevalier du Mérite Agricole. It's ironic that today Munson is better known in France than in Texas.

By 1900, Texas had more than twenty-five wineries. Though Texans saved the European wine industry from phylloxera, not a soul could save the Texas wine industry from a worse scourge—the federal government. The Eighteenth Amendment, implemented in 1919 by the Volstead Act, instituted Prohibition and effectively killed the Texas wine business. Of Texas wineries active when enforcement of Prohibition began, only Del Rio's Val Verde Winery survives.

The Texas wine business stayed dead until the 1970s, when Americans began to regain their taste for wine. Serious connoisseurs then knew that the best wines all came from France and Germany. But Robert Mondavi and a few cohorts boldly claimed that the United States could make great wine, too. Mondavi proved his point the hard way, making better and better wines and challenging other Californians to join him.

In the late 1970s, Dr. Bobby Smith in Springtown and a partnership called the Sandy Lake Growers Association in Lubbock started the first of a new group of Texas vineyards. If critics downplayed California's chances at wine greatness, they were positively insulting about Texas's opportunities. The climate and location were wrong. There was this problem with distribution. And much of Texas was still "dry"—no alcohol allowed.

To this day, 20 percent of Texas counties are dry and another 30 percent have large pockets that are dry, and by law no wine can be sold within their boundaries. The 1977 Farm Winery Act, pushed through by Bobby Smith and some friends, finally allowed grape growers to make wine in a dry county as long as the distribution took place elsewhere. But small producers make the majority of their money from folks who buy directly from the winery, and Texas wineries in dry counties still could not sell wines from their tasting rooms. To make matters worse, many of the state's best wine-grape growing areas were in dry areas and could sell only through distributors.

That changed when Susan Combs, then commissioner of the Texas Department of Agriculture, pushed her substantial political clout into an arena dominated by liquor distributors, who enjoyed a profitable three-tier system of distribution: most alcoholic beverages were sold from the manufacturer to a distributor, then to a retailer or restaurant, assuring that no winery, for example, could sell directly to consumers. Distributors thus got a percentage of all the business.

Combs proved better at political wrangling than many expected. On September 1, 2001, the law changed, allowing wineries in dry areas to sell wine at their wineries and to ship purchases made the wineries to or from either wet or dry areas. Consumers were allowed to place orders with wineries and pick them up at approved package stores. Texas has become the fifth-largest wine-producing state, with more than 300 commercial vineyards and more than 120 wineries.

Grapes Grown in Texas

People fight over the funniest things. Take grapes.

"French grapes are the only ones worth growing. All the others are inferior. They are inferior in the country they're from and they are inferior in Texas."

"Anyone who grows French grapes is crazy. Texas is too hot. Just look at it. Where does it look like Bordeaux or Burgundy in Texas? It's too hot here. We have to grow hot weather grapes. Grapes from Italy and Spain."

"We have to find a way to make good wine from Lenoir, Blanc du Bois and Cynthiana, the only ones that won't get killed by Pierce's disease. Anyone who plants anything else is just foolish."

These are all actual pronouncements. The names have been eliminated to protect the people. But the truth is, no one knows which grapes are going to work best at a certain site. Texans have tried hundreds of wine grape varieties in dozens of locations, searching for the Holy Grail of grapes.

The push for the last thirty years has been on the grapes that American wine drinkers know how to pronounce. Grapes like Chardonnay and Cabernet and Merlot. However, since the late 1990s, nearly every vineyard has started to grow Italian and Spanish grapes. Also, the grapes of Southern France, especially the Rhone varietals, have been widely planted.

This is a truncated list by necessity. Between the time this book goes to press and the moment you read it, someone will have planted new (to Texas) grapes. Nevertheless, the majority of Texas wines are made from the following grapes.

Cabernet Franc. With only a couple of exceptions, Texans use a Cab Franc grape for blending. Personally, I love it. The color is medium red, and it tastes like berries and vanilla. Try to get one of the wineries to let you taste a barrel sample.

Cabernet Sauvignon. A famous red grape usually referred to as Cab. In France it is the major ingredient in Bordeaux. Cab vines will readily adapt to most growing areas in Texas. Winemakers use it for everything from sweet red wines to rosés to French-style Clarets. Cabernet is capable of making some of the world's great wines. Unfortunately, with poor vineyard management it can end up tasting more like vegetables than fruit. Texas Cabs range from smooth and easygoing to lush and fruity. Good examples will remind you of black currants.

Chardonnay. Almost one-fourth of the wine made in the United States is Chard. The public loves it. Texas winery owners can be excused for wanting to get on the bus, but this is one of the toughest grapes to grow locally. The sharpshooters that carry Pierce's disease seem to love Chardonnay as much as the rest of us. Heat devastates it and a late spring freeze can kill it. Never mind. Several Texas wineries are making glorious Chards, but it requires a heroic effort. The grape is a chameleon; every winemaker's version is different from every other's. Taste around and see what appeals to you.

Chenin Blanc. This grape is a dilemma for wineries. On the one hand, it is robust and carefree and produces more tons per acre than any other good wine grape. The downside is the public seems to have zero interest in it. One winemaker told me he could leave an unprotected pallet of Chenin Blanc in front of a liquor store overnight and it would still be there the next morning. Most wineries use it anyway, sometimes as part of a blend, occasionally by its own name. Good examples can be anywhere from dry to sweet and usually remind you of pears and papayas. I think it deserves a lot more credit than it gets; those on the hunt for a bargain can hardly do better. I've seen major wineries sell their Chenin at $4.99 a bottle. Next time you want a Chard, try this instead.

Merlot. This is another grape, like the Cab, that demands a real artist to make it sing. A few bad versions taste like the leftover water from steaming asparagus and artichokes. But when a winery hits the mark, Texas Merlot can be world-class. The taste should be remind you of ripe plums and black cherries.

Muscat Canelli. Also sometimes called Muscat Blanc. Fruity, floral and very easy to drink. If someone traveling with you doesn't like wine, this is what to serve them. Texas versions vary from light and dry to golden and sweet.

Pinot Grigio. A white relative of the red Pinot Noir. This grape is just catching on in Texas, where it is usually made closer to an Italian style than an Alsatian style. In other words, it is generally tart and minerally instead of fruity and minerally. It's not easy to grow, so the winemaker has to be dedicated to its charms.

Pinot Noir. This is almost impossible to grow well in Texas. There are a few good versions, but in those cases I almost suspect alchemy. Pinot Noir has a red color that can resemble anything from light cherry to brick. Its smells can sometimes remind you of leather or soil. Despite those unattractive descriptions, you can fall in love with a good version. Just don't expect to find very many.

Riesling. This is another low-demand grape that does really well in Texas. Both German and French versions are well loved by chefs for their food-friendly demeanor. Texas versions usually have some sugar and go well with Asian foods. Good Texas Rieslings will be a little floral and "apple-y" with a light golden color.

Ruby Cabernet. This is a clone of Cabernet Sauvignon and Carignane. The winemakers' joke is that two beautiful parents had an ugly child. It's a cynical joke because, in the right hands, this grape can make wonderful wine. Texas winemakers use it for everything from syrupy sweet wines to bone-dry Bordeaux styles. Growers love it because it soaks up the sun like George Hamilton and puts out tons of fruit per acre.

Sangiovese. You know this grape if you've ever had Chianti. If the last Chianti you had came wrapped in straw, you are in for a big surprise. The best Texas versions, and that includes nearly all of them, carry tremendous cherry-like fruit with some complicated fragrances like leather and cedar. Colors vary from pink to garnet. For dry-wine lovers, this variety is always worth tasting. You should be seeing more and more of it, because Sangiovese loves Texas weather.

Sauvignon Blanc. If you like dry white wines but get tired of Chard, the Texas version of Sauvignon Blanc might offer you just what you want. Our version is quite different from the French (who call it Pouilly Fumé and Sancerre), Californian (where they usually oak it and call it Fumé Blanc) or the recently popular New Zealand style, which resembles grapefruit more than grape juice. In Texas the wine is light with a hint of citrus but also a little smell of herbs and olives. I love it. A few wineries are also trying a sweet version that is sometimes good. This is another wine that grows very well in Texas and has a terrific future.

Syrah. Also known as Shiraz. If I had to pick one grape to plant in Texas, it would be Syrah. Not because it's easy to deal with. It's not. But when the weather provides the least encouragement, it tastes like nothing else in the world. Good versions are so opulent that they'll stain your teeth red and leave your tongue feeling like it took a bath in Tellicherry peppers. Conventional wisdom is that Australia and the southern part of France grow the best Syrah. Someday Texas could be on that list.

Viognier. This grape is widely used in southern France. It makes marvelous wine, packed with apricot, apple and peach flavors. Viognier is a far more complex and interesting wine than Chardonnay. Every version I've tasted from Texas has been world-class. If the marketplace ever latches onto Viognier it could end up the centerpiece of Texas wine, much like Pinot Noir is for Oregon.

Zinfandel. Texas Zins come in dry red and sweet white. It's really hard to get the full-bodied red version in Texas. Usually they come out a bit light. Interesting, but not intense. There are a few outliers with a California-like richness. White Zins, made by taking the red Zin grape and taking the skin away from the juice, are dependent on the taste of the winemaker. They can be dessert-sweet with little Zin taste, or they can be fruity and refreshing.

The Texas Department of Agriculture has also recommended four grapes that are resistant to Pierce's disease: **Lenoir** (Black Spanish), **Herbemont, Blanc du Bois** and **Cynthiana** (Norton). I have had some stellar wines made from Lenoir and a few wonderful white wines from Blanc du Bois. Most winemakers choose to make these grapes into sweet wines, but not all. Even if you are a confirmed dry wine drinker, you might try these and see if you find something you like. For example, the Black Spanish makes a very good Port-style wine. In any case, you can be sure that these grapes will be getting more of an audience from vineyard owners who have had to face the heartbreak of losing their vines. Perhaps with experience, these grapes will make good wines.

And now, please excuse me while I get on the soapbox: We need the universities to quit the skirmishing and turf battles and get behind the industry. One of the reasons we haven't settled on the best grapes for local use is that none of our major universities have stepped up to the plate and taken a swing at the issues confronting grape growers in Texas: Pierce's disease, cotton root rot, geographical appropriateness for varietals, pruning and harvesting methods, trellising systems and the like. California's wine industry catapulted into fame with the help of the University of California at Davis. Among the University of Texas, Texas A&M and Texas Tech, the talent is available. We need the universities to quit the skirmishing and turf battles and to get behind the wine industry. As I said, people fight over the funniest things. I'll step down now.

🍁 Planning Your Trip

This book can provide valuable background if you want to visit just a single winery, but it is even more useful for planning a day or a weekend—or an entire vacation—visiting wineries. The seven geographic divisions are based on the Texas Department of Tourism's convenient "Unique States of Texas" (www.TravelTex.com).

To help you organize your trip, this book organizes wineries into regional groupings so you can visit up to four per day. Along with routing information you'll find recommendations for the best restaurants, hotels, B&Bs and attractions along the Wine Roads. A warning: the people who operate wineries, make your food in restaurants and create those nice B&Bs often live complicated and unpredictable lives. Save yourself aggravation. Call ahead.

After deciding which part of the state you want to travel in, the question is, how much time do you want to spend?

"I just want to go to one winery."

If you know which winery you want to visit, check the index and turn to the winery. If you know what area you want to travel to but don't have a clue which winery to read about, check the map at the beginning of the regional section you'd like to travel in to decide which one interests you most.

"I want to make a day of it."

Pick a place close to home and read the regional section. Two of the larger regions— the Hill Country, and Prairies and Lakes—are divided into one- and two-day trips. Check to make sure everything will be open and hit the road.

"We're going on vacation for several days and want to visit wineries."

Pick one chapter and do the whole thing. The Hill Country would take eight to ten days, Prairies and Lakes at least a week, Big Bend three days, Panhandle Plains three days, the Gulf Coast two or three days and the Piney Woods two days. Also, try combining parts. The Hill Country fits nicely with the southern part of Prairies and Lakes. The northern Prairies and Lakes fits well with the Piney Woods. For folks addicted to the wide open spaces, Big Bend and the High Plains would make a perfect week.

"We're here from France and we want to visit every winery in Texas."

Lucky you. With your average six-week summer vacation, you should be able to comfortably carry it off. Fly into Dallas, rent a car and take off. A votre santé.

A Texas Wine Calendar

Friends often e-mail Texas jokes to me, like, "It was so hot I saw a roadrunner trying to pull a worm out of the ground and he was using potholders."

Here's a calendar of "the six seasons" of Texas weather:

Spring, Feb. 16–Apr. 15
Summer, Apr. 16–Jul. 15 (90 to 98 degrees)
Super Summer, Jul. 6–Sep. 10 (100 to 115 degrees)
Other Summer, Sep. 11–Oct. 1 (90 to 98 degrees)

Fall, Oct. 2–Dec. 1
Winter, Dec. 2–Feb. 15

Most natives probably wouldn't care to argue, as there's some truth to it. Texas can get viciously hot, and in some places there's enough humidity to curl your hair. Driving trips in the summer, when the interior temperature of tightly closed cars can exceed 120 degrees, can ruin the wine you purchased in minutes. Bad weather can make the difference between a great trip and a miserable one.

Do a little planning, though, and you can travel comfortably in Texas year-round. While summer temperatures down by the Rio Grande near Presidio can get above 120, not that far to the north, in Fort Davis, the temperature even in the dead of summer can be in the 50s at night.

Here's a schedule of wine-related events that work around temperature extremes. Their focus and dates change, so check the Websites before you go.

FEBRUARY   *Wine Lovers Trail in the Hill Country. www.texaswinetrail.com/calendar.htm*
Southwest Wine Symposium, various locations. www.twgga.org
Boys and Girls Club of Laredo Annual Wine Tasting Gala. (956) 787-8866

MARCH   *Denison Arts and Wine Renaissance, Denison. www.ci.denison.tx.us/mainstreet/*

APRIL   *Texas Hill Country Wine and Food Festival, Austin. www.texaswineandfood.org*
Texas Wine and Food Festival, San Angelo. www.sanangeloarts.com/page5.html
Wine and Wildflowers Trail in the Hill Country. www.texaswinetrail.com/calendar.htm
Grand Wine and Food Affair, Sugar Land.

AUGUST   *Lone Star International Wine Competition. www.twgga.org*
Harvest Wine Trail in the Hill Country. www.texaswinetrail.com/calendar.htm
Kerrville Wine and Music Festival, Kerrville. www.kerrvillefolkfestival.com

SEPTEMBER   *Grapefest, Grapevine. www.grapevinetexasusa.com*

OCTOBER   *Texas Wine Month Trail in the Hill Country. www.texaswinetrail.com/calendar.htm*
Grape Camp, usually in Junction, but they're running out of room. www.twgga.org
Fredericksburg Food and Wine Festival, Fredericksburg. www.fbgfoodandwinefest.com

DECEMBER   *Holiday Wine Trail in the Hill Country. www.texaswinetrail.com/calendar.htm*

If you can't already tell, I love Texas. My family has lived here for more than 150 years. I'll be here 'til God is ready to take me to the only better place. Unfortunately, most travelers see Texas whirling by in a rush of freeways and amusement parks. You should try a different way.

Slow down. Get off the highway. Wander through beautiful country. Relax at picturesque vineyards operated by friendly artisans. Unwind in inviting restaurants. Enjoy regional foods accompanied by local wines. Take a day or a week to enjoy what Italians call *la dolce far niente*—the sweet doing of nothing.

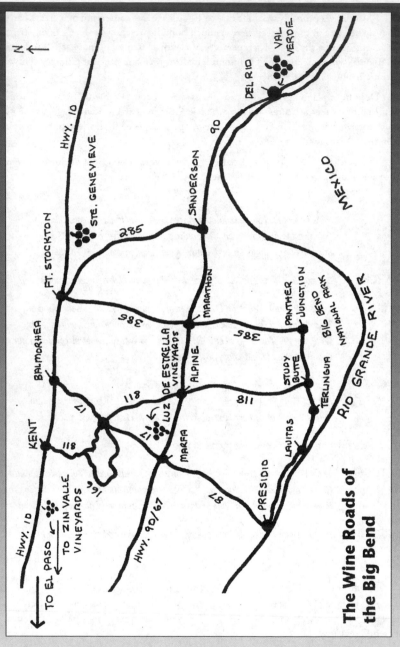

CHAPTER 1

**The Wine Roads of
the Big Bend**

The Wine Roads of the
Big Bend Country

I am a Big Bend sentimentalist. I'm not proud of it, I'm just warning you. In my opinion, two weeks in the country around Big Bend would be a nice start. A month would be better. The section from Fort Davis to Presidio, along the Rio Grande to Del Rio and back through Fort Stockton, is some of the most beautiful country on earth. It's also inhabited by some of the best people. So be warned: I'm not rational about this area.

Be prepared to put a lot of miles on your car. Traveling is measured in hours. Locals think nothing of driving two hundred miles for groceries. Or getting their car towed one hundred miles for service.

If you go in the summer, be prepared for hot weather. Presidio regularly captures the day's hotspot crown for the United States Down by the Rio Grande, the heat can get above 120 degrees. On the other hand, even in the dead of summer, Fort Davis will be in the 50s at night.

Don't even try to go out there for less than three days.

Here is the schedule I would follow for trips of up to seven days, staying at the Gage Hotel in Marathon, the most central location.

Day one, leave early. Drive down to Big Bend National Park, then across the park through Panther Junction and exit at Study Butte. Then take Texas 170 to Presidio. Give yourself some time, for you'll be stopping every five minutes to get out and look at the views. The seventy-mile trip next goes through Big Bend State Park and along the Rio Grande and ends up in Presidio. From there, take US 67

In the scenic Big Bend country, traveling time is measured in hours, not miles.

back up to Marfa. Have a late lunch, then head to Luz de Estrella Winery. Drive to Alpine and have drinks at Reata. Stay for dinner or head back to the Gage, where they have a great bar and decent food.

The next day, get up early and head for Del Rio. This drive will take about three hours, but you'll want to make two stops. The first is at Langtry, home of the legendary Judge Roy Bean. Then you'll want to go up to the lookout post above the Pecos River Bridge, about eighteen miles east of Langtry. Imagine trying to cross that little gully with a Conestoga wagon. Have lunch in Del Rio, go to Val Verde Winery and then head back to Marathon. After dinner, go see the mysterious Marfa Lights. A public viewing area has been built just east of town.

By the third day, hopefully, you will have figured out a way to time your trip to allow you to get into Ste. Genevieve—if you can get in. They are not set up for tours, though from time to time they allow Fort Stockton Chamber of Commerce access. So be sure to call the winery before trying to get a tour. You might get lucky. Then take time to go to Pacheco's for some chicken fajitas or to Le Petit Oasis for fancier fare.

If you can't get in to Ste. Genevieve, head for El Paso to try the wines at Zin Valle. Coming back on Highway 10, exit south on Texas 17 to Fort Davis. If you still have time and it's a clear day, take the Scenic Loop Drive. You'll eventually come to the McDonald Observatory, where, if you picked Tuesday, Friday or Saturday as your travel day, you can stop after dark for their fantastic Star Party. If not, turn left on Texas 166 and loop back around to Fort Davis. Head back to Marathon, appropriately named; after these three days you'll feel like you've run one.

If you have seven days, and you are in decent physical shape, don't miss the climb to Mount Emory, the Sand Slide in Boquillas Canyon or the guided hike to the four- to seven-thousand-year-old Seminole rock art at Seminole Canyon State Park.

Vines can thrive where the Rocky Mountain foothills meet the Chihuahuan Desert, as in this view of St. Genevieve's vineyard near Fort Stockton.

I started off by branding myself a Big Bend sentimentalist. Feelings over reason. Every person you talk to (except real estate agents) says something along the lines of, "This used to be a really nice place before _____." You can fill in that blank with just about anything from Republicans to Californians, scientists to the Sierra Club or country clubs to chili cook-offs. The grousers are probably right to some extent. The area has changed. But just like I'd be happy to take a Martin D-45 with a broken tuner, I'll take this area just like it is.

Luz de Estrella Winery

100 Starlight Way, Marfa, TX 79843.
Mon.–Sat. 10 am–6 pm, Sundays by
appointment. (432) 729-1819,
www.luzdeestrella.com

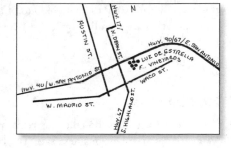

"She crushes the grapes and I crunch the numbers."

We're sitting in a mobile home on a windswept plain east of Marfa while John and Linda Armstrong delineate their division of labor. The vineyard is planted but is not old enough to produce fruit. Linda has a big glass of red wine in her hand. She's wearing cut-off shorts, while John looks more like a Houston lawyer on his day off.

Well, maybe not Houston. He actually practices law in LaPorte. John and Linda have been married for four years. They met after John's first wife died in 2001. Despite being somewhat newly married, they act like they've been married forever; they gently correct each other and act sweet, loving and happy.

"One day we were in Fort Davis and it was time to go back to Houston," John tells me. "I said to Linda that I wish we didn't have to go home, and she said, 'Why do we?' And I said, 'Why DO we?' It felt so free."

So they decided to start a winery, raise a few head of cattle and live their dream. John maintains his law practice while Linda learns winemaking from resident guru Patrick Johnson.

They have big plans for the future. Their goal is to reach 20,000 cases per year, something never accomplished before in this area. They are going to build what John calls "the largest wine cellar in the state." Once that's complete, they'll start having Friday night Italian dinners. (I hope they understand the level of Friday night football mania in Brewster and Presidio counties.) The Armstrongs have received substantial assistance from some of the best business minds in Texas wine—the folks at Haak and Messina Hof—so they're starting with a few checks in the plus column.

*John and Linda Armstrong
are raising cattle as they wait
for their vineyard near Marfa
to produce its first grapes.*

They both have a great sense of humor, something they'll need as they make their way up to 20,000 cases. Look out for a groaner or two from John. Example: "Two potatoes are standing on a street corner. One's a whore. How do you tell? One says 'Idaho.'"

Ouch.

The Best Wines

The Armstrongs bought the remaining inventory from Blue Mountain Winery's going-out-of-business sale. The best thing to come out of that is that they retained the services of Patrick Johnson as winemaker. Patrick is a bona fide Texas character who spent years at Blue Mountain refining his skills as a blender of Davis Mountains fruit.

We won't know until the 2008 harvest is released how well the Luz de Estrella vineyards will work in the potentially perfect climate—hot days and cool nights—around Marfa. But they are already buying grapes and releasing some very nice wines. Keep on the lookout for the **Paisano Blanco** and **Paisano Rojo.** They are Patrick's best shot at creating blends and should remain special wines as Luz de Estrella matures.

Ste. Genevieve Winery

IH 10 Exit 285, Fort Stockton, TX 79735. (432) 395-2417. Open to the public occasionally; check with the Fort Stockton Chamber of Commerce.

From the outside, Ste. Genevieve Winery looks as imposing as the business side of the Kremlin. Its security also mimics the Kremlin. Good luck picking the unmarked entry (it's the small door on the left). After entering, you find yourself in a sterile waiting room with an intercom for company and a sign announcing that there are no tours available. If you make it farther, you'll find there are no tasting rooms. This place is all business and no hospitality.

The biggest vineyard in Texas borders a huge building, stretching across the plains east of Fort Stockton for nine hundred acres. Ste. Genevieve outsells all other wineries in Texas combined. It's one of the twenty-five largest wineries in the United States yet sells only in Texas. But don't think this place is all about size. There are people here who care about quality.

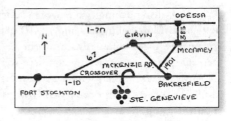

The University of Texas owns the vineyard. Mesa Vineyards owns the building, equipment and the operating entity. UT planted the vineyard between 1981 and 1984 as a way to stimulate income during the oil and gas bust. The grapes include Cabernet Sauvignon, Chardonnay, Gamay, Merlot, Chenin Blanc, Sauvignon Blanc, Pinot Noir, Zinfandel, Ruby Cabernet, Syrah, Viognier, Tempranillo, Malbec, Tinto Madeira, Trebbiano, Nebbiolo, Sangiovese and Semillon.

Mesa Vineyards is the brainchild of Pat Prendergast, a Harvard MBA with a background in marketing. Pat ran Gallo in northern Europe. He and his partners bought the already successful winery from Cordier in 2004 and kicked it up more than 80,000 cases. That increase is alone is almost the size of production at Fall Creek or Messina Hof.

Jen-Michel Duforat and winemaker Bénédicte Rhyne at one of St. Genevieve's 27,000-gallon tanks.

Pat is savvy enough to know that if it ain't broke, don't fix it. Ste. Genevieve already had one of the state's premier winemakers, Bénédicte Rhyne, a ten-year veteran of Ravenswood Vineyards in California. Pat has a simple goal: raise the grapes right, hand them to someone who knows what they are doing and get the wine on the shelves as quickly as possible. That speed may be more important than most people think.

"I don't think consumers think too much about freshness when it comes to wine," Pat says. "But I think they notice when a wine is fruitier and less oxidized." In a country where the average consumer stores a wine for less than seven hours (really), getting the wine to the consumer ASAP has its benefits.

Pat is also pushing two newer products. The new premium wine is named Peregrine Hill. Selling at under $10 a bottle, double the price of the Ste. Genevieve, these wines constitute the best work the winery can do with 100 percent Texas grapes. Many compete well in blind tastings with much more expensive international wines. Pat doesn't think he should raise his price; he thinks the others charge too much. That's Pat, the Harvard MBA, who's become a pure Texas populist.

The other focus is L'Orval, wine imported from the Languedoc-Roussillon. Bénédicte, born and raised in France, makes wonderful budget wine from a number of grapes. Priced just above the Ste. Genevieve ($9.99 vs. $7.99 for a 1.5 liter bottle), this is Vin De Pays D'oc level wine, and it constitutes a pretty good bargain.

My wife and I recently went to an Austin restaurant that has amateur belly dancers one night a month. Don't ask me why we went; we just thought it would be great fun. Since the belly dancers took over the whole restaurant, no beer or wine was being served. However, patrons were allowed to tote their own libations. I don't know if the crowd represented a cross-section of Austin—I'll grant you that Austin is weird—but I thought it might be interesting to see what folks were drinking. So I went walking around, surreptitiously computing. Almost 80 percent of the bottles on the tables were Ste. Genevieve. And that counts our three bottles from France and California. That's the kind of market penetration that would make any company jealous.

Mesa doesn't do much advertising. They don't use the predatory practices of some out-of-state wineries that slip money into the store manager's pocket— usually disguised as sales contests—to get better shelf space. Mesa does it by making good wine and selling it for a fair price. They've grown to the level they are at by making sure customers come back for more.

I love it when I find a large company with benign and quality-conscious people in the r's seat. That's Mesa.

The Best Wines

All Mesa wines are well made and accurately reflect what the grape tastes like. Complexity is not the goal. These wines are simple and straightforward. If you were traveling in Italy and found wines like this at a trattoria, you'd fall in love with their unpretentious nature. Fruity and fresh, as Pat says.

There are a couple of exceptions, wines of the quality you would expect in a fine restaurant. For instance, I had a wine tasting at my house where I pulled a dirty trick, not unusual in my house. I took **Ste. Genevieve Fumé Blanc-Chardonnay** and poured it out of its 1.5 liter Texas bottle and into a normal-sized French Bordeaux Blanc bottle, then served it to my unsuspecting guests. People loved it and guessed at a $15–25 per bottle price. When I showed them that it was a Texas wine at the equivalent of $3.99 a bottle, there were some shocked faces. One person started ordering the wine by the case. It's that good.

Ditto for the **Ste. Genevieve Sauvignon Blanc,** a quiet wine that neither shouts grapefruit—a la New Zealand— nor pineapple—a la California. Instead its charms whisper, gently, as you get varietally correct flavor and aroma in an easy drinking wine, closer to a Sancerre style than a New World style. I love it.

From the French side, the **L'Orval Syrah** is aromatic with vanilla and black pepper. The mouth feel isn't as rich as a Cotes Rotie, but it stands comparison with any Cotes du Rhone at twice the price.

Moving up the ladder, the **Peregrine Hill Chardonnay** is a wine my wife goes nuts over. To her, it carries just the right mixture of dense fruit and a hint of oak. She'll buy California or Washington Chardonnay if it's on sale cheaper than the Peregrine. Otherwise, the Peregrine goes in the shopping cart.

Personally, I think the **Peregrine Hills Syrah** is the winner of the line. Obviously, Bénédicte Rhyne learned something in all those years she worked with Joel Peterson at Ravenswood. There the motto is "no viño sin huevos," and the saying doesn't translate literally, if you know what I mean. Bénédicte's Syrahs are always models of what the grape should be: teeth-staining richness without any sense of being overly jammy, elegance with power. And at these prices.

Val Verde Winery

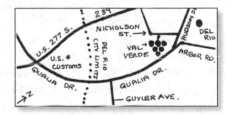

100 Qualia Dr., Del Rio, TX 78840.
Mon.–Sat. 10 am–5 pm. (830) 775 9714,
www.valverdewinery.com

We had just come back from lunch at Memo's Mexican Restaurant, owned by the late but still famous Texas piano player Blondie Calderón. Tommy was giving me the tour of Del Rio. If, like me, you've just passed Del Rio from the highway and have never been back along the irrigation canals, you are missing a truly beautiful place. Huge shade trees, beautiful old houses and nothing but green everywhere you look.

Tommy turns his Ford pickup down Qualia Lane. As in Tommy Qualia. I ask how he and the street had the same name.

"My grandfather, Frank, was eighteen when he left Italy," Tommy says. After an unhappy stint in Mexico, he and some of his friends moved north. "When Grandpa and the group of Italians got to San Antonio, they heard there was lots

Tommy and Linda Kaye Qualia's Val Verde Winery was for many years the only winery in Texas.

of water and land available down by the border, so they scouted it out and liked it. He got here to Del Rio in 1882."

Within a year Frank had found some Black Spanish grapes and was making wine for his family and friends. After a while, people were clamoring for his wine, so he opened a commercial winery. He never closed during Prohibition, but made wine for medicinal and religious purposes.

When Frank died, his son, Louis, took over and added some French grapes to the mix. At the same time, the family was developing a sheep farm in Mexico. Tommy figured he would be a sheep farmer and went to Texas Tech to get a degree in agriculture.

One day in 1969 Tommy and his future wife, Linda Kaye, were walking through Tech's student union and saw a table with information about the Peace Corps. "We were both interested, but they wanted us in July and we were getting married in August. They wanted me because I spoke Spanish and knew about sheep farming. They wanted Linda Kaye because she was from a farm family and had a degree in home economics. We had the bargaining power. We weren't going to go in as two individual volunteers. They finally gave up and took us on our terms."

The Peace Corps sent them to Bolivia. "Our families were scared to death for us," Tommy tells me. "We were pretty scared, too. Just a few days before we got to the country, the Bolivian Brown Berets killed Che Guevera, who was there trying to bring Cuban communism to Bolivia. In the cities, there were signs saying 'Muera los Yankees' ('Yankees die') and 'Go Home Gringos.' But the Indians out in the country didn't know Che Guevera from anyone and didn't care about communism."

Despite the scary circumstances, Tommy and Linda Kaye stuck it out. And they realized something that would help when they came home.

"One thing I learned from the Peace Corps," Tommy says, "is that when there is a problem, you go over it, under it, around it or through it, but you keep on going." The Peace Corps discipline paid off for Val Verde Winery and the Qualias.

"I was born and raised in this business all my life," says Tommy. "What it takes is someone who is willing to get up in the morning, roll up their sleeves and work hard. Then when the going gets tough, they need to stick with it."

Tommy's sentimental side starts showing.

"My dad gave me the winery in 1973. I was floored that he chose to give it to me because I had two brothers." Tommy shakes his head, still evidently amazed. "When I took over, we were the only winery in the state and no one was interested in wine." But he's hung in.

I ask him if he would do it all over again or do anything differently. "I'd probably go to UC Davis and learn about grapes instead of animal science," he answers. I can see his wheels turning. This is a kind and happy man.

"Every year has a new a challenge. During crush and harvest, we're already making plans for next year. Now that Linda Kaye has retired from being a teacher, we can spend a lot more time together. We've been married forty years and I still just love being around her. We get to share an office at the winery. Now when I come to work, I can do different things in the office or the lab. Or I can go work on the tractor." He comes up with a smile, looks me in the eye and says, "I love it."

There's a lot to love. Tommy Qualia is a well-respected man in both his hometown and in the wine business. He's the type whose handshake is a contract. When you look him in the eye you see straight shooting. During our visit for the second edition of this book, I saw a deep well of emotion come up twice.

A Val Verde wine won a medal in international wine competition at Houston's Livestock Show and Rodeo in 2005.

The first time was when he asked me to change the original introduction of the section about his winery. I had made fun of one of his deceased neighbors, Dr. J. R. Brinkley, better known as "the Goat-Gland Doctor." (See *Border Radio: Quacks, Yodelers, Pitchmen, Psychics, and Other Amazing Broadcasters of the American Airwaves* by Gene Fowler and Bill Crawford for that amazing story.)

Tommy explains: "We're so proud of living in this little oasis of West Texas where the water makes everything so verdant. Business is good. The whole industry just feels great. You know, from 1949 to 1976 we were the only winery in the state of Texas, and there were a lot of times I was scratching my head wondering if I made a mistake. But we've made it, and I just wish you would talk about the positive stuff instead of Dr. Brinkley."

It is a sincere request, one that I will honor.

The other emotional time was when Tommy started talking about Val Verde Winery's future: "Any time I get upset about how hard this business is, I remember Dad and Granddad going through Prohibition."

That 125 years of history is important to Tommy Qualia.

Tommy is the third generation of Qualias to run the winery. I ask him about the fourth. He looks at the table between us, and I feel an overwhelming sense of dignity.

"Our daughter Maureen went to UT Austin and got a degree in nutrition. Then she and a friend of hers went to Cuzco, Peru, and hiked to the tip, took the boat across to Bolivia and went to the place where Linda Kaye and I used to live."

You could see the pride well up, both in his daughter and in his past, the hard-earned pride you rarely see in a world where fifteen minutes of television face time indicates stardom.

Maureen's now at Fresno State University in a master's program in enology, prepared to follow in her father's footsteps.

The Best Wines

Val Verde Winery makes nine wines but only grows one grape: Black Spanish. Tommy uses the grapes to make the port named after his father, Don Luis. For his other wines he buys grapes from West Texas growers he knows and trusts.

His **Muscat Canelli** is a gorgeous, fragrant wine with a touch of sweetness and a cleansing acidity. Tommy also makes a good **Cabernet Sauvignon** in a Nuevo Rioja style featuring soft tannins and just a little oak. The star in Val Verde's crown is the same it has been for many years: **Don Luis Tawny Port** is one of the best wines I've ever tasted made from Black Spanish grapes. It is rich and unctuous, with a huge aroma reminiscent of the original Portuguese wine.

🍁 Zin Valle Winery

7315 Highway 28 at milepost 1,
Canutillo, TX 79835. Fri.–Mon. noon–5 pm
or by appointment. (915) 877-4544,
www.zinvalle.com

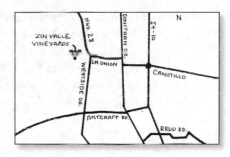

Well, Victor, you're not in Kansas anymore.

Zin Valle Winery owner Victor Poulos went to college in Kansas and on to law school on a Department of Defense scholarship. When he finished in 1976, the military had dibs on his next four years. By the time he got out his parents had retired to the El Paso area, and Victor loved what he saw.

He started his law practice in both Texas and New Mexico defending insurance companies, then saw the light and switched to doing plaintiff's work. During his time off, Victor studied West Texas history and was intrigued by the fact that back in the 1800s the Mesilla Valley was one of the top grape growing areas in the United States. In 1999, Mexican music superstar Juan Gabriel decided to sell a small ten-acre plot. Victor bought Gabriel's land and planted some of his favorite grapes, Zinfandel.

"My neighbor down the road has a winery in New Mexico," he tells me. "I just wanted to be a farmer and sell the grapes to my buddy. Then I really liked the grapes and decided to make some wine. Then I decided to share it with the public by opening my own winery. It was just a natural progression."

This description of the process is a little too pat. There's a lot more involved. Imagine the dedication it would take to tackle Victor's dilemma.

"I did some soil tests and found I had a lot of clay," he says. "So we dug 18 rows, 300 feet long and 39 inches wide, and I kept digging down until I hit sand, usually around four feet down. Then I brought in over 100 tons of sandy loam to give the vines a chance to grow."

Wow!

So how is he enjoying the fruits of his labor? (Sorry, I couldn't resist.) "I only have a few acres planted and, I can tell you, farming sucks. It's too much work." That's refreshing candor.

Consequently, instead of being a slave to stoop labor Victor has decided to purchase many of his grapes. He's in the lucky position of being in an appellation—the Mesilla Valley—that crosses state boundaries. He is currently growing Zinfandel, Malvasia Bianca and Gewurztraminer and purchasing grapes from New Mexico and California. Right now the winery is still small, producing about 1,500 cases per year. That means if you want a Zin Valle wine you'll have to get it in the tasting room.

In the near future, look for more Alsatian varietals in the Zin Valle portfolio. Victor will also be pushing pink wine, but this time it will be dry and mostly Mouvedre.

After spending some time with Victor, I'm sure he will continue to do well. He's pleased with his winery, his law practice continues to thrive, he is constantly trying to learn about new methods or new varietals and, most of all, he's a happy guy.

The Best Wines

You often hear about wines that are so aromatic they fill the room. This one is room-filling on steroids. I opened **Zin Valle's Malvasia Bianca** and walked away for a minute. When I came back the whole room had the seductive floral aroma of the grape.

I've often wondered why more Texas wineries don't use this terrific hot climate grape. I'm just glad someone has made a great wine with it. For German wine lovers this is done in a Spatlese style, with just a bit of sugar to give the natural fruit a boost. This wine smells so good it's almost a shame to drink it.

The other great wine is the **Dry Rosé.** I'm nuts for Mouvedre, a grape mostly from the southern part of France but one with a brilliant future in Texas. Zin Valle's wine is mostly Mouvedre, with some Cinsault added. This wine has the gusto and depth that you normally only get in rosés from the Rhone, Provence or Bandol. Don't miss it.

¶◎ FOOD
Alpine

Reata, 203 N. 5th St. Lunch & dinner, even later if one of several Hollywood movie stars is in residence. (432) 837-9232). Reata is Spanish for rope. More to the point, it was the name of Rock Hudson's ranch in *Giant*. Started in 1995 among a bunch of hype and hoopla, the place was doomed by its own publicity. No place could live up to the buildup it got. If you go just for great service in a charming location with inventively prepared "cowboy cuisine," you'll love the place. The only downside is the shockingly high-priced wine list. Expensive.

Del Rio

Memo's Mexican Food, 804 E. Losoya St. Lunch & dinner Mon.–Sat. (830) 774-1583). Blondie Calderón was a local legend as a musician and for his restaurant, Memo's. After he passed away the family kept the restaurant going, and it's still one of the top draws in town. My favorite dish is Blondie's Carne Guisada ($8.95). Folks love the Wednesday and Friday buffet lunch.

Avanti Italian Restaurant, 60 E. 12th St. Lunch & dinner daily, close at 7:30 pm Sundays. (830) 775-3363. The Italian food is good, especially the veal parmesan ($14.95). The real draw is the best wine list in town.

If you feel like going across the Rio Grande to Mexico, try **Lando's** cabrito or **Manuel's** steaks.

El Paso

The **Greenery Restaurant and Market,** 750 Sunland Park Dr. (915) 584-6706. Good seafood—try the Chilean sea bass—and the best wine shop in town.

Fort Davis

Marylou's Restaurant. Daily 6:30 am–2:30 pm except Saturday, when Marylou takes the day off. (432) 426-9901. Food and service here are just about perfect. Scrumptious huevos rancheros ($4.75) and an incredible lunch buffet ($6) are just the start. For a glimpse of heaven, try the cheese enchiladas with an egg ($5). Sounds crazy, tastes great.

Old Texas Inn, formerly called the Fort Davis Drugstore. Breakfast & lunch daily. (432) 426-3118. Remember what I said about being a sentimentalist? Of all places in the Big Bend area, this one hits my heartstrings more than any other. My childhood memories of sitting at the bar and having a cherry phosphate are overpowering. And the fact remains, this place makes great food. Try the wonderful hamburgers ($4–$6, depending on how loaded up), the best grilled cheese sandwich in Texas—says *Gourmet Magazine*, and me ($3.50)—or a gut-busting Biscuits, Sausage and Gravy breakfast ($5).

Fort Stockton

Pacheco's, 208 W. 10th St. Lunch & dinner Tue.–Sat. (432) 336-8727. Excellent Mexican food and great chips and dips. Try the chicken soft tacos or fajitas. Inexpensive.

La Petit Oasis, 1572 Blaine McCallister Ln. Lunch & dinner Tue–Sun. (432) 336-2050. Continental food in a nice location. Worth taking a little time out for.

Marfa

Maiya's Restaurant. Wed–Sat. 5–10 pm. (432) 729-4410 Maiya's is a revelation. I guess it's all those Yankees moving in and raising the property rates. They need a fancy place. Luckily, Maiya's is much more than fancy. There's inventive, tasty food here, and I usually end up going every time I'm in Marfa. Get reservations. One Hollywood star can fill the whole place.

The Brown Recluse. Daily. (432) 729-1811. The best breakfast for thirty miles and the best coffee you'll find until you get to Austin.

Study Butte/Terlingua

Starlight Theater, Terlingua. Dinner daily (late service Fri.&Sat.), brunch Sat.&Sun. (432) 371-2326. Inventive food for such a rural outpost. Venison sausage with roasted peppers is a good starter. Moderate prices and great atmosphere.

Los Paisanos Restaurant, Terlingua. Daily lunch & dinner. (432) 371-2101. My kind of place. Family run, plain but clean with killer good Norteño Mexican food. Everything from the sauces to the tortillas is handmade. Gorditas, chiles rellenos, enchiladas, crisp tacos. If you don't want to choose, get the Mexican plate, which includes all of them. Bring your own wine or beer.

⌂ SHELTER

Big Bend National Park

Chisos Mountain Lodge, in the basin at the park. (432) 477-2291. Location, location, location. In the dead center of the park and up in the mountains, where it's 20 degrees cooler. Rooms are clean and some have incredible views. Charges are reasonable and based on the number of people in the room. This place is booked *way* in advance, so make your reservations early. Ask for one of the historic stone cottages for the best experience. Inexpensive.

Fort Davis

Hotel Limpia, 100 Main St. (800) 662-5517. Right in the center of downtown Fort Davis. The main building of the Limpia was built in 1912. Since the tourist boom in Fort Davis started in the 1980s the hotel has expanded out of the historic building into three other sections, but all are filled with period furnishings. The owners have also been busy buying historic houses around town. On my last trip we stayed in the Trueheart House, a glorious late-nineteenth-century abode named for one of my Texas ancestors. The restaurant has good food and Texas wines. If you're really hungry, try one of the delicious chicken fried beef tenderloins. There's also a great Texas bookstore. Moderate price.

Indian Lodge, Davis Mountains State Park. (432) 426-3254. Owned and operated by the State of Texas. The Civilian Conservation Corps started building the lodge in the 1930s and it opened in 1939. It's an enchanting old building with eighteen-inch-thick adobe walls and timeless Native American–style architecture. It could have been built 150 years ago or yesterday. In the rooms you'll find hand-carved furniture made by the CCC workers. Once you've been here, you won't want to stay anywhere else. But you may not have a choice, as Indian Lodge is usually booked months in advance. Inexpensive.

Marathon

Gage Hotel, 101 U.S. Hwy. 90 W. (800) 884-GAGE. Rancher Alfred Gage built this hotel in 1927 and died the same year. No owner after seemed to have as much interest in it as he did, and the neglect showed, until J. P. and Mary Jon Bryan bought it, restored it to its original charm and then expanded it. The décor is comfortable cowboy chic. I felt it was a little fussy, but my wife loved it. The restaurant is kid-friendly; don't be surprised to find a bunch of little bandits yelling and running through the dining room. We loved the bar, a hangout for local characters. Expensive.

Marfa

Hotel Paisano, TX 17 between the courthouse and U.S. Hwy. 90. (866) 729-3669. Built in the 1930s and owned by the folks who have the Limpia in Fort Davis. The Paisano is refurbished and targeted at luxury travelers. The main attraction is staying in the same rooms that Elizabeth Taylor, James Dean and Rock Hudson stayed in while filming *Giant*. A bottle of wine on the patio with friends and you'll understand the draw.

☼ FUN

Big Bend National Park. (432) 477-2251

Chisos Mountains Basin. From the time you leave Panther Junction and you drive up into the Basin, you'll have gone up two thousand feet and down 20 degrees. The desert changes to forest as you meet vista after vista along the way. This is also the location of the only restaurant in the park. If you are in good condition and heights don't scare you, this is the departure point to climb Mount Emory. If you're in good shape but don't like heights, go for the South Rim. In either case, you will be treated to one of the most spectacular views you'll ever see. Check with the rangers first. Either hike will take all day.

Boquillas Canyon. After 9/11, the once freely flowing border between Boquillas and Big Bend was closed. It's a shame. Boquillas was a sweet little town that depended on Americans. But you can still walk back and see where the Rio Grande has cut a canyon. The rocks are gorgeous and tailor-made for photographers (go in the evening). For children of all ages, the sand slide is an experience you won't forget. I'm guessing, but I would say it rises almost five hundred feet. Once you've crawled to the top, just start rolling. Again, this is strenuous and dangerous. And fun.

Santa Elena Canyon. Walls 1,500 feet on either side of the river, and you can walk almost a mile into the canyon. You don't get the light show of sun on canyon walls that you get at Boquillas, but Santa Elena is even more massive. This is a must, and the walk is only slightly demanding.

Fort Davis-Marfa-Marathon Triangle

Scenic Loop Drive. This trip takes about two hours and runs some seventy-five miles. From Fort Davis, take TX 118 toward Kent. You'll drive through the Limpia Canyon, past the Davis Mountains State Park and along the highest mountain road in Texas. Near where TX 118 intersects TX 166 is the McDonald Observatory (432 426-3640), home of the third-largest telescope in the world. Even if you don't show up on Star Party Night (Tuesday, Friday or Saturday nights, weather permitting) there is still a fun visitor center and a beautiful view. Once you pass the wind generators, check the beautiful view of the Sierra Vieja Mountains in Mexico. You'll end up back in Fort Davis.

Marfa Lights. Depending on your level of paranoia, the lights could be anything from little green men sending secret messages to confederates bent on taking over the world to static electricity. People have been trying to figure these out since 1883. The University of Texas, *National Geographic* and the *Unsolved Mysteries* TV show all left scratching their heads. You have to try to see them while you're in the area. The best place is at the roadside park eight miles east of Marfa on TX 67. The lights look like cars in the distance, just above the horizon. Then they start showing up higher in the sky, so unless someone is living in an alternate universe where cars can fly . . .

Balmorhea State Park, on TX 17 between Fort Stockton and Fort Davis. (432) 375-2370. The little town of Balmorhea is famous for the San Solomon Springs, an underground gusher that pumps out 25 million gallons of water each day. Visitors don't stop to see the springs. They stop for the 1.75-acre spring-fed swimming pool. The pool covers over 77,000 square feet, is 25 feet deep and has a constant temperature of between 72 and 76 degrees.

Davis Mountains State Park, on TX 118 north of Fort Davis. (432) 426-3254. This is one of Texas's prettiest state parks, 2,700 acres of mountain air and cool temperatures. From the low part of the park to the top of Skyline Drive, you go up one thousand feet. This is also home of Indian Lodge, usually booked months in advance. This park is also a perfect stop for bird-watchers.

Fort Davis National Historic Site, outside Fort Davis on TX 17. (915) 426-3224. Ever wonder what it would have been like to be a soldier during the Indian Wars? This is the place to come. It's widely considered to be the best surviving example of a frontier fort.

Chihuahuan Desert Research Institute, four miles south of Fort Davis on TX 118. (915) 364-2499. Aimed at educating people about the fragile and diverse Chihuahuan Desert.

Along the Road from Marathon to Del Rio

Judge Roy Bean Visitor Center, Langtry. Daily 8 am–5 pm except holidays. (432) 291-3340. This place is more interesting than you might suspect. Judge Bean, the "Law West of the Pecos" and "the hanging judge," was equally famous for his quick justice and his unrequited love for the English actress Lily Langtry, " the Jersey Lily." High-quality, well-trained people help you out and show you around. For plant lovers, the cactus garden is fascinating. Not only is each type identified; you're also told a little about how Native Americans used the plants.

Seminole Canyon State Historical Park, nine miles west of Comstock on US 90, just east of the Pecos River bridge. (432) 292-4464. Call ahead to see about getting a guide to take you down into the canyon to visit Fate Bell Shelter, one of the oldest cave dwellings in North America, which also has some of the continent's oldest Indian pictographs. You can only go in with a guide's supervision, so be sure to call ahead.

CHAPTER 2

The Wine Roads of the
Panhandle Plains

S o you're sitting around one day, assuming the pose of Rodin's Thinker. Where will I go on vacation? New York? London? Paris? Munich?

How about Lubbock?

That's right. While Lubbock may not be your first choice for a vacation, I found it captivating. I like the weather. It's the same kind of weather that grapes like—dry, with warm days and cool nights. The altitude of 3,241 feet means the sun burns intensely, but get in the shade and the weather's fine. The air is usually clean, unless the Feed Lot Inversion is taking place. Then gas masks are required.

But our purpose is wine, and Lubbock is the home of some of Texas's best wines. La Diosa is right in town and Pheasant Ridge, Llano Estacado and Cap*Rock are all just minutes away. For those of you interested in the farming aspect of wine, many of the state's best vineyards are within an easy drive of Lubbock.

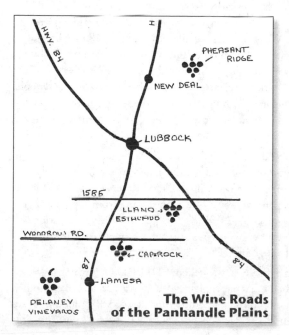

**The Wine Roads
of the Panhandle Plains**

Bobby Cox, the founder of Pheasant Ridge and a famous local character, claims that if you draw a circle with a twenty-mile radius around the town of Brownfield you'll encompass the majority of great red wine growing land in the state.

While there may be only four wineries, the Lubbock area has more than forty vineyards. Most of the owners simply sell their grapes to wineries; they aren't really equipped for tours. But I've found that if you take the time to call and ask them if you

An advanced system of subsurface irrigation helps Newsom Vineyards produce rich-tasting grapes in subarid soil.

can come see what they do, many are gracious and generous with their time. The best bet is to ask someone in the Llano Estacado or Cap*Rock tasting rooms if they know of a vineyard that you can go see.

Vineyard land may look flat and uniform, but the High Plains Appellation is actually quite diverse. As Bobby tells me, "How do we communicate the differences inside our AVA? There are nearly 1,000-degree days of variability from north to south and 4,100 to 3,000 feet of elevation. Think Carneros to Alexander Valley."

If you do get the chance to visit, Neal Newsom, Cliff Bingham and Larry Young own the three most beautiful vineyards I saw. Larry has a place in his vineyard that's about ten feet taller than the surroundings. From there you can see many of the best vineyards.

Cliff's vineyard, just outside of the town of Meadow, is an organic farmer's dreamscape. Cliff babies his grapes into uniform excellence. We were guests at a luncheon at the Binghams' house with the cream of the crop of High Plains farmers: Neal Newsom, LaVerne Newsom (eighty years old and still going strong), Cliff Bingham, Bobby Cox. We even had the parson there for prayers. Cliff's wife, Betty, home-schools their eleven (!!) children, and based on what I saw—loving, cooperative children that were intelligent and would look you in the eye while talking—I'd say we should try to bottle Betty and send her out to fix our schools. The topics were far ranging, but one thing is certain: these farmers, after getting beaten down by commodity pricing and stupid federal government systems, see grapes as a way to literally save the family farm.

We next went over to Neal Newsom's house—his wife, Janis, wanted to give us a bottle of home-made preserves—and were startled to see how simply and modestly they live. If any single vineyard in the state deserves the title Grand Cru, it would be Neal's. Nearly everyone who makes wine from his grapes gets something outstanding. As of 2007, Neal is shifting his farming operations to grapes only, giving him more acreage for vines. If there's any justice, the Newsom family will soon be living the high life.

The Newsoms are also pioneers in the field of SDI PRD. Before you go cross-eyed over what that stands for, let me explain. Water is a precious commodity. The standard way to irrigate used to be flooding the vineyard. But flooding loses a lot of water. When drippers became cheaper, vineyard owners moved to drip irrigation; much more efficient. The Newsoms are using a system that is buried and staggered so the vines can be stressed by lack of water but still kept alive. This makes the richest tasting grapes you can find. SDI PRD Subsurface Drip Irrigation and Partial Row Drying.

Try to meet one or two farmers while you are traveling the "wine roads." When you taste a wine that says Cliff Bingham Vineyard or Newsom Vineyard, or any of the other vineyards good enough to claim a place on the label, you'll have the experience of knowing the person who grew your grapes. Tasting Orange Muscat from Newsom Vineyards—whether it's made by Llano Estacado, or Flat Creek or Light Catcher—will always taste like Newsom fruit. It's such a great experience to go to the source.

It's possible to make all four wineries in one day, as long as you start early and it isn't Sunday. Start at Pheasant Ridge, then go to Llano Estacado and Cap*Rock (they are very close to each other), then finish at La Diosa for food, wine and entertainment.

But why pressure yourself? Spread it to two days and be leisurely. Llano and Cap*Rock one day, Pheasant Ridge and La Diosa the other. Spend some time listening to Scotty tell stories at Great Scott's Barbecue. Go have a beer with the students. Walk around Texas Tech.

If you have the time and money, I'd recommend trying to hire Bobby Cox (BobbyGrape@aol.com) to take you on a vineyard tour. He's a consultant in the business of selling his knowledge and experience, so even though he isn't normally a tour guide, if you catch him at the right moment he might do it. But he is in high demand, so if you're interested, call him as far in advance as possible. Wrapped up in one person, you'll get a history lesson, (probably) a chance to meet some farmers otherwise not available to you, an understandable explanation of how vineyards and governments work and an opportunity to meet a genuine Texas Wine Character.

Bobby Cox believes the majority of the best red wine growing land in Texas is within a twenty-mile radius of Brownfield.

🍁 Llano Estacado Winery

On FM 1585, 3.2 miles east of U.S. 87,
Lubbock, TX 79452. Mon.–Sat. 10 am–5
pm, Sun. noon–5 pm. (806) 745-2258,
www.llanowine.com

Llano Estacado is one of Texas's oldest, largest and best wineries. Chartered in 1975, its first wine came out in 1976. By the mid-80s production had increased to 15,000 cases and Walter Haimann, ex-president of Seagram Distillers Company, was hired to run the winery. He passed away several years ago, but people still remember his hardball negotiations and take-no-prisoners competitive style. He probably doesn't get enough credit for his professionalism and hard-business approach. Under his stewardship, Llano Estacado angered some people. But while other West Texas wineries were going bankrupt, Llano was flourishing. His first wise move was hiring a gifted veteran winemaker—Greg Bruni—in 1993.

Greg's family owned California's San Martin Winery, one of the state's top ten wineries during the 1960s and 70s. He had worked at the winery since he was twelve, and thought the work too hard for too little payoff. He wanted to go to medical school but didn't have the grades. Thankfully, the California wine business was starting to take off and he reconsidered his career choice. He was accepted into the University of California at Davis and eventually earned his B.S. in enology.

After spending time at the family winery, Greg struck out on his own and went to Bandiera Winery in Sonoma County, where he was head winemaker. When a conglomerate bought San Martin, they asked Greg to come back and run it. Then Byington Winery offered him the chance to build a state-of-the-art winery from the ground up. Greg loved this chance, and his first wines won some big awards. His wife, Sharendale, was also having a successful career in Silicon Valley. They had everything except time to enjoy each other. They wanted out of the California rat race. He started putting out feelers. Someone told him about Texas. He was skeptical. Then Walter Haimann made him an offer he couldn't refuse.

The Texas wine business attracted Greg for personal reasons. "When I first visited Llano Estacado Winery," he told me, "I found everything that had first inspired me to fall in love with winemaking: challenge, enthusiasm and an industry, much like California in the 70s, just bursting with potential." The other aspect that excited him was being able to quit worrying about management and marketing and focus on what he loves, making wine.

Good managers care enough about their organization to make sure someone is always available to take their place. Haiman's second wise move was hiring Mark Hyman, then area manager for the Heublein Fine Wine Group, in 1994.

In Llano Estacado's laboratory are, from left, Chris Hull, winemaker; Greg Bruni, vice president and executive winemaker; and Jason Hook, lab manager.

Mark gravitated to marketing, sales and management, while Greg loved the day-to-day tasks of a winemaker. The duo has gone on to become something of an odd couple. Mark offices in Grapevine, close to the Metroplex action and near the big distributors. Greg works at the winery, checking samples and also going out to contracted vineyards to evaluate harvest times and conditions. Each respects the other's talents and turf. One may occasionally want something different than the other, but when it comes down to final decisions, their mutual support is solid.

Llano Estacado has grown in market share (it's now the second largest winery in Texas), and, more important, its quality gets better each year.

In 2004 I took a group of New York restaurateurs and writers on a barbecue trip. They said they'd like to try some Texas wine. Whenever I get a request like this, I always require that all tasting is blind and that there will be ringers from places like California, France and Australia. That keeps everyone honest, and, after all, Texas wines have to be able to compete on a world stage.

The winner that afternoon was the Llano Estacado Cabernet Shiraz. The writer from *USA Today* was so amazed that he featured the wine in his weekly column.

Greg and Mark are on a run. Greg's dream is to have Llano Estacado play the role Robert Mondavi played in California.

"When I was growing up in California, Robert Mondavi's was the Test Tube winery; they always wanted to do better and would experiment like crazy. I look at Llano as the Texas experimenter," he explains. "We view our role as being a leader, fully knowing that there will be other wineries that do better. But Mondavi stimulated me, and I hope that we can stimulate a lot of competition from the smaller wineries. When another winemaker says they can beat us, I love it. As far as I'm concerned, the best wines in the state of Texas haven't been made yet."

The Best Wines

Llano Estacado produces more than 120,000 cases of wine per year, and Greg and his staff make thirty-three different wines. The big seller is their **Blush,** a wine they try to downplay. "What we have to come to grips with is that blush is in demand from our consumers," Greg says. "So we make the best Blush we can, and it gives us the money to buy the best barrels and the best equipment."

It also allows them to keep prices in line with the world marketplace. Although Llano Estacado makes a few expensive wines, I love tasting Greg's stabs at midpriced perfection. Take, for example, the **Signature Red Meritage** (by the way, the word rhymes with heritage; it is not French-ified as you usually hear). I avoided this wine for years based on prejudice. How could this cheap red wine be good? I was eating at a steak house in Lubbock and Llano's Red Meritage was the only red wine on the list. I bought it, not very happy and with expectations of thin and sour wine. Surprise! It was exceptional, one of my favorite bargains in wine (not just Texas wine). It's a blend of Cabernet Sauvignon, Merlot and Cabernet Franc with youthful vivacious fruit, good mouth feel and richness that will have you scratching your head at how they can do this for the price. These are the kind of wines that wine writers live to discover—cheap and delicious.

At the same price point and IMHO a harbinger of what is possible with Rhone varietals in Texas, the **Texas Signature Rhone** is a blend of Carignane, Syrah, Mouvedre, Grenache and Viognier. It's spicy, fragrant and easy to drink, especially at true cellar temperature (57 degrees Fahrenheit). You can get a great concept of Texas terroir by getting a bottle of this Llano wine and putting it next to a similarly priced Cotes du Rhone.

If you have some money to spend, Greg's Tête de Cuvée is called **Viviano.** It is a super-Tuscan-styled blend of Cabernet Sauvignon and Sangiovese, with the occasional addition of Merlot and/or Cabernet Franc. Both Greg and Mark know they will be evaluated on the success of Viviano, so it gets the Rolls Royce treatment, from buying the best grapes available to using small French and American oak barrels. The wine is not a California, in-your-face style. Here there is both elegance and structure. Each year, this vies for recognition as one of Texas's top ten best wines.

Cap*Rock Winery

408 E Woodrow Rd. Lubbock, TX 79423.
Mon.–Sat. 10 am–5 pm, Sun. noon–5 pm.
(806) 863-2704, www.caprockwinery.com

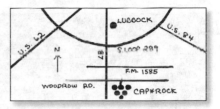

Cap*Rock has invested a lot of money in its facility. The 26,000-square-foot winery is gorgeous, designed in a southwestern mission style that makes you relax the second you walk through the door. The tasting area is set up like a living room with a big stone fireplace, overstuffed seating and a beautiful bar. The business end is equally impressive. Forty-foot ceilings cover 13,000-gallon stainless steel tanks. The capacity is 95,000 cases, should the market ever be there. The lab is state-of-the-art, as is the crushing, fermenting and bottling equipment.

Houston-based Saragossa Wine Group bought Cap*Rock in 2001, and word comes as I write this that they have entered into a joint venture with an Italian wine company, Cantine Matchesi Fumanelli. They have a good name to work with and a first-rate facility. Their future looks bright.

Cap*Rock's winery operations are housed in a southwestern mission-style building.

McPherson Cellars

You'll notice there is no address or phone number listed, nor will you find hours open. The reason: McPherson Cellars is a winemaker without a winery per se. Kim McPherson uses the facilities of other High Plains wineries, buys grapes from the best sources he can find (including his father's gorgeous old vineyard) and uses his years of skill and experience to produce some of Texas's best wines. In the hands of an amateur, an operation like this might not warrant inclusion in this book. But this is Kim McPherson's winery, and his presence makes it important.

The McPherson family's winemaking roots run deep in the soils of Texas and California. Clinton McPherson, Kim's father, was a founder of both Llano Estacado and Teysha (a prior name for Cap*Rock). Kim's brother Jon is a winemaker at

Kim McPherson's Texas winemaking roots run deep.

Thornton Vineyards in Southern California. Kim and Jon own California labels Cucamonga Cellars and Il Fratello. As if that isn't enough, Kim finds time to make the wine at La Diosa.

Kim grew up in Lubbock and went to Texas Tech, where he got a degree in food science. He worked as a researcher at Anderson Clayton Foods until the wine bug bit. He decided to go to UC Davis. After his time there, he worked at Trefethen Vineyards in Napa. In the meantime, his father had started Llano Estacado. When Llano's Australian winemaker got deported in 1979, Kim came home to be the winemaker at Llano. Five years later he won a Double Gold Medal—signifying that judges were unanimous in their votes—for his Llano Estacado Slaughter-Leftwich Vineyard Chardonnay at the San Francisco Wine Competition. One year later he went to Texas Vineyards in Bonham. It made some good wines but shortly went belly up. So he went back to California and started Chansa Vineyards. Then he got the phone call from a winery needing some help and came home.

Kim is one of Texas's bona fide characters. He is always willing to speak his mind, no matter whose toes get stepped on in the process.

His assessment of Texas wine: "Warm climate fruit doesn't age well. If you are really good, it lasts maybe three to five years. Instead of trying to sell big, expensive wines, we should be making $8 to $15 wines and be happy. Then if a big, incredible wine comes, so be it."

On grape choices: "We need to quit trying to make great Cabernets and Chardonnays. We can make competitive wines at low prices, but we need to find the grapes that really work for Texas. Oregon is known for Pinot. What are we known for?" "Viognier," I say.

"Yeah, maybe," he says. "Viognier and Syrah do well in the Hill Country. Have you tried Greg's Pinot Grigio?"

He's referring to Greg Bruni, winemaker at Llano Estacado, whose Pinot Grigio indeed turned out to be wonderful but very limited. I tell Kim I haven't had it yet.

"Well, it's wonderful. You need to encourage him to make more of it. But this is great wine. Why aren't we growing more of it?"

Good question.

On the joys of fatherhood: "My daughter is at UT. All I do is shell out $50 bills."

He should be developing a nice collection of $50 bills for his daughter's education. Between McPherson Cellars (which sells every drop it can make, usually without trying) and his wife's La Diosa Cellars, Kim is a busy guy.

If you want to meet Kim, there is a chance—just a chance, mind you—that you might find or meet him at La Diosa in the Depot District. Even if you don't get the opportunity to meet him, you can usually find all his wines at La Diosa. They are all worthwhile.

The Best Wines

Picking Kim's best wine is a challenge. First of all, he'll make a wine one year because he likes the grapes but not make it again. The wines you can count on are the ones he sources from his father's vineyards, the best of which is his **Sangiovese.** It is always elegant and unfussy, the type of wine you might find in a trattoria in the town of Greve in Chianti. Kim frequently makes a dry **Syrah Rosé,** which has all the fruit and spiciness you expect from the Syrah. Finally, Kim does a splendid job with Viognier. His version is more reminiscent of a French Condrieu with elegance and restraint, rather than a big bruiser.

To really understand the breadth of Kim's abilities, you also have to try the wines from La Diosa, especially the **Sparkling Chenin Blanc** and **Sangria.**

🍁 Pheasant Ridge Winery

Two miles west of New Deal on FM 1729,
mail to Route 3, Box 191,
Lubbock, TX 79401.
Open Fri.–Sat. noon–6 pm,
Sun. 1 pm–5 pm.
(806) 746-6033,
www.pheasantridgewinery.com

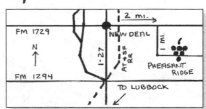

You know the old question about who ate the first oyster? The standard answer is, whoever it was had to be pretty brave or pretty dumb.

The oyster question is the first thing that strikes you when you drive up to Pheasant Ridge Winery. Who on earth thought this would be a good place for a winery? It's flat even by West Texas standards, open to the elements and surrounded by the red-hot Texas sun. Bobby Cox disagreed and built Pheasant Ridge. A lot of people thought he had lost his mind.

That was until his Cabernet Sauvignon won the Gold Medal at the 1986 San Francisco Fair. Then Bobby looked brilliant.

Winning the gold was the culmination of a dream and a vision. The dream was to develop a French-style winery and operate it in the estate tradition, using only grapes grown on the property. Bobby worked hard, put his sweat and blood into the fields. Unfortunately, as he explained, his ability to manage the funds didn't quite keep up with his ability to manage the wines. In 1992, in a heartbreaking moment, Bobby lost the winery. No one

Bill Gipson left the oil patch to make wine.

loses something they've put that much work into and feels okay about it. Though he takes it like a man, you can still tell it grates on him.

The person who took it over is oilman William Gipson, one of the original investors. He's ceded day-to-day operation to his son, Bill, a man who cares about doing it right. Bill Gipson followed the family business and worked in the oilfields for years. When the winery came up, he offered to be the full-time manager. Though far less lucrative than the oil patch, he loves Pheasant Ridge and claims nothing would take him away from it. "I can make a lot more in the oil and gas business, but I'm in love with this place. I love the fact that we are creating something from nature. I love that we do everything internally and control our own destiny. Plus," he explained, "I love building a business."

Right now Pheasant Ridge makes 10,000 cases per year. There are enough grapes to get to 15,000 to 20,000 cases, which is what Bill would like to do.

A couple of elements separate Pheasant Ridge from most wineries. First, you will never see a Pheasant Ridge Cabernet Sauvignon less than three years old. Every vintage of its Cab spends a minimum of two years in the barrel and one year in the bottle. As you might guess, Bill believes that he is on the right side of this decision and that all the rest of the wineries should be letting their Cabs rest longer. Then, to make sure he's putting his money where his mouth is, Bill sets aside a substantial percentage of each year's Cabernet production and ages it until he's satisfied it is at its peak, then sells it in limited quantities from the winery. These older wines constitute almost a third of his business, so he has a big investment wrapped up aging wine.

You might expect to pay a lot for the privilege of drinking these older wines, but one of Pheasant Ridge's commitments is to keep the price at a level where wine drinkers feel they are getting a bargain.

The Best Wines

The weather at Pheasant Ridge is extreme. It is dry, hail is a constant problem, tornadoes occur fairly often and the temperatures can range 120 degrees in a year. On Halloween 1991 the temperature dropped 75 degrees in one day, and the vineyard lost one-third of its vines. Despite these problems, most of the vines seem to do well. Bill believes that the cold winters stress the vines and are a good thing that, as with humans, it gives them more character.

At 3,500 feet, the altitude combines with the ultra-low humidity to allow hot days but cool nights. In summer months, temperature will range from the mid-90s to the upper 50s. This gives better hang time than we usually get in Texas. Pheasant Ridge usually picks white grapes in late August and red grapes in mid-September. When they harvest, everyone carries five-gallon buckets into the vineyard and hand picks each cluster based on whether it's ready.

The best white wine Pheasant Ridge makes is also the cheapest. The **Dry Chenin Blanc** is an incredible bargain. It is a medium-bodied, bone-dry, exotic, smoky and fruity. Serve it to a French wine lover without telling them what they're drinking and watch their amazement.

Pheasant Ridge made its name on **Cabernet Sauvignon,** and that's still its main strength. The beauty of going to the tasting room is that you'll have the opportunity to buy older vintages. Most Texas wines are happier drunk young, but the Pheasant Ridge Cabernet Sauvignon likes a little resting time before it joins the party. Right now the best vintage is the 2001.

🍁 La Diosa Cellars

901 17th St., Lubbock, TX 79401.
Tues.–Fri. 11 am–midnight,
Sat. noon–1 am. (806) 744-3600,
www.ladiosacellars.com

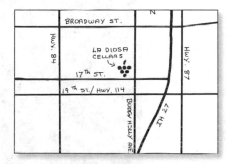

You walk into the La Diosa Cellars location in the Depot District of downtown Lubbock and are immediately transported to a different world. For years, due to the archaic laws in Texas dividing dry and wet precincts, Lubbock was a vast wasteland when it came to adult beverages to go. It was legal to get juiced-up at a restaurant.

But then those people got behind the wheel of a three-ton truck. If you wanted to have something to take to your house, you had to drive south on Highway 87 to "the strip," the only wet place in the county. Of course, plenty of folks had a few drinks before deciding to make the run to the strip, and quite a few accidents occurred over the years. And anyway, none of those stores has a very good selection of wine.

Then the laws changed in Texas. Now anyone who owns a producing winery can put it anywhere they please. It didn't take too long for the two goddesses, Sylvana McPherson and Catherine Traxler (the Diosas in the name) to figure out that they could place a winery right in the middle of downtown Lubbock and take advantage of the ability to sell wine for off-premise consumption.

Others have tried a similar formula around the state, but this may be the best of the lot. Step through the door and you'll think, "Wow, Toto, I've got a feeling we're not in Lubbock anymore!" The place is gorgeous, comfortable and inviting, almost like it was designed by a professional interior designer with a vision. Then you notice the aromas of delicious food wafting through the air. This is a winery?

It turns out the impressions are intentional. Sylvana is a successful interior designer, and Catherine previously owned a health food restaurant. Now all that was missing was finding the right winemaker. Sylvana didn't have to go too far. Her husband, Kim McPherson, is counted by some as the best winemaker in Texas. When asked, he did what any smart husband does, and said, "Whatever you say, dear."

With the team together, they forged ahead on opening a winery in the old but suddenly trendy Depot District. It opened in 2004 with a splash and has

Lubbock's Kim McPherson is also the winemaker at La Diosa.

stayed busy ever since. Though the menu is more comforting than haute cuisine, La Diosa has the best food in Lubbock. Tapas, panninis and wraps are the main categories, but everything is made with care and the best ingredients. There's interesting music Wednesday through Saturday evenings. Besides tables, there's nice furniture, reading spots, and a burnished glow that just relaxes your senses.

If you get the idea I like this place a lot, you're right.

How about the wines?

Kim McPherson and I were sitting at a table with my wife and a couple of friends. Kim never brags, but he also feels confident in his abilities. Talking to him is like talking to a mature athlete, one who's been around long enough and doesn't feel like he has anything to prove. He's now at the winemaking level where he can focus his wines in any direction he chooses. "I'm big on mouth feel and finish," he tells me. "I don't want to sound sexist, but I'm trying to make wine for women."

What he means is, he's not going for long aging blockbusters; he's going for immediate pleasure, the type of wine a person can enjoy as soon as it's released. The fact that 75 percent of La Diosa's wines are consumed on the premises shows that Kim is doing something right.

The Best Wines

The first thing you should know is that La Diosa has a great selection of Texas wines made by other wineries, so you'll have a wide selection of wines. Their fellow winemakers have to be happy that they are sharing the wealth.

La Diosa is currently making eleven wines, and all have their positive traits. I'll save the stunner for last.

Two reds really stand out. Both are made with High Plains fruit from farmers Kim has known for years. The **Cabernet Sauvignon** needs a little time to open up in the glass, but when it does, you get rich aromas of red berries and black pepper. Their **Syrah** has a luscious mouth feel and a long peppery finish.

For whites, the La Diosa **Viognier** is a no-brainer, a little light compared to the Hill Country bruisers but fragrant and an easy quaffer. Kim once famously said that Chenin Blanc is so tough to sell that you could leave a palette of it on the street corner by the Salvation Army and it would still be there the next day. Well, he may have found the answer in **Sparkling Chenin Blanc,** a classic in the making.

The stunner, by the way, was something I never would have guessed. Turns out the ladies thought it would be a good idea to have a **Sangria**. Kim wasn't thrilled about the idea but decided that if he was going to do it, he was going to do the best he could and try to make it a wine he could be proud of. He has stumbled on a great recipe, with lemon/lime and a flavor just made for a hot Texas evening. Amazing stuff. Don't be snobby and miss it; this is really good wine.

⚭ FOOD

"People in Lubbock don't dine out. They go out to eat." Words from one of the winemakers, who shall remain anonymous to save him from his neighbors.

I understood what he meant. I found some wonderful food. In two cases, the food was beyond wonderful. But don't expect a dining experience.

Luckily, Lubbock has some great places to go out to eat.

The Best

La Diosa, in Lubbock's Depot District. (806) 744-3600. The best food in town. See the chapter on their winery.

Cagle's Steakhouse, West 4th St. at FM 179. (806) 795-3879. Home to one of the four or five best restaurant steaks I've ever had. You can get any kind of steak you want, as long as it's a rib-eye. Your only choices are how thick and how well done. They cook it, weigh it and charge you by the pound. For fish eaters they do a grilled salmon. Service is by well-intentioned students who operate on a different clock than most of us: s-l-o-w. Don't let the Disneyland décor turn you off. The meat makes up for it. So do the prices.

Great Scott's Barbecue, Ranch Road 1585 at US 87, close to both Llano Estacado and Cap*Rock. (806)-745-9353. This will be another constant for me. Nobody recommended it to us; we came upon it accidentally. The Great Scott Burger ($4.50) is a smoked hamburger that is melt-in-your-mouth delicious. The Shawn Special Frito Pie ($5.25) had my wife so happy she could hardly talk. Scott also handmakes yummy sausages. Even if the food were awful, I'd still pay just to sit and listen to Scotty telling tall Texas tales. Don't miss it.

Also Good

Café J, 2605 19th St. Lunch & dinner, closed Monday nights. (806) 743-5400. The nicest place to eat in Lubbock. Attentive service, creative American food and moderate prices help. But the corker is the wine list. Everything is available by the glass. The prices are upper moderate. Try the pistachio crusted pork tenderloin ($15.95). Now, J, how about more Texas wine.

Chez Suzette Fine Dining, 4423 50th St. Lunch Tues.–Fri., dinner Mon.–Sat. (806) 795-6796. www.chezsuzette.com. A popular romantic dining spot serving mostly French but also some Italian food. Prices are upper moderate.

Ugh!

One of the most popular and frequently recommended Mexican food places in Lubbock is **Abuelos Mexican Food Embassy** at 4401 82nd St., (806) 794-1764. The whole experience was awful. Two examples. While we were waiting (for an hour) to get in, I decided to order a Margarita. It had no discernable Tequila. Rather than fix it, the waitperson tried to sell me an extra shot. I asked for the manager, who seemed totally uninterested in me or anything else to do with his job. When we went in, the service was slow and our waitress had the kindness of Ebenezer Scrooge crossed with the social skills of Mariah Carey. Then the food came. Cold, tasteless and made with the same spirit and sentiment we had already seen in the waitress and the manager. The only reason I go through this rant is that if you ask for a Mexican food recommendation in Lubbock, I guarantee you it will be for Abuelos. I wouldn't go.

🏠 SHELTER

Lubbock is stuffed with every chain hotel you can imagine. Large, impersonal and boring. Best of the lot is the **Hawthorne Suites,** 2515 19th Street, (806) 765-8900. It is saved by a delightful heated pool, an excellent free breakfast and spacious rooms with full kitchens. Expect to pay $100–125 a night.

Small, intimate and interesting places are nonexistent, with one exception. The **Woodrow House,** 2629 19th St., (800) 687-5236, is across the street from Texas Tech. David and Dawn Fleming are trying hard to inject some personality in the Lubbock market. Their property is new, but their attitude is definitely B&B-style. Prices run from $85 on up.

☀ FUN

Lubbock has charms besides the wineries and vineyards. Like all good college towns, Lubbock has great music. If you caught the music allusion in the introduction, you probably already know about the incredible music history of Lubbock. Buddy Holly, Waylon Jennings, Mac Davis, Pat Green, Jimmie Dale Gilmore, Joe Ely, Butch Hancock and Kimmie Rhodes all lived in Lubbock. If their names are familiar, you probably will want to go to the **Buddy Holly Center** (19th and Avenue G), a surprisingly nice cultural arts museum that focuses on much more than Buddy Holly.

History of another era comes alive at the **Ranching Heritage Center** (Fourth Street just east of Indiana Avenue, (806) 742-0498). It is a sixteen-acre site with thirty-five real structures from the 1800s, giving you the opportunity to see how you would have liked to live back then.

A more up-to-date experience is the **Omnimax Theater,** 2579 South Loop 289, (806) 745-6299. If you've only experienced IMAX, you're in for a surprise. Omnimax is to IMAX is like a Corvette to an Impala. The theater is attached to a science museum with lots of stuff for kids.

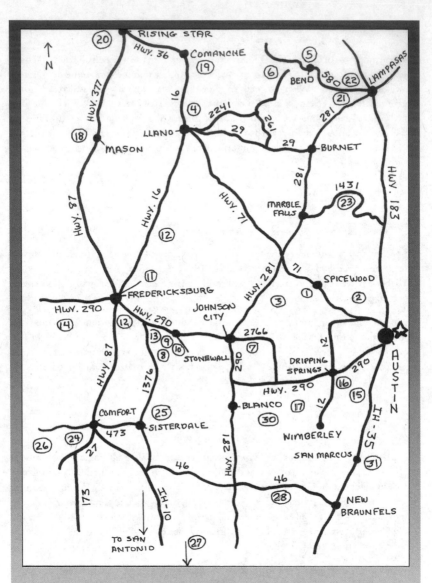

1. Spicewood Vineyards
2. Stone House Vineyard
3. McReynolds Wines
4. Lost Creek Vineyards
5. Alamosa Wine Cellars
6. Fall Creek Vineyards
7. Texas Hills Vineyard
8. Becker Vineyards
9. Torre Di Pietra
10. Woodrose Winery
11. Fredericksburg Winery
12. Bell Mountain Vineyards/Tasting Room
13. Grape Creek Vineyard
14. Chisolm Trail Winery
15. Mandola Estate Winery
16. Driftwood Vineyards
17. Bella Vista Ranch
18. Sandstone Cellars
19. Brennan Vineyards
20. Rising Star Vineyards
21. Pillar Bluff Vineyards
22. Teas Legato Winery
23. Flat Creek Estates
24. Comfort Cellars
25. Sister Creek Vineyards
26. Singing Water Vineyard
27. Poteet Country Winery
28. Dry Comal Creek
29. La Cruz de Comal
30. Fawn Crest Vineyards
31. Three Dudes Vineyard

CHAPTER 3

The Wine Roads of the
Hill Country

T he Texas Hill Country has the largest number of Texas wineries in the smallest amount of space. One-fourth of the state's wineries are in the Hill Country and three of the state's ten viticulture areas are there, as well.

To many Texans, the Hill Country is a version of paradise. The area is beautiful, especially during the spring wildflower season. Three of the prettiest drives in the state are in the Hill Country. The old trees, limestone cliffs and ever-present spring-fed swimming holes endow the area with a relaxing grace that attracts hundreds of thousands of people a year. But for those of us who live here, the pull goes beyond the beauty.

The Texas Hill Country is a melting pot of cultures, all having left their mark. Whether it is Austin's vibrant Mexican community, the Germans in Fredericksburg and Comfort and Walburg, the Poles in Bandera or any of the scattered Moravian, Czech, Scottish or Irish conclaves in the area, the Texas Hill Country is alive with diversity.

It's also the place where hippies and rednecks decided they like the same music, kind of an amalgam of western swing, folk, blues, polka and Tejano. To this day, whether it's the dance hall at Gruene, the stage at Luckenbach, or Poodie's Hilltop in Spicewood, artists like Gary P. Nunn, Jerry Jeff Walker, Asleep at the Wheel, Pat Green and Willie Nelson pack in the locals to dance and drink longnecks.

The Hill Country is also an artist's haven, alive with musicians, writers, painters, photographers and the occasional Hollywood type. The size and influence of the state's universities mean that you are as likely to live next door to a professor as a plumber. With the exception of the Houston area, the Hill Country has the highest concentration of great restaurants in the state.

Once you've seen Czechs teaching cowboys to polka, shared a shade tree with someone from a different culture or seen an old woman and a young man talking about Bach at Barton Springs, you'll understand why those of us who live here love it. But don't expect to come to the Hill Country to soak up the charm in a day or two. Give it time to unfold and you'll love it, too.

For this section, I've separated the wineries into nine tours. The Hill Country is small enough for you to set up your home base anywhere. Austin and

Fredericksburg are the easiest, but Marble Falls or Bandera are also possibilities. The best Austin hotels have astronomical prices, but you can find bargains. For fans of B&B's, Fredericksburg will seem like heaven. If you don't mind moving around, you could stay at Horseshoe Bay Resort for the first two trips, Fredericksburg for trips three to six and somewhere between Austin and New Braunfels for seven to nine. If you want to unload your bags just once and don't mind driving longer distances, Fredericksburg is the best choice. Austin is almost as convenient and has all the amenities of a hopping city. Each of the nine trips is manageable in one day and allows you time for food and a non-wine stop. But get an early start!

TRIP ONE

🍁 Spicewood Vineyards

1419 Burnet County Road 409, Spicewood, TX 78669. Wed.–Sat. 10 am–5 pm, Sun. noon–5 pm. (830) 693-5328, www.spicewoodvineyards.com

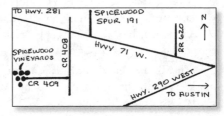

I hope that anyone interested in creating a winery will read this chapter carefully. Ed and Madeline Manigold own Spicewood Vineyards—as I write this. They are both unusually thoughtful and bright. Both had Ph.D.s and were in highly responsible positions in education. But Ed and Madeline wanted to retire from their education jobs and look at a second career. One night in 1987, while having a glass of wine at Louie's on the Lake in Austin, they decided to be winemakers.

Neither had any training in winemaking, but after twenty-one years of education between them the last thing they wanted was to pursue still another degree. They took a few hands-on classes from the University of California at Davis but found the Californians didn't understand Texas weather. They tried to get help through the County Extension Agency but got more help on cattle and sheep than Vinifera. Finally they tried the program at Grayson County College and found out that a lot of other winery owners would lend a hand. By 1990 they had the beginnings of their winery.

They started with just 1.5 acres and eventually decided to expand their vineyard to 17. After being bonded in 1995, they began marketing Spicewood Vineyards wine. That developed some acclaim almost immediately. They started winning medals in competitions and soon were making enough money to hire some help. Everything looked rosy.

Ed and Madeline
Manigold taking
a rare break from
winemaking.

That's when the winery's responsibilities overtook their desire to travel, and the daily travails of owning a business began to eat away at the dream they had started with. They had a lot to be proud of, but one day they woke up and, as Madeline says, "We've achieved our dreams. We made award-winning wine on our own estate and built a solid reputation for good wine. But it's not all easy. The problem with being an estate winery is you have to be able to ride out the bad years."

A patch of bad years that came in the early part of the millennium was financially tough on everyone in the Hill Country.

It's evident that they are still getting used to the idea of selling Spicewood Vineyards. They trip over each other to make sure I understand what a bittersweet decision this is. This winery has been a big part of their identity and has taken twenty years of their lives. Like an embattled CEO retiring from his company while it's on an upturn, you can see the emotion in their eyes when they look at one another and talk about selling. It's like they are still trying to convince each other it's the right thing to do. Then they both face forward, strengthened, and look like great quarterbacks retiring after a Super Bowl.

I use that Super Bowl simile on purpose, because Ed is making the best wines of his life. He's going out on a bang, but I am going to miss his further development as a winemaker. "Our wines are getting better because we've focused on water management," Ed says. "When we learned viticulture, it was about getting the vines up and healthy. Water management, almost on a vine by vine basis, has really increased the quality of our wines."

Madeline adds, "Our early training was to keep the pH really low, and in the Hill Country, you can't get really ripe fruit with really low pH's." Ed agrees: "Sugar, pH and TA were supposed to be perfect, and if you had to pick one, pick pH. But if you handle everything right, you only have a three- to five-day window of opportunity for picking, and your pickers may be in Missouri by then."

What about machine harvesting? "Machine harvest is an alternative," Ed says. "But when you do it, you have to check the clusters, and if you get a bad cluster at the bottom it can ruin your whole crop. So we've stuck with picking by hand."

I can feel they are getting themselves convinced again, but when I tell Ed he's making the best wines of his career they turn pensive. Then Ed's resolve strengthens again. "I'd do it over again in a minute," he says. "But I wouldn't have grown it to the point where it was so big. The model we've been drug into in Texas is you have to make 3,000 cases or you can't make it. Our decision is whether to take it to the next level, 20,000 cases, and if I was ten years younger, fine, but I'm 70 now and it's just time to retire."

Madeline squeezes his hand, looks at him lovingly. She looks over to me and says, "Our goal is to travel and spend more time with family and friends."

The lesson I hope prospective winemakers come away with is that it is easy to get swept away in a whirlwind. You start with a dream, then you either go belly up, tread water or get successful. If you make it to the success stage and win a few awards, you'll see the demand for your wine going up. Unfortunately, there is a great range of sizes that are just not financially feasible. Three thousand cases or less, selling everything from the tasting room, and you can have a nice little money-making hobby. Then Ed is right you are in limbo until you get over 20,000 cases.

Jumping from 3,000 cases to 20,000 is a big step. You have to have mighty deep pockets because you'll have to use a distributor, which means that a wine that today is paying you a profit margin of $4 a bottle in the tasting room tomorrow will only be breaking even. Once you get to 20,000 cases, you might find that you're earning less than you were when you were making 3,000 and selling it all through your tasting room. Then you wake up one day and find the winery owns you instead of vice versa.

Ed and Madeline did everything right. They are good, decent people, widely respected, always willing to help out a charity. Ed's wines started good and progressed to the point where they could compete in the nationwide marketplace. They were frugal but never stingy when it came to putting money back into the business. Sadly, the winery wasn't allowing them to have a personal life.

As I write this book, Spicewood Vineyards on the market. Whoever buys it will have a beautiful place with an established reputation. As for Ed and Madeline, I wish them the best. I'll miss them a lot.

The Best Wines

Ed and Madeline make their wines solely from grapes grown at Spicewood Vineyards. Once crushed, most of their wines are stored in French oak—young barrels if they want a stronger oak aroma, older barrels if they don't. Though they make a number of very good red wines, their real strength is in the whites. Their **Chardonnay** is 100 percent barrel fermented and aged for at least six months.

The wine has a nice mouth feel, good acids and delicious flavors. Their **Semillon Reserve** comes from a very small patch of grapes. Just a hint of oak adds complexity. This is spectacular wine.

The real star at Spicewood Vineyards is the **Sauvignon Blanc.** Where New Zealand versions can taste like grapefruit juice, and California versions like pineapple juice, Spicewood's tastes closest to the gold standard—Sancerre. It's varietally correct. You will get hints of those tropical fruits; you just won't get sledge-hammered. This is one of the great wines of Texas. I hope the new owners can keep it up.

🍁 Stone House Vineyard

24350 Haynie Flat Rd., Spicewood, TX 78669.
Fri.–Sun., noon–5 pm and by appointment.
(512) 264-3630,
www.stonehousevineyard.com

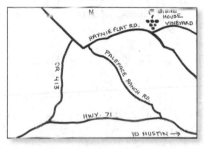

Angela and Howard Moench wanted some land on Lake Travis. They were simply scouting for a nice place to build a second home. Neither had any idea of planting a vineyard, but in hindsight it was a predestined path.

Angela and I are standing in her tasting room. It's a gorgeous day outside, cool and clear. A few folks are sitting outside on the patio, enjoying a glass of wine and looking over the vineyard. Angela is, as always, gracious, forthright and just slightly formal. I ask about how she found herself an owner of an award-winning winery.

"I come from the Barossa Valley," she said of the home to some of Australia's greatest red wines, "and my family has vineyards there. I've always had a huge interest in gardening. When I was a child and other children wanted toys, I wanted garden tools." Her love of playing in the dirt took a giant step sideways when her father was asked to be the Australian High Commissioner to the Court of St. James. She had lots of formal meals, and, in the European tradition, they always served wine.

Living the life of a diplomat can be exciting and prestigious, but it had one downside for Angela. "When I was growing up, I never cooked. We always had staff that did all the food preparation. So at twenty, I couldn't even scramble an egg." Her mother decided Angela needed to have a grasp on the art of the kitchen and sent her to the Cordon Bleu Cooking School in London. It opened

Australian-born Angela Moench with a bottle of Claros, one of her finest wines.

a completely new world for her. "Suddenly I was able to produce these wonderful foods. Then I started to really understand the importance of wine with meals, and it became a central part of my life."

Angela married Howard Moench, a radiation oncologist, and settled in to a comfortable life in the River Oaks area of Houston. She again had a place to do a little gardening and helped design a few showpieces in the River Oaks Garden Club's garden. She created a foundation to set up traveling art exhibitions from the United States to Australia.

Her name gets attention in Australia, not only for her own valuable work but also because of her family. Her brother is Alexander Downer, MP, the Australian Minister for Foreign Affairs, the equivalent of our Secretary of State. Her father was Sir Alec Downer, High Commissioner to London. Her grandfather, John Downer, was the premier of South Australia.

When she and Howard bought the land in Spicewood, they started thinking about how much they enjoyed food and wine and decided to join the evolving world of Texas wine. That way Angela could be a second-generation vigneron. There was a side benefit, she explains: "Howard is a frustrated architect, so it's been wonderful for him to be able to design the winery."

They decided to focus on Norton grapes, a varietal notorious for off-putting aromas in the hands of normal winemakers. Angela and her consulting winemakers have figured out the key to making great wine from Norton: grow great Norton grapes. I don't mean to sound glib, but Angela is careful and very protective of her grapes. Even her husband is not permitted to work in the vineyard. "Howard is allowed to walk in the vineyard and admire my work," she says, with just the hint of a smile. She's not joking.

I ask her if she would do it all again. This is the most animated she's been during our time together.

"Definitely, absolutely, with no question. The whole thing is such an adventure. I love it. I wish I had planted even more in the beginning. I don't know anything about marketing, but I do know you have to love what you are doing and do the best you can do. Then the wines sell themselves." She pauses, and you can see some of the grit that allows her to spend time in the hot Texas sun doing stoop labor, all for the love of the wine. "I am determined to do better every year."

I bet she will.

The Best Wines

Angela produces two types of wine from her Norton grapes. I first learned about **Stone House Claros,** her dry Norton, when I got a couple of breathless phone calls from sommeliers and restaurateurs asking if I had tried the wine. What has them so excited is the divine juxtaposition of Burgundy-style acidity and Sonoma Zinfandel-style richness. Wrap in a little bit of the interesting and idiosyncratic Norton flavor and you get a very nice drink.

Stone House Screaming Beagle is the Port-styled Norton. Many winemaking sins can be and are covered with sugar, especially with non-vinifera grapes. Not here. This wine has a density and richness that make it more like an Australian Shiraz Port from McLaren Vale. By the way, the EU has stepped in to protect the name "Port," so expect to find new names for these sweet fortified wines.

Stone House is also, not surprisingly, an importer of Australian wines. Though the focus of this book is Texas wines, Angela's are made to her specification and, after all, she does have some history in Australia. The less expensive line is called **Lyre.** All are worthy wines. Step up to the Stone House Special Reserve series and you are in a different world. **Stone House Special Reserve Cabernet** is big-boned enough to drown out the flavors of the Shiraz, and that's nothing short of miraculous.

The last wine Angela poured for me made me go weak in the knees. Simply called **XO,** it is the essence of a solera wine, like Madeira or Sherry. Syrupy in texture, with honey and floral aromas, it has a mouth-coating sweetness and just enough acidity to keep it from being cloying. Even at its elevated price—around $60 for a .500 liter bottle—it's a bargain.

McReynolds Wines

706 Shovel Mountain Rd., Round Mountain,
TX 78663. Usually Fri. and Sat. 10 am–6 pm,
Sun. noon–6 pm and by appointment.
(830) 825-3544, www.mcreynoldswines.com

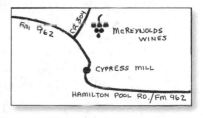

All I knew about Mac and Maureen McReynolds was that they had made a delicious Shiraz from grapes they got from the University of Texas and that Mac had fallen off a pickup truck and been hurt badly. My interview time with them was so fascinating that I encourage you to go and meet them. Their story is incredible.

Mac and Maureen met at the University of Chicago in the early 1960s. She was pursuing a Ph.D. in biochemical genetics and he was a Ph.D. student in

Maureen and Mac McReynolds in his new Kawasaki Mule.

geology and working in the university's Institute for Computer Research. After she graduated, they moved to Austin so that Maureen could do postdoctoral research at UT. Mac helped Tracor develop instrumentation troubleshooting methodologies. When Maureen's major professor died, she became a research assistant at Stanford with Dr. Paul Ehrlich, author of *The Population Bomb*. That was when she and Mac fell in love with wine.

"There were a lot of vineyards in the area," Maureen said. "We made friends with the folks that worked at Mirassou and started working in their tasting room. They asked me if I knew anything about wine chemistry. I didn't know wine chemistry, but I knew chemistry. So I started working for them on Saturdays and Sundays doing their lab analysis." She loved it.

In the meantime, Mac started helping out at Ridge Vineyards, where his penchant for creative solutions to mechanical and engineering problems was needed. While there he developed a system to hold the cap below the surface of the wine, making wines richer and darker. At the same time, Maureen was getting so enthused about wine that she thought about it as a career. When her position at Stanford ran out of funding in 1971, she went to Charles Krug Winery and asked for the job of winemaker. "The owner rudely assured me that no woman would ever be able to do the job," she remembered, still obviously frustrated. Shortly thereafter Robert Mondavi proved the owner of Charles Krug wrong when he hired Zelma Long. Interestingly, the owner of Charles Krug was Robert Mondavi's brother, Peter.

Maureen was offered a job with the City of Austin in their environmental office. She and Mac liked Texas and decided to come back. Mac used his skill with airplanes to run the airport in Smithville. In 1982 he met a local entrepreneur who was interested in making wine on some land west of Austin. Based on a handshake, Mac entered into a partnership.

Working whenever he could find some spare time, he built the building, put in all the equipment and devised the cooling systems. He had 7,000 gallons in juice and $12,000 in bills. That was when his partner called and said he was not going to go through with the project. Even though it is years later when he tells me the story, Mac gets a tear in his eye. "I now know what a woman with a stillborn child feels like."

But justice triumphed. When his partner went bankrupt, Mac and Maureen bought the property on the courthouse steps. It was the fall of 1989. By the next spring, their life would be forever changed.

They were on a trip to Australia. Friends there knew Mac was interested in wine, so they took him with several others on a vineyard tour. Mac was sitting in the back of the pickup when they hit a bump. He was thrown out of the truck; he landed on his head and was knocked unconscious. He spent the next six years going through therapy. By 1995 he was in good health again, though his memory was somewhat hampered. He decided, for a second time, to pursue the wine business.

Then lightning struck again. Maureen was ready to retire from working for the City of Austin. She was driving home and didn't notice a stop sign. When she ran through it, she was hit broadside. Maureen spent five months in the hospital recovering.

In the meantime, they'd had calamities in the vineyard. Mac planted good rootstock, intending to graft. But the summer was extremely hot, and they lost a lot of their vines. Then their well gave out. They planted again and again for the next three years. Finally, everything was working and they looked forward to their first big homegrown vintage. But a plague of birds and raccoons ate all the grapes. Since then, they've been mostly buying grapes.

They are proudest of having been able to survive and adapt. I think they should be proudest that they are still smiling and looking forward to a new future. Mac is proud of his new Kawasaki Mule and wanted me to take his picture in it. After all they've lived through, they still focus on the little things. "At night when we lay in bed and listen to the critters singing and see the moon come up"—Mac hesitates, then smiles. "It's a very pleasant life."

The Best Wines

On average, the McReynoldses make about 2,000 cases of wine per year. They make a number of one-off wines, which suits Mac's personality—curious, inquisitive and restless. One wine to watch out for is the **2006 Chardonnay.** Mac sourced the grapes from a vineyard that had been hit hard by weather, so the yields were just 200 pounds per acre from vines that generally produce over 6,000 pounds per acre. It is an intense wine with substantial body and just a hint short of the right amount of acid.

Also, be on the lookout for any **Syrah** that Mac makes. He once made a Syrah from grapes at the UT Experimental Vineyard that was world-class.

TRIP TWO

🍁 Lost Creek Vineyard

1129 Ranch Road 2233, Sunrise Beach, TX 78643. Mon.–Sat. 10 am–5 pm, Sun. noon–5 pm. (325) 388-3753, www.lostcreekvineyard.com

An elegant white swan glides on the pond next to the winery. Twenty yards away, a romantic couple shares a bottle of wine under a shade tree. Walk through the front door, turn right, and there's a stunning hand-carved bar, about fifteen feet across. It's a relic, built in the 1880s by the Brunswick-Balke-Collender Company, better known for its billiard tables. In 1884 the company

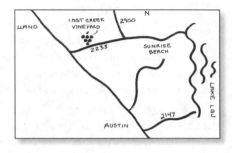

started a lucrative side business, making outsized flamboyant neoclassical style bars for prosperous saloons. These bars sold for a mere $298, the equivalent of just under $5,000 today. Of course, today we'd never find the craftsmen. So take a minute and enjoy the elegant workmanship.

The owner of Lost Creek Vineyard is David Brinkman. David grew up in the military, living all over the place. He started a security company and built it into a profitable business, then sold it. (Don't confuse it with Brinks Home Security; David's operation was strictly Central Texas.)

David's interest in wine came about slowly. "I drank Michelob and Coors most of my life," he says. "My first wine was a box of Zinfandel that lasted me a month." When he finally developed an interest in wine, he decided to try his hand at making it. He spent twenty years making wines in car-boys, the small plastic containers used primarily by home winemakers. Friends said the wine was good and encouraged him to make it commercially.

"It became a passion for me," he says. "I wanted to be a little old winemaker. When I sold my company, I had to have something to do. I can't just sit still. I have to be doing something." That "something" turned into Lost Creek Vineyard.

Lost Creek's David Brinkman at his 1880s tasting bar.

David now has a three-acre vineyard with Cabernet and Shiraz. He buys grapes from around the state to build his annual production to 3,000 cases. Working with the red wines is where his passion lies. "It's probably because they are so work-intensive and more difficult to work with than the whites," he explains.

He's doing something right. His Shiraz took Texas Champion and then placed second to a Penfold's in an international tasting. But it hasn't been easy. He's had to buy things little by little, financing on a shoestring. When I ask if he would do it all over again, he hesitates before saying yes. Just for a second his face is a jumble of contradicting emotions. David pulls himself out of it and smiles.

I change the subject and ask about the future. David brightens up. "Right now, we sell almost 100 percent of our wine here at the winery. My long-term goal is to keep it just like it is, but I'm looking at adding a weekend restaurant and event center."

He just can't sit still.

The Best Wines

The Lost Creek Shiraz sells out so fast I've never even tasted it. I think David's best wines are his red wines. **Buddy's Blend** is a combo of Shriaz, Cabernet Sauvignon and Merlot. It's named for David's dog, and a portion of the proceeds go to the Hill Country SPCA. For a dog lover, that's probably enough. Anyone who'll put a canine family friend on their label is all right in my book. Luckily, the wine is good, too, with smoky spicy aromas and nice long finish. His best wine is his **Merlot**, a rich, dense, deeply colored version with crème brulee aromas and an unusual amount of tannic grip.

🍂 *Alamosa Wine Cellars*

677 County Road 430, Bend, TX 76824.
Fri. and Sat. 10 am–5 pm, Sun. noon–5
pm, during the week by appointment.
(325) 628-3313,
www.alamosawinecellars.com

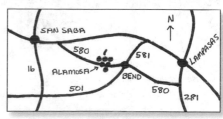

In 1989, at age forty-two, Jim Johnson took a big chance and left his career in purchasing to pursue a dream: enrolling in the wine program at the University of California at Davis. Two years later, he graduated with honors in fermentation sciences. He interned at both Iron Horse and St. Francis, then went to work with Heitz Cellars. He could have stayed and worked at some of California's best wineries, but he had too much Texas dirt in his boots to stay away from his home state.

So in 1993, Jim returned to Texas. He became the winemaker at Slaughter-Leftwich, where he learned how different Texas fruit is from California fruit. The winery started having financial problems, so Jim jumped to Becker Vineyards while searching for some of his own ideal vineyard land. He found it near Bend, Texas, on a 41-acre plot. He planted his 10-acre vineyard in 1996 while still working for other wineries. He was going to call the business Cottonwood Cellars, but that name was already taken in Colorado, so he gave it the same name in Spanish: Alamosa, which translates as "big cottonwood."

When Jim planted, he decided to avoid the more popular French grapes, like Cabernet Sauvignon and Pinot Noir. Instead he went straight for the grapes that thrive in dry, hot weather: grapes from the Rhone, Spain and Italy. "Everyone told me that there wasn't any demand for grapes you couldn't pronounce," he says. Jim bulled his way ahead anyway. Now he's considered one of the pioneers in what he calls "climate-adapted varietals."

Jim Johnson relaxes with a glass of Alamosa's Jacques Lapin.

A perfect example of a climate-adapted varietal is Tempranillo, a Spanish grape that loves hot weather. "We are the first and so far only Texas producer of Tempranillo," Jim says. "I figured Texas looks like Spain, so it should work." Most wine industry people didn't think Americans would buy the Spanish version, let alone a Texas version. So Jim had a bright idea. He didn't call it Tempranillo, he comically called it "El Guapo."

Comically because El Guapo, which translated means a lady's man, has a label with a picture of an ugly toad. Jim just thought it was hilarious. It turned out that TCU alumni loved the image, which reminded them of their beloved mascot, the Horny Toad. TCU alums tried to buy his entire stock! Now it's all Jim can do to save some of it for us wine-lovers. El Guapo is delicious proof that Alamosa's devotion to hot weather grapes was right.

Jim's wants to establish a tradition of wines that reflect Texas. You could call it the pride of a native, but I think it goes further. He hates anonymous wines. "Kendall Jackson, for example, makes decent wines," he explains. "But, to me, they lack a sense of place. When you taste my wine, I want you to know it's from Texas."

One way he achieves the flavors and aromas he wants is by using pre-fermentation blending. Most winemakers ferment their juices and then blend them until they get tastes and aromas they like. Not Jim. He decided on his blends when he ordered the grapevines from the nurseries. "I saw a piece of research at Davis where they compared lots blended pre- and post-fermentation. Folks always preferred the field blend because of the added complexity and synergy." This brings some degree of risk, but he believes the added character is worth it. "There is only one 100 percent varietal wine at Alamosa: Viognier. Every other wine we make has something added." Jim believes that this increases complexity, fills in holes and makes the wines more interesting.

Jim is getting a little philosophical as he's watched the Texas wine industry grow. "I think we validated the concept of warm climate varietals," he says. "I'm proudest of opening everyone's eyes to Tempranillo. And we weren't the first to plant Sangiovese, but we were the first to bottle one [1998]." He also is proud of the direction the Texas wine industry is going and the high-quality wines that are being made in a number of places around the state. He especially singles out Kim McPherson as a masterful winemaker.

They've been open for ten years now, a good point for pondering past successes. In the beginning money was tight, and the years have been tough on their vineyard, with a daunting fight against late freezes and Pierce's disease. But Jim and Karen are survivors. The new tasting room is a booming enterprise and the business is flourishing. Karen says, "We stuck our neck out and took a chance. Now we've built something we're proud of, and we did it from scratch."

The Best Wines

Jim makes some great red wines, but I always gravitate to his whites. I almost hate to tell you about his **Orange Muscat** because that means one less bottle for me. Jim has managed to take this fragrant grape and make room-filling aromas and smooth, delicious, luxurious wine, even though the wine is not very sweet (2 percent) and has an enormous alcohol kick (15.2 percent is the label claim, but it may be a tad higher). If you know the wines of Beaumes de Venis, you'll get this.

Alamosa's first wine to achieve some fame was the **Viognier**. Today, Jim makes two versions, one from his own Tio Pancho Ranch and the other from High Plains fruit. If you favor the Rolling Stones, the High Plains version is for you. Prefer the Beatles? Go for the Tio Pancho.

The final white wine I want to bring to your attention is Jim's flight of fancy called **Jacques Lapin**. It is a Chenin Blanc from Andy Martin's vineyard close to Lubbock. Chenin Blanc is a tough grape to make into a great wine. Fall Creek has done a great job, as has Pheasant Ridge. But Jim's wine is a different animal, closer in character to a dense, rich Vouvray. It's quite special and definitely worth your attention.

Fall Creek Vineyards

1820 County Road 222, Tow, TX 78672.
Mon.–Fri. 11 am–4 pm, Sat. 11 am–5 pm,
Sun. noon–4 pm. (325) 379-5361,
www.fcv.com

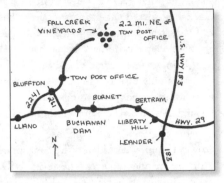

We were at a small gathering. Sitting across from me was Denman Moody, ace wine critic and owner of one of the best wine tip sheets in America (www.moodysweeklywinereview.com). The rest of the gathering included Denman's wife, Mary Jo; Ed and Susan Auler, owners of Fall Creek Vineyards; and my wife, Emily. Ed was having fun pulling bottles of wine, putting them in brown bags, then making Denman and me guess what they were.

Now this is a tough test for anyone. I once had a double-blind tasting at another winery that included a panel discussion. A Texas winemaker (the name withheld to protect the guilty) ridiculed one of the wines as being defective, saying it never should have been bottled. You guessed, he was tasting his own wine. I tell you that story so you understand how hard it is to get a correct guess at this blind tasting stuff.

One of the wines Ed poured was a beautiful red. It was obviously old enough to knit all the details together perfectly. I immediately tasted something in it that reminded me of a Bordeaux. The quality was so intense I knew it had to be an '82. Boldly, I proclaimed it to be a 1982 Bordeaux. I was feeling pretty proud. Denman said, without a trace of hesitation, "It is 1982 Palmer." Pretty bold statement. Ed unveiled the wine . . . a 1982 Palmer. Wow. Now that was impressive.

I tell you that story so that you know Denman and I are at least somewhat adept at recognizing our wines.

Ed poured a white wine. I looked at it and tasted it. There was that hint of a slightly toasty and nutty aroma, bracing acidity on the palate and that finish you can only get from a Burgundy. "Mid-1990s Corton Charlemagne," I proclaimed. Denman said, "1996 Coche-Dury Corton Charlemagne." Was this guy on fire or what? The last bottle I saw of that wine was at an auction where the opening bid was $1,700!

Ed Auler is normally taciturn and prone to understatement, but a grin formed from ear to ear. He showed us the bottle. It was a Fall Creek Reserve Chardonnay. Denman and I were stunned. A Texas wine performing to Burgundy standards. What's next? Cats and dogs sleeping together?

Ed wasn't surprised. He believes Fall Creek makes world-class wines, and further, that Texas can make wines as great as any. But one thing bothers him. "Texas faces both an opportunity and a threat from the consolidation of the retail business in Texas. There's going to be an industry here even if they give us a cold shoulder, but if they get behind us, we could grow quite a bit. But if we don't get more wineries interested in getting in the stores, wine will stay a cottage industry in Texas."

Ed has put a lot of thought into the whole issue of Texas wine's future. With the third-largest winery in the state, the outlook matters. "The real challenge is to push market acceptance a lot further than we've got. We ought to be able to go into any retailer or restaurant and see Texas wines. That's not gonna come from wineries pushing their tasting rooms. The tasting room is just the tail on the dog. It's a nice tail, but it's still the tail."

I switched the subject to the history of Fall Creek. "We put in the vineyard in 1975," he says. "By 1982, we decided to expand the vineyards and do a winery. We were winning a lot of competitions and they helped convince people that we were serious and could stand on the same plane with the big boys." Ed was lucky that Fall Creek wines came along at the same time that southwestern cooking was becoming popular. Stephen Pyles (Routh Street Café in Dallas) and Robert Del Grande (Café Annie in Houston) started featuring Texas wines. The future looked bright.

Then, in December 1991, the temperature in the vineyard dropped to 12 degrees below zero. They lost most of their vines. That was good, in a way, because it forced them to find other sources for grapes. They replanted, but by 2001, Pierce's disease had devastated the vineyard. "We had a healthy vine next to a partly sick vine next to real sick vines next to dead vines. It just couldn't work. So we pulled everything up and are drawing most of our fruit from other Texas vineyards." Now they buy all of their grapes, some of them from other states, when necessary.

Fall Creek's Ed, Susan and Chad Auler, from left, have had a great impact on Texas wines.

This happens to all the largest wineries. Texas grape growers still haven't caught up with the demand of Texas winemakers. The big winemakers–Ste. Genevieve, Llano Estacado, Fall Creek, Messina Hof, Becker–have all fought hard for their places on wine shop and grocery store shelves. One bad year in the Texas vineyard, like 2006, and any winemaker dedicated to making wine solely from Texas grapes might have to tell the retailers they are out of wine. Then the shelf space goes to a mega-corp wine from California.

As you can tell, the wine retail business is a tough, time-consuming business. Ed is happy that his son Chad will be gradually taking the reins of Fall Creek. Chad's already showing the Auler genetics, starting right off by creating a new wine called Caché. It's a wine aimed at the Conundrum lovers. "I told my dad that we have all these white varietals left over after bottling—why don't we make a blend?" Caché has gone on to be one of their top sellers.

Susan is proud of her husband and son and happy to let the men do most of the talking about the winery. But she's a fascinating person, worth several chapters of her own. With her cheerleader good looks and gracious demeanor, she often surprises people when they realize she's also one of the formidable powers in Texas wine. When Susan decides something will happen, it does. If you like the TV show based on this book, send Susan a thank-you note. It was frozen in funding limbo when she decided to make it happen. Six weeks later, it was funded.

The bottom line is the Aulers have had a dramatic impact on the last thirty years of Texas wine, one they are planning to continue. Ed once told me: "Life is a journey, not a destination. If you had asked me in 1985 if I would be happy when I got to this level, I would have said yes. I think we've been instrumental in getting a new industry here in the state. We've been able to do some things that people didn't think we could do. I want Fall Creek to get to the point where it is known as a national wine. I want to take this business to a different level."

The Best Wines

I asked Ed to describe his wines. "European tradition with California technology adapted to Texas conditions" is what he said. Succinct, and a great goal. The European and Texas part are simple to understand, but what about the California reference?

Ed was referring to the famous Andre Tchelistcheff, enologist at Beaulieu Vineyards from 1938 to 1973. "He was such a great guy," Ed said. "Virtually all the white wines we made were great, but our reds weren't doing so good. We let Andre taste the fruit from the first vintage. He told us to keep going and that he tasted hints of real quality. Andre was extremely helpful to me because he was encouraging and he taught me things about red wines no one else knew."

Fall Creek makes a lot of very good wine. Their portfolio is diverse enough that almost anyone could find a Fall Creek wine they like. But I have a few long-term favorites. Their **Granite Reserve** is one of Texas's great bargain wines, a red with depth and character, and it's under $10. Their **Chenin Blanc** is cold fermented and has a little bit of sugar left in to balance the acidity. This is the wine to choose with spicy Asian food. Of course, I've already discussed their **Reserve Chardonnay**, aimed at a Burgundy style by going for nuance over force. Then the wine goes into French oak, with French yeasts. It's long lived and quite a bottle of wine. Finally, try to get a taste of their **Meritus**, Ed's take on the classic Meritage concept of Bordeaux grapes grown outside of Bordeaux.

TRIP THREE

Texas Hills Vineyard

Ranch Road 2766, one mile east of US 290, Johnson City, TX 78636. Mon.–Sat. 10 am–5 pm, Sun. noon–5 pm. (830) 868-2321, www.texashillsvineyard.com

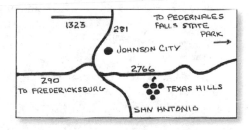

"I haven't had a day off in the last 120 days, and I'm still loving every minute of it," says winery owner Gary Gilstrap. He and I are sitting in front of their beautiful Tuscan-styled winery and tasting room. It's a nice fall day, dogs are lying around us and kids are playing on the lawn. He looks placidly content. I ask Gary to do a little reflecting on what he's learned.

"First, I'm so excited that we are getting some more wineries around," he tells me. "We're becoming a real wine trail." Then he looks me in the eye. He's got a kind demeanor, but he tends to look at you while he's thinking. It's a bit distracting until you understand what's going on. The wheels are turning. He looks down into his wine glass, then looks back up.

"We've really seen a huge shift over the last three years. I think Texans are finally getting to the point where they really want to buy Texas wines."

Part of the reason is the adoption of the blind-tasting strategy at a lot of wineries. That takes the bias—"prophets without honor in their own land"—out of the tasting. Gary has a favorite: "I do blind tastings all the time and match our

Winemaker Gary Gilstrap trained as a pharmacist.

wines up against the best, things like Santa Margherita Pinot Grigio versus our Texas Hill Country Pinot Grigio, or our Newsome Vineyard Kick Butt Cab against Silver Oak." He shoots a little understatement my way. "We do pretty good."

Texas Hills is an interesting experiment because it is owned by two scientists. Both Gary and his wife, Kathy, are pharmacists by trade. In the early 1970s, Gary got interested in personal computers and how they might help him keep track of inventory and customers for his pharmacy. He ended up writing software for a field that desperately needed it. IBM liked it enough to start sending Gary all over the world to demonstrate it. Then, in the early 80s, he married Kathy. They sold the pharmacy and entered a new phase of life.

But Gary had to spend so much time on planes that they decided to move closer to an airline hub. Chicago, Dallas or Atlanta? They chose Dallas. After the kids graduated from college, they started thinking about doing something else. Why not wine?

"It's all Gary's fault," Kathy says. "We loved the whole wine culture in Europe," Gary adds. "We thought it would be a very nice way to spend the rest of our lives. It really uses all of our talents. We used to fly into Paris and, after a few days, take the train to Florence. We noticed that the wines were okay and the food was okay, but when we combined the two, it was magic. We decided we wanted to live that life." That was 1993. They immediately started looking for land.

"We looked at several sites," Gary said. "This was the first. We sent out soil samples and they came back exactly like Tuscany." Gary and Kathy decided they wanted the property, made an offer and found out it had already sold. Both were heartbroken. Two months later, they got a call from the broker asking if they were still interested. Gary dropped everything and got in his car; four hours later, he dropped off the deposit check. They bought the land in 1994 and planted on April 15, 1995. From concept to completion, less than two years.

"Gary never dallies," notes Kathy.

Over the last decade, Gary, Kathy and Dale Rassett–Kathy's son–have taken the dream to the point that they are actually making money and getting occasional time off for a trip. And they've learned a lot about making wine. "If I knew then what I know now, I build a bigger winery. We don't want to be huge, but I'd like to be selling 10,000 cases someday. Mainly, I always want to be known as a classy winemaker. I guess 'boutique-y' would be the word."

Soil samples from Texas Hills Vineyard tested the same as soil in Tuscany.

As befits a person trained in chemistry, Gary is not one of those winemakers who believes you shouldn't touch the grapes once they've been pressed. He sees the role of winemaker as an activist. "We respect tradition, but we're more interested in figuring what really works." He does ion exchange to control pH and micro-oxygenation to smooth out any bitter phenolics. Gary is also partial to oak tea bags as opposed to oak barrels. "You can control it much better that way," he says.

Through ups and downs, all of them still love what they're doing. "We're always a day late and a dollar short," Kathy says. "But I love the wine business. When people came into the pharmacy, they didn't want to be there. They were sick and hearing about medicines and side effects. Here, people come to have fun."

Gary agrees. "I've never had this much fun."

The Best Wines

"Wines in the style of Italy" is how the Gilstraps describe Texas Hills Vineyard. After a few joyous trips to Italy, they noticed that the wine and food had a symbiotic relationship: both improved the other. Their goal is to make wine that lights the palate when served with a meal. Gary is proud of one thing above all else: "I feel most gratified by the fact that we don't have a bad wine."

"Bold statement," I say.

"Now don't get me wrong," he says. "I'm not saying everything is perfect, because not everything is perfect. But we don't make a bad wine."

I do have a few favorites. Year after year I've loved their **Due Bianco,** a blend of Pinot Grigio and Chardonnay. It's never over the top but always has a subtle hint of green and tropical fruits, kind of like smelling a thin slice of pineapple with a ball of honeydew resting in the middle from about six inches away. My two other favorites are from Neal Newsom's vineyard. That **Cabernet Sauvignon** is dark, intense and long lasting. And just like everyone else using Newsom fruit for an **Orange Muscat,** Texas Hills hit a home run. It's a little sweet (usually less than 5 percent sugar), soft and rich on the palate, and dizzyingly aromatic. It also packs a punch at over 13 percent alcohol, so watch out!

🍂 Becker Vineyards

Off Jenschke Lane, Stonewall, TX
78671. Mon.–Sat. 10 am–5 pm,
Sun. noon–5 pm. (830) 644-2681,
www.beckervineyards.com

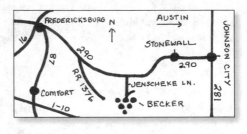

Richard and Bunny Becker were looking for a little house in the country to store some antiques. Nothing fancy, nothing big. Just a little house on an acre or so. What they found was a pretty little house on 180 acres. But it caught their fancy, so they bought it. Richard's days were spent practicing medicine (endocrinology) in San Antonio, but he loved gardening, traveling, eating great food and drinking wonderful wines. Plus, he had had a little experience making some of his own wines. What could be better than planting a little French Vitis Vinifera and trying his hand at making some wine?

Bunny pushed for a slow start, maybe an acre. Richard decided to plant thirteen acres. He asked for some help about what to plant, where he might sell his crop. Folks told him that no one could grow good-quality French grapes in Texas. But one person gave him a piece of advice that he thought was more powerful than the pessimist's message.

"I was talking to Robert Mondavi and he told me that I shouldn't let anyone dissuade me just because I was at the wrong latitude to make world-class wines. He advised me to never cut corners and always make the best wine I can. And that's advice we've always followed."

Luck was on their side in a couple of areas. When they tested the soil, they found that they had a nice mixture of sand and granite that provided great drainage

Bunny and Richard Becker with Jesse Mendoza, their manager at the Ballinger Vineyard.

Becker Vineyards
is headquartered
in the remake of a
nineteenth-century
stone barn.

and pH levels. They also found a good source of limestone-filtered water, perfect for drip irrigation, about three hundred feet below their land. Next up was the decision of what to plant.

Dr. Becker doesn't mince words about why he has stuck with classic French grapes. "All the others are inferior! They don't taste good in their native land and they won't taste good in Texas."

Now they grow sixteen different varietals, including Viognier, Grenache, Mouvedre, Syrah, Chardonnay, Sauvignon Blanc, Malbec, Petite Verdot, Cabernet Sauvignon, Cabernet Franc and Merlot. Again, the skeptics told him to avoid most of the grapes. "If no one can pronounce it, no one will buy it," they said.

Texas winemaking is full of mavericks who do it their own way, come hell or high water. Richard Becker thumbs his nose at the cynics with more force than most. Which is somewhat surprising, because he and Bunny are two of the most warm and gracious people in the Texas wine business. Even when they are not at the winery, their thoughtfulness and civility show up in one of nicest tasting room staffs in the state. But, as we've said, you have to have a stubborn streak a mile wide to even try your hand at the tough business of Texas wine. Somehow, the Beckers pull off the "steel hand in a velvet glove" without ever losing the power of either.

The winery is a gorgeous, old-Texas-style place. A remake of a classic nineteenth-century German stone barn, it is surrounded by wildflowers, lavender and vines. On one side is the little house they originally loved, an 1890 log cabin they renovated in 1997 and now rent out as a B&B. The winery is about 10,000 square feet with plenty of underground storage for their barrels of red wine. They can store 64,000 gallons of wine and ferment another 35,000 gallons. The tasting room is on the ground level and features a mid-nineteenth-century bar from San Antonio's Green Tree Saloon. Out back is one of the loveliest lavender fields in Texas. On the porch, you're likely to hear someone playing a little soft music. It's a testament to the beauty of the grounds, the quality of the wine and the friendliness of the staff that more than 75,000 visitors drive out of their way to tour Becker Vineyards each year.

The Best Wines

The Beckers are justifiably proud of their wines. Their wines have been served at the Governor's Mansion and at the White House. Becker wines have been chosen four times for dinners at the James Beard House.

Since the first edition of this book, their production has grown from 15,000 cases per year to 45,000 cases. Many of their grapes come from the Stonewall vineyard, but they also have a high-yielding vineyard in Ballinger. All vintages are aged in new French oak along with some new American oak, then stored in one of the largest underground wine cellars in Texas. As Dr. Becker says, "We have over 1,500 barrels in this winery, and you must use barrels, and good barrels, to make good wine. We buy more than 500 barrels a year. We follow Robert Mondavi's advice to us: Cut no corners in winemaking, and do *not* bottle wine that's not good."

Something's working because, even with the three-fold increase in production, Becker's wines, if anything, have gotten even better. That's a big statement when you're already talking about one of the best wineries around. And notice I didn't limit that to Texas.

When I do panels around the state to show some Texas wines, I always require the bottles to be placed in brown paper bags so no one knows what they are. Then I throw in wines from California, France, Australia and South America and make the Texas wines compete on a world table.

Three wines continually show up as winners in those events–**Becker Reserve Cabernet,** Llano Estacado Viviano and Fall Creek Meritus. The Becker Reserve Cab is nearly perfect. Rich dark color, perfectly integrated oak, big fruit flavors and a finish that can be counted in minutes instead of the normal ten seconds or so. At its price of under $25, it's a miracle.

Trying to narrow down the best wines from the Becker portfolio is like trying to pick the best of Tiger Woods's rounds. One wine you absolutely must try is their **Viognier.** I don't know if Becker had the first bottling of Viognier in the state, but that sure helped put the varietal on the Texas map. It tastes like a more muscular Condrieu. The peach, apricot and apple aromas fire out of your glass like lightning. The mouth feel is almost oily—it's that dense. And the finish features a cleansing acidity you don't always find with this grape.

One more wine deserves special attention. Beginning with the 2005 vintage, the Beckers are sourcing some of the best **Barbera** I've tasted outside of Italy. The nose on this wine is an incredibly mesmeric combo of cinnamon and sandalwood, and the flavors are just lush. Don't miss it!

Ken Maxwell, having trained in the semiconductor field, is not intimidated by his latest winery equipment.

Torre di Pietra

10915 East US 290, Fredericksburg, TX 78624. Sun.–Thu 10 am–6 pm, Fri. and Sat. 10 am–7 pm, later in summertime. (830) 990-9755, www.texashillcountrywine.com

"I'm a Texan. If you don't want to know the answer, don't ask," says Ken Maxwell—owner, vineyard manager and winemaker all rolled into one. He's just finished raking another winemaker over the lexicographic coals. He's proving true to his word: nothing in our interview is off-bounds. His occasional flights of thought take us into novel concepts of his business, his fellow winemakers and his customers. Having Ken regale you with stories is like sitting down with someone as folksy as Jimmy Stewart, as opinionated as James Woods (both Woods and Maxwell are vocal Libertarians, in case the comparison is a little obscure) and as entertaining as Will Rogers. We show up on a Saturday with the intention of staying for an hour and end up staying for three.

Ken has had a successful career in the semiconductor business, working with both Sematech and Applied Materials. When he got the call to move to Silicon Valley, he balked. "I decided to stay here and start a winery."

The statement comes out as a flat fact, with none of the normal concerns over financial solvency, overtime hours or future success. When I push at him about the financial strains, he answers me with the direct confidence of an MBA (University of Texas): "It's a good investment. In the past three years, the property values here in Stonewall have gone up 500 percent. Plus, being close to Fredericksburg is a great place for a winery because so many women like to come to Fredericksburg and, demographically, women buy the most wine." He must be right. Women buy 85 pecent of his wines.

So how do you go from the semiconductor business to making wine, and good wine, at that? "I always made wine. My granddad and great-granddad had mustang grapes, and they made wine. My dad also made wine. In fact, that's where I developed my taste for wine. My dad never kept inventory on his stock, so I was always in there getting a little wine. He never noticed it being gone."

Ken has built one of Texas's most beautiful tasting rooms and one of the state's most modern wineries. A tour through Torre di Pietra allows you to see the current state of the art in equipment. After that, there are comfortable tables both inside and out where you can enjoy a glass of wine. The place feels comfortable, friendly and rustically elegant.

Torre di Pietra is a real family affair. Ken's wife, Jenise, helps design and work the front of the house. Their five-year-old son even works with them. "He planted 1,000 vines. It was incredible to see. I had to pay him, so I gave him $2 a row."

When you go by the winery, ask to meet Ken. He's one of the Texas wine industry's real characters.

The Best Wines

"We have a bimodal distribution of wine buyers," Ken tells me. "We have the first group that comes in knowing what they like, and they are the ones who regularly buy the sweeter wines. The other group is the aficionados who want to know what methods we use to the last detail. 'What yeast did you use?' 'What brix did you pick it at?' 'What kind of barrels do you use?'" Ken and his staff are equally adept at talking with either type of customer and love getting newcomers, too.

There is a house style at Torre di Pietra: "Fruit forward. That's the style of the future. I'm trying to get the grapes to express themselves," Ken says. But that doesn't necessarily mean he doesn't use any winemaker tricks with the wine. In fact, he has nothing but disdain for the normal California mission statement of doing nothing to the grapes and having the wines made by the time they hit the crusher. "I worked in high technology and I'm not afraid to use technology on my wine," he says. "I use reverse osmosis, ion exchange, whatever I need to do to make great wine."

Torre di Pietra makes about twenty different wines. All are competently made, so anyone should be able to find something that appeals. Ken's biggest sellers are **Red Flirt,** a slightly sweet red wine, and the **Hill Country Reserve Cabernet Sauvignon.** On the latter, Ken adds a touch of Petit Sirah which adds color and a little intensity, making a spectacular bottle of wine. Reds seem to be Ken's real strength. His **Hill Country Primitivo** is a big, intense wine with dark berry aromas and cleansing acidity. The **Hill Country Sangiovese** gets butterscotch and crème brulee aromas from the barrels, and intense strawberry and raspberry aromas from high-quality fruit. And the **Classico,** a blend of Cabernet Sauvignon, Carignane, Sangiovese and Syrah, has gorgeous color and good tannic grip.

Woodrose Winery

662 Woodrose Lane, Stonewall, TX 78761 Wed.–Sun. noon 6 pm. (030) 644-2539,
www.woodrosewinery.com

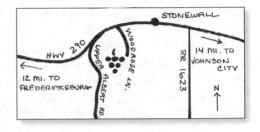

Michael Guilette is a soft-spoken guy whose successes have come from hard work, smarts and an affable personality. He grew up in Chicago. The day he graduated from college he drew a line across the United States dividing snow states from non-snow states and vowed he'd seen the end of the white stuff.

His best job offer came from Motorola, which landed him in the temperate climate of Austin. He never left.

As we sit in his tasting room, sipping wine and chatting about the business, he recalls the circuitous route he took from semiconductors to wine. "Being in high tech, I spent a lot of time in Northern California. One day I cut out of a conference and decided to go see Napa and find out what all the fuss was about Napa wine. I found this guy selling his wine at a tasting room. I meant to just get a taste of wine, but I ended up spending the day helping him in the vineyards and in the winery. By the end of the day, I was hooked. I was twenty-five years old, and I knew that some day I would have a winery."

Michael Guilette on Woodrose's tree-shaded tasting deck.

Fast forward twenty years, when a tragedy struck that helped Michael achieve his dream.

Brian Wilgus had worked on getting Woodrose built and in business for eight years. "I was always looking for the perfect cottage industry," was how Brian put it. "The people I knew who had little wineries always had a smile on their face." In 1995 he started work on Woodrose Winery, a task that would cost him money, time and a marriage. By 2003, he was up and running, and making good wine. Then one day, while working in the vineyard, Brian had an aneurism that left him chronically ill. He would never be able to operate the winery again.

Michael found an ad in the Austin newspaper offering a winery for sale. He had intended to wait until he retired to open a winery, but this deal seemed too good to be true. Brian had built a good operation to start with, but Michael brought additional design panache and added a gorgeous, tree-shaded deck out back (dogs welcome).

For Michael, the whole experience has been right out of a late-period Frank Capra film. "The first time I held a bottle of wine where I did the bottle, the label and the wine, I just felt so proud, almost like a father holding a newborn child," he says, clearly still moved by the experience. "I'll come out here on a weekend, roll out of bed at seven and work until the sun goes down, get up the next morning and do the same thing. When I drive back to Austin for my other job, I'm just as happy as I can be."

The Best Wines

Michael is making a number of good wines, but he has in his possession one of the best **Cabernet Sauvignons** ever to come from a Texas winery. Everything about it is fundamentally correct. From the deep color to the dark berry aromas, to the tannic grip (sweet tannins, not harsh), to the endless finish, everything is just right. And here's the good news: the wine comes from grapes grown in the vineyard you'll see about two-hundred yards from the tasting room. Which means there's a bright future ahead.

TRIP FOUR

🍂 Fredericksburg Winery

247 W. Main St., Fredericksburg, TX 78624. Mon.–Thu. 10 am–5:30 pm, Fri. and Sat. 10 am–7:30 pm, Sun. noon–5:30 pm. (830) 990-8747, www.fbgwinery.com

Fredericksburg Winery is a family-owned operation: three brothers, wives and families— Bert, vineyards director; Minerva, tasting room manager); Mark, age 12, junior assistant winemaker; Jene, winemaster; Sandra, sales;

Chardonnay, age seven, junior assistant winemaker; Cord, G-1; Sandy, general manager; and Oma, grandmother. Throughout this book I've been telling you about the wonderful set of characters, the mavericks and iconoclasts involved with Texas wine. If there ever was a poster boy for the maverick contingent, it has to be Cord Switzer. His title, G-1, stands for "Go for Number One."

Cord has a new title to append. It's now G-1, PII. What? "Politically incorrect individual," he tells me with that signature, understated grin. Cord loves to drop pithy comments. Here are a few of his better ones:

Cord Switzer holding court.

"Wine snobs usually last about five minutes in here until we offend them enough that they leave."

"The only reason you age wine is because there is something wrong with it."

"We do wine one on one, WHP (without the horse pucky)."

"We have the greatest job on earth: drink wine all day and harass customers."

"The only rule in wine is to drink what you like when you like it and tell everyone else to go take a flying leap."

"Cell phones disturb the wine. I told a guy to leave his cell phone off and the guy said he would leave. I told him, 'Bye.'"

"We have fun with wine. We tell customers that if they want to be serious, they should go down the road to one of the other wineries. They're serious. We like to play and be creative."

Half the fun of visiting the Fredericksburg Winery is the experience. Cord's family doesn't just tolerate his bodacious views—they egg him on. I wish I could sit in the corner all day and listen. Here are a couple of encounters I missed.

In walks a potential customer. He wants to taste a Cabernet Sauvignon. Problem is, they aren't making Cab that day. Cord offers him a Merlot, saying they taste similar. The customer refuses, sniffing at an affront to his gilded palate. "I can always tell the difference between Cab and Merlot," he claims.

Cord goes to the cash register, takes out a $100 bill, places it in front of the customer and challenges him. "You put down a $100 bill and I'll go buy three bottles of Cab and three bottles of Merlot. You blind taste and separate them

The Switzer family's winery on Main Street in Fredericksburg.

correctly and you can have both $100 bills. But if you can't, I take the money and you pay for the wine."

The customer stares at Switzer in disbelief, sets a clammy look on his face and storms out. The family nearly falls on the floor laughing every time this story gets a replay. So do I.

Then there was the time a customer came in and asked to taste the Chardonnay. They pulled out the bottle and the customer commented that they had incorrectly put the wine in a Bordeaux-style bottle instead of a Burgundy-style bottle. The family told the customer that he was in Texas, not in France. The customer left in a snit, and the Switzer family howled.

I love telling these stories because this family is interesting, but story-telling aside, family members are dead serious about their wine. Beneath that mocking exterior lies good business brains and a sincere desire to give customers what they want. When I asked what made him proud, Cord told me, "The fact that we're a family business that started from scratch and it has worked. It really is a family business, started on a shoestring."

That's probably my favorite part of the Fredericksburg Winery experience. I think it's fascinating watching this tight-knit family with just a touch of "us-against-the-world" foxhole mentality. When you throw a roadblock in their path, you'd best step out of their way. Especially when it comes to politics. When you hear about legislation regarding the wine industry, you can be sure Cord's finger will be in it somewhere.

"I'm really proud of the industry and how everyone works together," he says. "Especially the grassroots efforts to keep legislators involved. Now we have to make sure we don't lose what we've gained." I doubt they will. Cord won't let that happen.

Once the jokes stop, Cord becomes more reflective. "You know, the biggest thing that has happened for us is the industry having gotten so much better. So many more people are going to Texas wineries. Twenty years ago no one gave us any credibility. We're now getting new people coming because they are out for a day tasting wines. But, thankfully, our loyal customers come year after year, and God bless them."

The Best Wines

There is really no way to discuss Fredericksburg Winery's regular offerings because the Switzer family changes them as fast as they sell. I've never seen them selling less than twenty different wines, all handmade. All wines are fermented in small tanks and stored right in front of the customers. When it is time to bottle, they do everything from filling to corking and labeling by hand. They make their sparkling wines in the traditional methode champenoise, with riddling and disgorging done by hand. Even with all this work going on right in front of the customers, they still have the time to sell over 7,000 cases per year. Every single bottle is sold only from the winery.

Many of the wines they sell retain residual sugar. Try them and you may find that a touch of sugar is nice. Ask and you might find a dry wine among the day's offerings.

I've had some wonderful dry red wines from Cord. My favorite, a stunning bottle of wine that could be placed on the table at any three-star Michelin restaurant, was a 100 percent **Petit Verdot.** This grape is seldom made into an individual wine. It is mostly used as a blending grape. Alone it is a massive, dense, peppery wine with dark red color. The folks in Bordeaux use it to give color and tannic grip to their wines. Fredericksburg's version is teeth staining, spicy and delicious. Cord likes to make a great dry wine now and then just to prove that he can. He can.

🍃 Bell Mountain Vineyards

463 Bell Mountain Rd., Fredericksburg, TX 78624. Sat. 10 am–5 pm or by appointment. (830) 685-3297, www.bellmountainwine.com

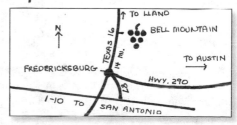

Bob Oberhelman's career was in the food technology business in Dallas. But he and his wife, Evelyn, had a keen interest in the country life. They were also fans of wine, especially those of France and Germany. In the early 1970s they started to look for property around Texas and finally focused on the Hill Country because of the soils and climate. They looked at a lot of places but never felt any magic. Then they found Bell Mountain. Bob

Bob Oberhelman owns the entire Bell Mountain appellation.

described it: "I felt like I was struck by lightning." He thought he had found a nice, cool getaway from big city life. What he didn't realize until later was that he had also found a beautiful spot for vineyards.

Still working in Dallas, Bob and Evelyn drove down to their property on weekends and during vacations. They worked the land, clearing mesquite trees and pushing rocks. During 1974 and 1975 they built a small building to stay in and store things. By 1976 they had cleared enough land to plant their first small vineyard. Two years later they were making wine to drink themselves and share with friends. The tech side of Bob led him to constantly work on improving the growing techniques in the vineyard. He also studied and traveled, soaking up knowledge on winemaking everywhere he went.

By 1983 they were ready to take the plunge and open a winery. Over the next two years, they worked harder than ever, searching out and planting the best clones, installing irrigation systems. By 1986 they had achieved two more dreams. First, they built a beautiful German-style home. Second, with resounding importance to the Texas wine business, they succeeded in having their property and about 10,000 surrounding acres designated as Texas's first wine-growing appellation. This ended up being very important in the growth of the Texas wine business.

Bell Mountain is 2,000 feet above sea level, which helps it stay eight to 15 degrees cooler than Austin. Bell Mountain is actually cooler during the day than large parts of Napa and Sonoma. Also, even though surrounded by land that is predominantly sandstone, Bell Mountain is against the Llano uplift, which gives it a granitic soil almost 150 feet deep.

Because of these near ideal conditions, Bob is able to produce wines through principles closely allied to organic farming. During the first part of the decade, Bob ripped out the majority of his vines. "We're replanting with ideal rootstocks," he says. "We're still focusing on making the best wines we can with our own grapes, but we're also buying some from other Texas growers. Wine is not made by a person. It's made by the vines, so we put all our emphasis there."

The Best Wines

Bob Oberhelman made his name on his Riesling, and that's still the best place to start. I like his Auslese-style **Late Harvest Riesling,** a wine with about 8.2 percent sugar and nice acidity. He also makes a **Mead** under the Oberhof label from pure Hill Country wildflower honey. It's delightfully floral and delicious as a dessert wine.

🍃 Grape Creek Vineyard

Vineyard Lane Highway, US Hwy. 290 East, Stonewall, TX 78761. Mon.–Sat. 10 am–5 pm, Sun. noon–5 pm. (800) 950-7392, www.grapecreek.com

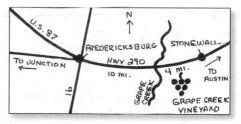

Grape Creek has a remarkable history. Ned Simes, the original owner of Grape Creek Vineyard, was a true Texas wine character. The first time I interviewed him, he appeared to be in his mid-sixties and was wearing shorts and a short-sleeved shirt with a few leftover breadcrumbs stuck to the front. Soon he reached into his pocket, produced some fingernail clippers and started clipping away while waiting for my computer to cycle on.

I asked why he was in the wine business. He smiled at me and said, "Well, it keeps me out of the pool hall." That's when he told me he was eighty. I thought he had to be invincible.

Ned started drinking wine while in the offshore drilling business, traveling to places where you couldn't drink the water. He worked his way up to chairman and CEO of Diamond M Company in Houston, then decided he'd like to break away from the big city and move to the Hill Country. He'd flirted with the idea of a winery and, in fact, the Chilean government had encouraged him to put one there in the early 1980s. But in 1985, he finally decided on a seventeen-acre plot of land just outside Stonewall. The next year he planted his vines.

Brian Heath has taken over Grape Creek Vineyard.

Things went beautifully for ten years. Grape Creek Vineyard was producing about forty tons of grapes and buying as many more. It won awards and sold out every vintage. Even better for a hard-nosed businessman, it was all done without the help of a distributor ("I don't want a distributor and they don't want me. It's kind of a mutual admiration society," he told me), and without borrowing any money ("We aren't in business to make the banks rich," he groused). Then, echoing a story heard many times in Texas, heartbreak hit.

In 1997, Grape Creek Vineyard was devastated by Pierce's disease. Almost the entire vineyard was decimated. Growing stopped for three years, and grapes were bought from other growers just to stay in business. Grape Creek was lucky to maintain its customer base and continued to sell over 5,000 cases per year, almost all sold at the winery.

Ned died in 2004, leaving a hole in the industry and a family that wasn't sure it wanted to continue in the wine business. Enter Brian Heath, president of the US Advisor Group for Ameriprise Financial (they're the ones using Easy Rider Dennis Hopper to appeal to post-hippie investors on TV commercials). He purchased Grape Creek and has been busy making improvements to the wine and the winery. Heath has a history of taking big companies and building on their success, so I anticipate big things from Grape Creek.

The Best Wines

I've always felt the best wine from Grape Creek is the **Cabernet Trois.** It is a nice combination of three Cabernets—Sauvignon, Ruby and Franc. The blend is delicious, sort of like cherries and plums with a tiny touch of tobacco. The best white wine is **Fumé Blanc,** a dry Sauvignon Blanc with vanilla aromas added from a little time in well-toasted oak barrels.

🍁 Chisholm Trail Winery

2367 Usener Rd, Fredericksburg, TX
78624. Thu.–Mon. noon–6 pm.
(877) 990-2675,
www.chisholmtrailwinery.com

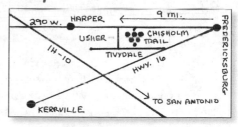

You drive down a small back road through some beautiful trees. Cows wander around. Idyllic, pretty, relaxed. A perfect getaway for a tired Texas attorney.

Paula K. Williamson wanted to get out of the big city (San Antonio) and try country life. And she wanted to do something else besides law. After traveling to the Germany and Italy wine countries, she started making wine at home. Everyone loved it and told her to take a try at the business.

So in 1992, Paula found land outside Fredericksburg that she thought might be just the ticket for making her own wines. Then she hired the best consultant she could find—Vernon Gold, who had over twenty years in Texas wines. He encouraged her to plant Chenin Blanc, Cabernet Sauvignon, Merlot and Cabernet Franc. He also recommended that she sell the first three harvests, reserving a small amount of juice for experiments. Paula found out pretty quickly that there is a huge difference between home and commercial winemaking. The learning curve was steep.

Unfortunately, Vernon Gold passed away in 1999 and never had the chance to taste the final product. Paula then had the good fortune to meet Robert Pepi, one of California's best producers of Italian varieties. He agreed to help and has been her consultant ever since.

Paula has blossomed into a good winemaker. Her personal life has had its share of drama, but through it all she's remembered to take care of the grapes. As her assistant Linda Matlock says: "Paula really babies her grapes. We were

supposed to go to this real important festival, but six tons of Merlot showed up. Paula decided to stay here and take care of those grapes right away."

Chisholm Trail Winery's
Paula Williamson.

Paula has also learned a few things, like the importance of having a nice tasting area. And that a lot of folks who visit wineries like sweet wines. "I really had to make a sweet wine," she tells me. "Even though it's not my favorite, so many people want them. So I thought about it and decided I'd make the best sweet wine I could."

Like almost everyone I've talked to in the Hill Country appellation, Paula has nothing but praise for her fellow winemakers. Competition is friendly and help is always a phone call away. While not organized as a co-op, winemakers in the Hill Country act like one. Each lends the other equipment, knowledge, time and muscle power.

Paula has a good heart. She's well-liked in the Hill Country and respected by her fellow winemakers. Her dream is becoming a reality. As she tells me, "My whole life is so much better than it's ever been." The smile on her face is all the proof I need.

The Best Wines

Paula knocked the ball out of the park with her **2000 Merlot.** Dense, chocolaty, with black pepper tastes and an endless finish. It is sold out, but watch what she does with Merlot. Lightning may strike again. My current favorite Chisholm Trail wine is **Belle Star Blanc de Bois,** a wine with huge fruits and acids and a nice floral character to the finish.

TRIP FIVE

Mandola Winery

13308 Farm Road 150 West, Driftwood, TX 78619. Daily 10 am –5 pm (512) 858-1470, www.mandolawines.com

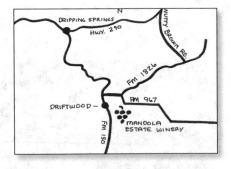

I originally stopped by the Mandola Winery to visit with ace veteran winemaker Mark Penna. I figured Damian Mandola, the name behind the winery, would be too busy. Between filming his new PBS cooking show (*Cucina Siciliana*), doing PR for his three books (*Ciao, Y'all*, *Ciao Sicily* and *Ciao Tuscany*), getting his new concept grocery-restaurant going (Mandola's Italian Market) or making sure the new winery meets his standards, he's on a hectic schedule. Lucky for him he sold his interest in Carraba's Italian Grill to his nephew. Damian has plenty on his plate.

Cookbook author, restaurateur and winery owner Damian Mandola, left, with Mark Penna, his veteran winemaker.

So I was surprised to see Damian in the tasting room, chatting up old friends and making new ones. If you've seen him on TV, you already know what to expect. He's a happy, outgoing guy, always on the verge of laughter. The shirt he's wearing says, "1 Ton o' Fun," which makes light of his girth, the result of his obvious enjoyment of the food he tries around the world. The operative word on the shirt is fun.

When I ask about his creative side, the guy who loves to teach the world to cook the foods he grew up with gets serious, as he is about his goal to create a showplace for food and wine in Driftwood. Damian and his wife, Trina, and a couple of Houston doctors, Stan and Lisa Duchman, have sunk $6 million into the Mandola Winery. This is the most beautiful winery in Texas, and the money they spent shows everywhere you look.

The walk up to the winery from the parking area passes picnic tables and gorgeous gardens before you cross a footbridge. The winery looks like a Tuscan villa. When you walk in, instead of feeling the imposing weight of a slick designer you get a gemütliche feeling. Is there an Italian translation? Perhaps we should say più cosier, but that doesn't quite catch the homey, comfortable, alluring feel you get when you walk in the door. You know the feeling you get when you visit a beloved grandmother? That's the feeling you get when you step through the doors of the Mandola Winery.

The tasting room is spacious and friendly. You can sit at a table or stand at the bar. Italian groceries line the walls. There's a cooler for Pellegrino water. The people behind the bar know what they are talking about. You can tell I am impressed.

Damian, Mark Penna and I sit down to do a little talking and wine tasting. Why on earth would a successful restaurateur with a hit TV show want to start a winery? "I've always just loved wineries," Damian says. "In the beginning, my goal was to do a small little boutique winery. But we all talked and decided that if we're gonna get in business, let's do it right. So we're aiming at 20,000 cases of Texas-grown wine made from Italian varietals." Mark is smiling through his big beard. He is clearly having the time of his life.

The well-equipped Mandola Winery looks like a Tuscan villa.

A little background. Mark has been making Texas wine for twenty years, starting in the high plains with Llano Estacado and Cap*Rock. Then he moved down to Fort Stockton, where he took the reins of the biggest winery in the state, Ste. Genevieve. While he was there, discerning wine folks started to find great value wines, like the still memorable Fumé Chardonnay. Mark left to work in the Hill Country.

When Damian went searching for his winemaker, he got a recommendation from one of Texas's ranking nonconformists, the cigar-chomping master sommelier Guy Stout, who sent Damian to Mark. Damian is happy with the association: "Mark's making really good wine. We're lucky to get him."

Mark is more contented than I've ever seen him. "This is the most relaxed and pleasant place I've ever worked," he says. "I love being involved in every phase. I can crawl in and clean a tank and not feel like I'm goofing off. And while the front of the winery is homey and pretty, my part of it is very utilitarian. I have everything I need, but it's all so simple."

I've been in wineries all over the world. This is one of the best designs I've seen, from the well-equipped and spacious labs to the fermenting room with a washable ceiling. (Tanks do occasionally go super-nova during the heat of fermentation.) I'm reminded of Einstein's quote: "Everything should be made as simple as possible, but not one bit simpler." The designer at Mandola's Winery understood that concept.

I ask Damian what the future holds. "In ten years, we hope to have a portfolio of great wines, all Italian varietals, and a restaurant with a statewide, regional and, hopefully, even national reputation. I want to focus on braised and roasted meats, have a trattoria-style place. We'll also have a great banquet facility and a place for classes."

Damian is happy. His house is right on the property, so he can walk to work. He gets to spend more time with his wife and two children. And he's having the opportunity to enjoy a much slower, simpler life. As he says, "The whole process is fascinating. I love just sitting back and watching the grapes grow."

The Best Wines

While the vineyards grow, Mark is making wine sourced from other vineyards, both in and out of Texas. Vintage 2007 or 2008 is when they should start making estate wines.

Mark has always had a great touch with white wines. I tasted his un-oaked **Pinot Grigio** and was amazed at the depth and richness, even to the point of tasting a little vanilla. It is so easy to make a thin, acidic wine from the **Pinot Grigio** grape that getting a smooth, quaffable wine like this is a delight. There was also a **Syrah** sourced from the Hill Country, maybe from Guy Stout's new vineyard. The wine had good color— overcoming a frequent problem for Texas reds—and carried some chocolate and spice flavors, along with well-integrated acids. This wine should be a treat with Damian's cuisine.

🍁 Driftwood Vineyards

4001 Elder Hill Rd., Driftwood, TX 78619. Daily 10 am–6 pm. (512) 692-6229, www.driftwoodvineyards.com

Gary Elliott is still amazed he's made it in the wine business. In fact, Gary is still amazed he even got into the wine business. It all started when he was looking around for something to do with his land.

"First, the cattle didn't make any money," he tells me while laughing at some private joke. "Then the hay business didn't make any money. Raising horses didn't make any money, so I gave up on that, too. I wanted to make some money and my family in California sells grapes to Beringer, so I thought I'd try it here in Texas."

His background? "I was born in California, Orange County," he says. "I've been in agriculture since I was a kid. My parents had oranges and avocados and alfalfa and grapes. Then I majored in ag in college. It was pretty easy. I have a photographic memory so I remember everything."

From there he was in the military, served as a fireman and then found his calling. "I was a ski instructor in the winter and a tour director traveling around the world in the summers. I taught skiing in Japan and California. Traveled all over the world. I met my wife, Kathy, in Tibet. After we got married we were living in California, where I was a ski instructor. Then I started a commercial aviation business." He enjoyed ferrying movie and TV stars around but found

Gary Elliott at the counter at his Driftwood Vineyards.

that he couldn't quite squeeze a profit out of it. Then two things happened at once.

"Kathy's dad passed away and, at the same time, I was offered a job flying for Continental," he says. "I had a choice between the Hill Country or Newark. I would have only been able to fly for a few years because of mandatory retirement, so we moved to her family ranch." He started laughing and shaking his head. "I gave up being a professional skier, travel guide and commercial airline pilot to sit here and grow grapes."

The family farm is 880 acres of fertile and hilly land, crisscrossed by creeks and streams. Gary spent the first few years as a farmer, selling grapes from his fifteen-acre vineyard to Texas Hills, Fredericksburg, Becker and Dry Comal. He also made wines and entered them as amateur offerings in several contests, usually placing very high. So he decided that, as of October 2002, he would start selling his wines.

He likes the whole idea of being a winemaker. Plus, he thinks Texas is reminiscent of California during the development of the wine industry. "We are like California in the 1960s and 70s. Back then you couldn't give away California wine. Everyone thought the French wines were the only good ones. It was the people like the Mondavis and Sebastianis who turned it all around." When I mention that he must really love what he does, he looks up in the sky, as if trying to decide whether he wants to tell me the truth. He decides to go ahead.

"If I could go back to before I started, knowing what I know now, I wouldn't have done it. It is so expensive and takes so much work." He looked out across his vineyard. "But I've gotten to the point of no return. I have too much money and time in it. If it wasn't on the family ranch, I'd sell it. But I keep hoping so that eventually I'll be able to make enough money that I can enjoy it."

Putting a vineyard close to a creek is usually an open invitation for Pierce's disease. Gary has to drip the chemical Admire most of the year, and he has to, as he says, "nuke the floor of the vineyard to get it completely clean." He also wisely removed all of the native grapes from beside the creek, as they are carriers of Pierce's sisease. "I didn't realize how expensive all that care was going to be, but you have to spend the money to save your vineyard."

"Now I live with money worries. My stress level is much higher than it used to be. I keep hoping I'll see some light at the end of the tunnel before the tunnel falls in on me. People come to talk to me about starting a winery. They want to be in it for the 'romance.' Sure, I have a beautiful vineyard. In fact, an owner from Napa told me it was as pretty as anything in Napa. But it has cost a lot of money and taken a lot of work."

The Best Wines

Gary grows four reds and four whites. Cabernet Sauvignon, Syrah, Sangiovese and Pinot Noir; Viognier, Chardonnay, Chenin Blanc and Muscat Blanc. He believes that "the secret to everything is good fruit. Nothing you can do in the winery can make up for bad fruit. That's why everyone who makes wines with my fruit has had good success." He has chosen to avoid the over-oaked style of California wines and aims at a style that's ready to drink early. Light and fruity.

Gary's best wine, and consistently one of the best wines Texas produces, is his **Viognier**. Gary goes for a more elegant style than some others in the state. The dominant apricot and peach aromas blend seamlessly into the multiple other flavors—flint, grapefruit, honey, plum, I could go on. This is complex wine that rewards thoughtful sipping.

Gary's red wines are usually crowd pleasers. His ready-to-drink style favors fruit over anything else. Recently, my favorite has been his **Alamo Red**, made from 100 percent Syrah. It's a really nice version with a little tannic grip and nice acids. It's a great food wine.

Also, if he has it, try his sister's **Dry Merlot Rosé.** It's from her vineyard in Paso Robles, California, and provides a great opportunity to try a fresh, high-quality, dry rosé.

🍁 Bella Vista Cellars

3101 Mt. Sharp Rd., Wimberley, TX 78676.
Thu.–Sat. 10 am–5 pm, Sun. noon–4 pm.
(512) 847-6514, www.bvranch.com

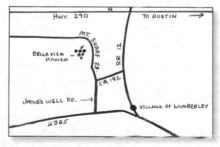

I show up for my meeting with Jack Dougherty and he is in a cantankerous mood, probably a side effect from suffering through a bad cold. Plus some of his equipment is on the fritz, and he's having to watch the repairmen. On top of that, I think he's a bit of a curmudgeon. When I set up my laptop for the interview, he stops me and says he wants to go outside. Where I can't take my battery-dead computer. I beg off, but he insists.

Bella Vista's Jack Dougherty among some of his 1,000 olive trees.

Jack was among the wave of Californians to arrive in Texas during the high-tech boom days. When I ask about his work in the computer business, he tells me it's too complex to explain, and wants to emphasize his years growing up in Santa Clara County. Though it's mostly known as the home of the Silicon Valley, Jack remembers the agriculture, particularly the orchards.

We step out and are standing in the midst of his gorgeous olive tree plantation. He talks to me about the history of olives and how much trouble he had getting the trees and convincing Texans that he can grow good olives. "Everybody told me I couldn't grow olives here. They thought I was some dumb Californian without a clue. I thought, well, I'll show them."

So he bought an old ranch down a country road in Wimberley and, based on a hunch that the area looked parched and hot like the areas surrounding the Mediterranean, he decided to plant over 1,000 olive trees. The trees are now all bearing fruit and yielding enough oil that he can blend some with the Italian oil he sells at the winery.

Now he feels he has shown the disbelievers. Because his harvest is still small, he's importing oil to mix with his own so more people can get a taste of Texas olive oil. He thought it might be a good idea to grow grapes as well, so he started Bella Vista Cellars. It's a very small winery, making under four hundred cases of wine per year. Jack has purchased good-quality equipment. One of the best uses you can make of Bella Vista is to watch the olive harvest and press during late September and early October. Call ahead to confirm.

The Best Wine

Jack sources most of his grapes from neighboring vineyards. His goal is to focus on Italian varietals. On my visit, we taste blends of Syrah, Cabernet Franc and Sangiovese. The best wine is, surprisingly, not one he makes a big deal out of. It is a **Blackberry Wine,** made only semisweet, and filled with the gorgeous aromas of the fruit. This is another example of the fight Texas has to achieve a good reputation for its wines. Put Jack's blackberry wine in a fancy bottle with an Italian or French label and folks would pay twice what he's asking. As it is, a lot of people turn up their nose at fruit wine. That's a shame. This is good wine.

🍂 Wimberley Valley Winery

Dean Valentine keeps threatening to open a tasting room at his winery in Wimberley. If he does, you can be sure it will be an interesting place in a beautiful location. You might ask Gary Elliott at Driftwood Vineyard whether Dean has decided that he'll be open for tasting.

TRIP SIX

🍂 Sandstone Cellars Winery

211 San Antonio St., Mason, TX 76856.
Thu.–Sat. 11 am–6 pm,
Sun. 11 am–2 pm. (325) 347-WINE,
www.sandstonecellarswinery.com

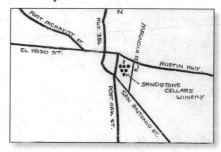

Mason is one of the Hill Country's most romantic and creative towns. A friendly stroll around the square will remind you of the Hill Country before tourism. Just off the square you'll find one of the Hill Country's best—and most authentic--Mexican restaurants, Santos Taquería (open for lunch only; don't miss it). Santos Silerio, mother of half the ownership of Sandstone Cellars, makes everything from scratch, by hand. Want a nice gordita? Santos grabs a handful of masa and makes it right in front of you. The place reminds me of the best taquerías I've eaten at, in Aguascalientes, Mexico. As you might guess, Sandstone Cellars wine goes great with Santos's cooking.

Scott Haupert and Manny Silerio own Sandstone Cellars. They met in college in San Antonio. Manny had come from Mason, Scott from Des Moines, Iowa. After college, they both went north. Scott went to Yale for a master's in music and then headed west, where he became a studio musician and played viola on filmscores like those for *Titanic* and *Jurassic Park*. Manny went home to Mason.

Winemaker Don Pullum uncorks a bottle at Sandstone Cellars.

Scott's royalty payments allowed him to invest in a project that he and Manny had talked about for years. Manny's mother, Santos, came from Durango, Mexico, in the 1960s. Not only did she raise eight children; she became known in the community as a stellar cook. Scott and Manny wanted to create a restaurant around Santos's traditional recipes. By 1998 they were in business. They also had an itch to create a winery. Mason is a dry town, but wineries can exist and sell products in a dry town. Vineyards were spouting up all over Mason County, which meant there was an opportunity to get good fruit.

Enter Don Pullum, an incurable experimenter, owner of a great vineyard and a good winemaker to boot. He can also claim Edgar Cayce as his great-great-great uncle, which accounts for the name of his vineyard—Akashic Vineyard. Don signs on to make the wine for Sandstone.

All three have the same motivation. They want their wines to be driven solely by Mason County terroir, so much so that if they can't get enough fruit for a vintage they'll just sit it out. They want each bottle to be a work of art, not just the wine inside but the look as well. They commissioned world-famous artist Bill Worrell to create their labels.

Manny and Scott have everything right where they want it. They're having fun and at least breaking even, while Scott's royalties pay for the everyday necessities. Don, a recovering private banker, loves getting out in the sun and getting his hands dirty. His understanding wife maintains her career while Don enjoys the fruits of a hard day's work. The overall effect is entering a kind of pastoral retreat. Everyone is working hard, and the serenity is calming.

Sandstone Cellars is worth a side trip.

The Best Wines

You mostly have to go to the winery to try the wine. Sandstone's production is a scanty four hundred cases. And I can't really tell you what their best wine is because they change every year, based on what's available and what stimulates their interest. They offer tastes, so you can make up your own mind. I tend to like anything Don makes with Touriga or Syrah, so you might ask about those two grapes.

This should be your plan: get to Mason at about 11 am, taste through the Sandstone wines; they also sell many other Texas wines. Finish just before noon, take your bottle and a couple of glasses over to Santos, sit outside at the *muy auténtico* metal tables, let the breeze blow through your hair and see if you don't start wondering about the cost of property in Mason.

🍂 *Brennan Vineyards*

802 S. Austin St., Comanche, TX 76442. Tue.–Sun. 11 am –5 pm. (325) 356-9100, www.brennanvineyards.com

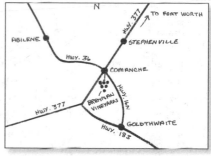

When Texas wine pioneer Bobby Cox gets up about six inches from my face and gives me that look, the one that looks like he just swallowed the Cheshire Cat and received enlightenment from Buddha all at once, I know something big is up. "You need to taste the Viognier from Brennan Vineyards," he says. I nod and agree to taste it. "No!" he says and raises the volume ten notches. "Look at me. You need to taste this wine!"

Now Bobby is occasionally prone to hyperbole, but it's generally when he's condemning the federal government for wasteful practices and attempting to destroy the American family farm. When he's talking about wines, he normally at least makes an attempt at understatement, even if it's the winking type aimed at letting you know it's thinly disguised irony.

We're at the Buffalo Gap Festival, one of the best wine and food gatherings anywhere, and Bobby grabs me by the arm and leads me to a table with the aforementioned wine. He pours me a glass and just stares at me. Well, he is right. When he sees my face light up, he starts laughing and bobbing up and down. "I told you," he says. "Isn't that great wine?"

It turns out Bobby makes the wine but didn't want me to know it until I tasted it. It is a tour de force.

Bobby takes me to meet the Brennan of Brennan Vineyards: Pat Brennan. He's a tall man with wire-rimmed glasses and a kindly manner. Three years prior, he had retired as a nephrologist—a kidney doctor— after thirty years of practicing medicine in Fort Worth. Pat and his nurse wife of thirty-nine years,

Pat Brennan retired from medicine and started a winery.

Trellise (perfect name for a winery owner), bought thirty-three acres and didn't have a clue what to do with it. Pat is friends with the most successful doctor in the Texas wine business, Richard Becker. When Pat heard of Richard's success, he decided to try it out himself.

"My wife and I have been wine fans for our whole marriage," he explains. "We started with Mateus and Lancers, then moved up to better wines. We eventually helped establish the Cowtown Enological Association."

The love of wine, intersecting with Richard Becker's encouragement and their inactive farmland, led to Brennan Vineyards. By 2002 the Brennans had decided to get into the wine business. Reality started sinking in after about a year. "It suddenly struck me that we grossly underestimated both the work and the investment," he says. "We're in our sixties and were looking forward to retiring. Now we work every day, weekends included." He gets that look I've seen on so many winery owners, the "oh my God, what have I done?" look. It passes quickly.

"Don't get me wrong. Truthfully, if I had it to do all over again, I'm not sure I would. But I'm in too deep now, and we are having a lot of fun. I'm never bored, and even though we are early in the game, we are making good wine.

The main building of Brennan Vineyards in Comanche.

As we walk across the yard from the tasting room, Pat greets a couple of wine lovers raving about his wine. When we get to the event center, about twenty people are there tasting. The vibe has a nice friendly buzz. This is the manna that feeds Pat's winery-owning soul.

Suddenly, all the effort, money and hard work seem worthwhile.

The Best Wine

Bobby Cox is right. Don't miss the unctuous, perfumed and perfectly balanced **Viognier**. I've often said that if the world ever develops a taste for this grape, Texas could be as famous for it as Oregon is for Pinot Noir. Taste Brennan's version for a crash course in what I mean.

🍁 Rising Star Vineyards

1001 County Rd. 290, Rising Star, TX 76471.
Sat. 11 am–6 pm, Sun. noon–4 pm.
(254) 643-1776,
www.risingstarvineyards.com

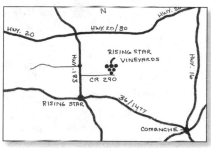

It's a cool, sunny afternoon. Michael Ourbre and I are sitting at RO's Outpost feasting on great barbecue and drinking our way though his portfolio. He's a tall guy, clear blue eyes, good disposition. I notice he's clean-shaven, and it dawns on me. You can tell winery owners that do it full time versus the ones who still have day jobs. Check for a stubbly, I-haven't-shaved-since last-Thursday kind of look. Michael, obviously, still has a day job.

And his day job is pretty high level, working for the Dell Information Technology Global Systems Engineering Process Group (take that, acronym lovers). He's spent thirty or so years in information technology, mostly working around the state.

Michael grew up in the Valley. It would be an understatement to say that wine didn't play much of a role in his family life. "No, there was never any wine around my house," he tells me. "My father was a Baptist preacher."

Michael worked his way through high school and college as the evening deejay at KRIO, the top-rated rock station in the Valley. Once he graduated, a friend with a steak house in McAllen asked him to help figure out how to put together a wine list. Michael was hesitant. He didn't know anything about wine. Then his friend said Michael would be able to sample everything before he bought it. That sounded like fun. During the process, Michael got hooked on wine.

Michael Ourbe with a bottle of Rising Star.

He moved to Austin in 1974 and found some land on the San Gabriel River outside Georgetown that he thought might make a great little vineyard area. Nothing happened, and as his career took off he never had time to get back to that plot of land. Then he took a job in the Bay Area. Suddenly his love of wine, his location and his desire to start a winery all aligned. One problem: vineyard land in California is the special preserve of hedge-fund operators and CEO's of Fortune 500 corporations. No one else can afford the freight. So Michael and his wife, Vicki, decided that someday, somehow, they would have their own winery.

When Michael went to work for Dell, he decided to buy some Hill Country land to grow grapes. "We made all sorts of mistakes, putting seven feet between the rows and planting with four-foot spacings," he says. "We also found that we weren't the only ones who loved grapes. We lost a big part of our crop to coons, birds, foxes, deer. We got sixty coons the other night, and that was just part of the population. Then there's the late frosts—" He stops and gets another bite of barbecue. I wouldn't want to talk about all those losses either.

Then his natural optimism returns. "We are finally doing the part of the business I got into the wine business for," he says. "I love having a tasting room, talking to people, teaching them about wines. But the real surprise for me was how much I loved working in the vineyard. It's sweaty, dirty work, and I love it."

Michael later had the opportunity to pick up a good vineyard near Rising Star. The vineyard was in pretty good shape, but Michael and his folks babied the vines into submission, yielding great fruit that has him excited for the future. Right now, he only has a six-hundred-case capacity so he's going to have to figure out a way to expand, especially since he's looking forward to the day he can be a winemaker full time. "We will grow," he tells me. "We're just so encouraged by the response we're getting. So far, we just love what we're doing."

The Best Wines

Michael is intent on letting the grapes speak for themselves. No micro-oxygenation, no added acids or sugars, no coloring or extracts, no reverse osmosis. He's keeping the whole thing pure. His grapes are good enough that two of the best wine minds in the state—Richard Becker and Greg Bruni—have asked Michael to sign long-term contracts for his Chardonnay and Cabernet. At the Rising Star vineyard, he has healthy eighteen-year-old Cabernet and Merlot plants. In other words, the future looks bright.

There are several good wines at Rising Star, but the best are reds. **Rustler's Red** deserves a little story. "We had a home winemaker come out looking to buy eight hundred to a thousand pounds of grapes," Michael says. "We agreed on a price. He was going to get some friends and come back the next morning to get the grapes. The next morning he called me hopping mad and said, 'You dog, you sold my crop out from under me.' Turns out someone had backed a truck up overnight and picked all the grapes they could by the moonlight. All we could do with the vineyard was pick what was left and coferment all the different grapes together. It came out delicious, so we decided to bottle it and call it Rustler's Red."

Every year since, they take what's left of the red grapes after making their main wines and throw them all in so the post-theft cuvee is a tutti-frutti mix of Syrah, Barbera, Merlot, Zinfandel and whatever else seems to make sense. Imagine my surprise. It's really good. The wine is light and the tannins are very soft. Try it just a little cold, like a Beaujolais, and you'll love it with barbecue or burgers.

The other wines to pay attention to are the **Merlot**, a peppery wine with just the right amount of tannic grip, and the **Reserve Cabernet**, a wine aimed more at fans of Bordeaux than of Napa Cab.

TRIP SEVEN

🍂 *Pillar Bluff Vineyards*

300 Burnet County Rd. 111, Lampasas, TX 76550. Fri. and Sat. 10 am–5 pm, Sun. 12:30 pm–5 pm. (512)-556-4078, www.pillarbluff.com

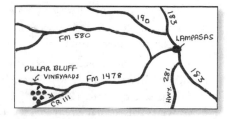

Everyone in the Texas wine business likes Gill Bledsoe. He's a kind man, ready with a smile and a good sense of fun. He's also thick-skinned enough to take a ribbing now and then. When I was going to meet Gill for the first time, I got a phone call. "Ask him about being a deacon in the Baptist Church." That was Ed Manigold of Spicewood Vineyards calling. He was laughing. "You're kidding," I said. "No." "Ask him. He'll tell you."

And he will tell you. He's proud of his association with the church, and he doesn't get too many disapproving stares from his fellow parishioners. "I look to the Bible," Gill tells me. "In First Timothy 3, it says a deacon is a man 'not double-

Gill Bledsoe relaxes at his Pillar Bluff Vineyards.

tongued and not given to much wine.' I believe that wine in moderation is not bad, only when it is taken in excess." I was impressed with his direct manner in staving off double-tonguing. As we went deeper into the subject, Gill came off as an interesting and sincerely religious man.

He was born and raised in Texas. After spending twenty years in the service, he decided to retire as a major in the Army. He and his wife, Peggy, bought a small tract of land just south of Lampasas. They built a house and planted fifty vines. They flourished, so they bought more land. They faced hordes of problems starting with bugs and pestilence and moving through terrible weather. Despite the problems, they ended up winning a handful of prestigious amateur-level winemaking awards. They decided to go commercial.

After toiling through the BATF and TABC quagmire, Pillar Bluff received the okay from the government to make wine. But there was one problem. They couldn't sell wine from the winery because they were in a dry area.

Then, in a bolt from the blue, the laws changed, allowing them to sell their wine.

In the meantime, Gill had accepted a job with a defense contractor that sent him to Iraq. He'd had about all the fun he could stand there, so he retired again in order to be a full-time winemaker.

Pillar Bluff's first vintage, 1999, was just eighty cases. They sold out almost immediately. That's a tragedy for us wine lovers, because their 1999 Merlot was one of the best in the state. They've ramped up to two hundred and fifty cases, but the best wines still sell out after just a few months.

Gill has a twin brother, Bill, who helped make wines with Peggy while he was in Iraq. That's when the good news/bad news scenario hit. "It was really hard for me to take the fact that the first two double gold medals our winery won were from wines made by Peggy and Bill while I was in Iraq." Gil has this angelic smile when he tells me the story. I can't tell if he's pulling my leg. Then it makes sense. It's just a little competition to keep him interested. This is one big happy family.

The Best Wines

Since the first edition of this book, the Bledsoes have created a new wine, one of the best they've made since the 1999 Merlot. They call it **Boardoe** (cute take on Bordeaux), and it is a combo of Cabernet Sauvignon, Merlot, Cabernet Franc, Petit Verdot and Malbec—all the principal Bordeaux varietals. It is a well-structured estate wine with a nice acidic kick, a velvety mouth feel and skillfully integrated oak.

And just so I don't put too fine a point on the small production aspect, when Gill and I sit down to taste wines the Boardoe is all he has left. The Cabernet Sauvignon, Viognier, Chardonnay and Chenin Blanc are all sold out.

Buy them when you see them, because you may not see them again.

🍁 Texas Legato

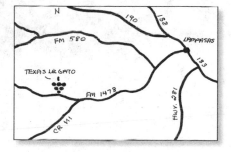

2935 FM 1478, Lampasas, TX 76550.
(Hours being decided upon at press time. She says "Wine Trail Weekends." He says "every weekend." Call ahead to be safe.)
(817) 313-9565, www.texaslegato.com

If you stop first at Pillar Bluff Vineyards, then take the two-hundred-yard drive over to Texas Legato, you might think you are seeing double. That's because Bill Bledsoe of Texas Legato is the twin of Gill Bledsoe of Pillar Bluff.

Bill and his wife, Sulynn, had been enjoying helping out at Pillar Bluff so much that they decided to buy the land next door and plant a vineyard of their own. From that point, it didn't take much encouragement to get them to start their own winery. Bill has worked most of his life either for or in the oil patch. Now he works at Bank of America in Dallas serving the petroleum industry. Sulynn also works there, in the charitable giving department. When retirement time comes (soon), they plan to spend most of their time at the winery.

Bill's hoping to see some of the same reactions his brother gets. "We spent so much time working with him," Bill says. "What I really like is when people taste your wine and their eyebrows go up. It's an immediate sense of accomplishment."

The work has been tough. They've made planting mistakes. Getting all the governmental agencies to approve their enterprise has been much more taxing than they expected. But when I ask if they would do it all over, Sulynn answers for Bill: "It depends on the day, but I think he would. He loves the vineyard work so much." Bill agrees. "I love the vineyard work, but putting in the winery has been a huge challenge."

Sulynn and Bill Bledsoe in Texas Legato's cellar.

Bill also learned a few lessons along the way, good information for folks interested in starting their own winery. "I would have planted more grapes and have good acreage of grapes already going," he says. "The real money is in the winery side of the business, but I love growing grapes, and a good supply on the day you open means you have something to show customers."

Bill planted some good varietals for the Hill Country—Malbec, Petit Verdot, Merlot and Petite Sirah—and he'll have plenty of help and support when the winery opens. As Sulynn says, "There are so many people who want to work with us and help us. And this has been such a great thing for our family."

My guess is Bill and Sulynn will be permanent residents before too long.

The Best Wines

I had a chance to taste through some barrel samples, so these aren't final evaluations, but I was impressed with the **Malbec**, a wine with a nice dark fruit and vanilla aroma and a long finish. Bill ferments in open top tanks and ages in new oak, six months in French and six months in American, which accounts for the strong vanilla aromas. The other wine that shows a lot of promise is his **Chardonnay**, a wine with nice intensity and the substantial mouth feel you find in good versions from the West Coast.

Flat Creek Estate Vineyard and Winery

24912 #1 Singleton Bend E., Marble Falls, TX 78654. Tue.–Fri. noon–5 pm,
Sat. and Sun. 10 am–4 pm. (512) 267-6310, www.flatcreekestate.com

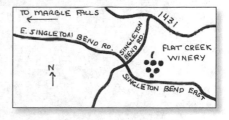

The first thing that strikes me about Flat Creek Estate Vineyard and Winery is the incredible loveliness of the place. The view as you approach the property is one of the most beautiful of Texas wineries—carefully manicured vines, rolling landscape. The winery is state-of-the-art, with every piece of test equipment you could want. The event center and tasting room is as beautiful as any in Napa. But, as usual in the Texas wine world, the owners are even more interesting.

Rick and Madelyn Naber led a peripatetic professional career. They grew up in Iowa in farming families. Rick supervised major construction sights around the world, but the traveling got to him. They decided to retire at a very young age. They loved the Texas Hill Country and decided to move to the north side of Lake Travis. After a few years of water skiing and riding their Harley, they decided they needed a new challenge. Plus, there was a nice eighty-acre spot just over the hill from their house that they were afraid would fall to the chop-a-block developers jamming the north shore with McMansions.

They thought about fruit trees, pecans, mushrooms, raspberries. Wine wasn't at the top of their list. They liked it but had no great passion for it. Then they got some help and encouragement from Ed and Madeline Manigold (Spicewood Vineyards), Jim and Karen Johnson (Alamosa Wine Cellars) and Ed and Susan Auler (Fall Creek Vineyards), and finally opted to try vineyards. But they weren't going to do it by themselves. They decided to hire an experienced, full-time winemaker.

Enter Craig Parker, a feisty, opinionated perfectionist from Australia and one of the true characters in Texas wine. He started in the wine industry at the age of five, sweeping shavings from a cooper's shop in South Australia. Craig received

The rolling Hill Country landscape provides the entrance backdrop to Flat Creek Estate Vineyard and Winery.

Madelyn and Rick Naber at the counter of Flat Creek's tasting room.

a degree in viticulture and enology and then spent fifteen years as a professional winemaker in Australia, the Champagne area of France and New Zealand. He landed a job with Robert Mondavi and worked on all his lines from Woodbridge to Opus One. Lovestruck, he followed a woman to Texas, where he'd also heard there was a burgeoning wine business.

He described his initial view of Texas wines: "I went to a lot of the wineries in Texas and wasn't impressed. The wines were musty and vegetal with too much volatile acidity. Then I met Bobby Young, who grows the best Cabernet in Texas. He told me to go to the Grape Camp run by TWGGA in Junction, Texas." Gary Gilstrap (Texas Hills Vineyards) was there and introduced Craig to his future boss. Craig also met some of the best growers in Neil Newsome and Bobby Cox.

Finally, Craig found grapes he thought were convincing proof that world-class wines could be made in Texas. "Fruit quality in the better vineyards is second to none in the world. The Cabernet Sauvignon in Lubbock, the Viognier and the Sangiovese in the Hill Country are excellent."

Though Craig and the Nabers have parted company, Rick and Madelyn intend to keep pushing the quality envelope. Rick says that they are now making world-class wines (they have the medals to prove it), but "the most exciting thing for me is developing the retail side," he says. "We have to have a presence in restaurants and in wine shops. I've already had the accolades of a successful career. Now I want to help drive the whole industry forward."

Rick has been working with the Texas Department of Agriculture to help fund Texas A&M or Texas Tech to deal with Pierce's disease. "People have to realize that if we're going to get recognition, we have to really push the industry toward more professional—not amateur—winemaking."

The Best Wines

Everyone at Flat Creek shares a standard: if it's not good, they won't release it. They realize they will get one good shot from the Texas market, and if they put out a substandard product they will lose the consumer's trust. So far they have an enviable record, with a number of awards and a strong portfolio.

The awards have mostly come for the red wines. Their **Travis Peak Reserve Cabernet Sauvignon** is a great bottle of wine, big-boned with plenty of tannic grip and a gorgeous color. Their **Prim Rosetti Secco Dry Rosé** is exactly as advertised. I can't imagine many Texas winery visits any better than getting a cold bottle of Rosé and sitting on the porch at Flat Creek enjoying a picnic lunch.

As good as those wines are, the stunner in the Flat Creek collection, a wine as good as any in the world, is **Travis Peak Orange Muscat** from Newsom Vineyards. Between the superior grapes (Neal Newsom grows unbelievable Muscat) and Parker's terrific winemaking, this wine is one of the best in Texas.

TRIP EIGHT

🍁 Comfort Cellars Winery

723 Front St., Comfort, TX 78013.
Sun.–Wed. noon–6 pm,
Thu.–Sat. 11 am–6 pm. (830) 995-3274.

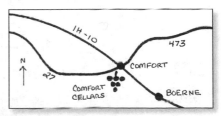

When you first arrive at Comfort Cellars Winery, you'll notice both the multitude of tchotchkes and the cutest little dog named Raisin. But the real story here is the owner, Cathie Winmill. She is a survivor.

I've watched her build this Comfort Cellars Winery from nothing and face some very tough circumstances, always with her head up. The fact that she can run a business, make the wine, work the vineyards and still have time to hand-make all those tchotchkes is astonishing. Even more so when you understand how she's wound up where she is.

Cathie was a major in the Army. She and her husband, who was also in the Army, dreamed of life after the military, for after living wherever Uncle Sam decided he needed them they wanted to settle down. Cathie had grown up in Illinois helping her father make wine, and she loved it. So they decided they would plant a vineyard in Arizona. Then tragedy struck. Her husband died and Cathie had to settle on what to do with herself. She decided to stick with her dream of a vineyard, but in the Hill Country, close to the San Antonio base where she had been posted. She faced another hurdle: the land she had was on a steep, rocky hill.

"The land just had to be terraced. It turned out to be grief therapy for me. Now I have a two-acre vineyard that is completely terraced," she says. Then the military love of acronyms comes out. "I call myself an RRS, rock relocation specialist." As she laughs at her little joke, I sense something deeper—a strength of purpose grounded in the concept that you can work your way out of pain if you push yourself hard enough. Think about the work that goes into terracing two acres of limestone. This is a survivor.

The vines were planted in 1997. But she couldn't do everything by herself. Her brother Robert decided to move down from Wisconsin and take over some of the chores. For three years she ran the tasting room and the vineyard and he made the wine. "My brother is the mushroom and I'm the sunflower. He likes to stay where it's cold and damp, and I like to stay where it's sunny."

Then he left suddenly in 2003, and Cathie had to show her survivor mentality again. There wasn't anything for Cathie to work from. No recipes, no order sheets, no vendor lists. She had to learn to make the wine herself. "Everyone at all the wineries around here stepped up to help me learn the trade fast," she says. "Cathy and Gary Gilstrap and the Switzer family came in and showed me all the stuff my brother had done, from where to order things, how

Comfort Cellars Winery's biggest sellers are sweet wines.

to file the reports. Danny at Sister Creek and Franklin and Bonnie Houser at Dry Comal—" She stops as tears well up.

"Without these people, I would have been dead. I was just clueless about the winemaking." She feels such deep gratitude for the kindness of her neighbors. "My mom and dad, in their eighties, came to help me do bottling. And my dad invents tools to help me like that punch that is light enough for me to use." She points into the corner at a homemade plunger.

Though she doesn't say so, my guess is she was scared she might have to face another death, her winery. No wonder she's emotional. Generosity in other human beings is rare enough that when you see it in the kind of help Cathie got it touches you.

"The other winemakers all take care of each other. We act as each other's therapists," she sums up. She sees the other wineries not as competitors but as all-purpose support groups. Oddly, for an Illinois native who has lived all over the world, Cathie exudes an old-style, rural Texas charm. Gracious, sweet and plain speaking, but with the obvious grit.

How does her longtime dream compare to the reality? "It's been a lot of hard work, but I don't mind hard work. There's a lot of variety. People come in from all over the globe, and I love talking to all of them. I also love working outdoors, which is what I do every morning. And I don't have to go to a gym; I climb hills, move rocks and pick weeds."

The only downside is that she wishes she had more money, at least enough to hire some help, and a little free time. "If someone has got a dream, then they should follow it. But I'd like to let them know they won't make any money at it for a long time. And you will work seven days a week almost 365 days a year." She is proud to be surviving, and she has riches beyond money in her wealth of friends.

The Best Wines

Cathie has a full line of wines ranging from dry to sweet. Given her location in the antique shoppers' town of Comfort, you might predict that her big sellers are the sweet wines, and they are. The wines I find most interesting are her stabs at blending *vitis vinifera* and non-grape products. They aren't your standard wines by any stretch of the imagination, but they are fascinating studies in what you can accomplish if you think outside the box. My favorite is **Orange Chardonnay**. I was surprised. The idea of a sweet Chardonnay doesn't appeal to me, and the idea of fermenting it with oranges doesn't turn me on, either. But I have to say this is a marvelous dessert wine. I'm not surprised to hear that this is the number one seller for repeat customers. Her other interesting flight of fancy is **Jalapeño Wine**. Yes, you read right. This stuff is only for folks with cast-iron guts, but I know a lot of you really like your food *muy picante*. Cathie's Jalapeño Wine will definitely open your sinuses.

🍂 Sister Creek Vineyards

1142 Sisterdale Rd., Sisterdale, TX 78006. Mon.–Fri. 10 am–5 pm, Sat. 10 am–5:30 pm, Sun. noon–5:30 pm. (830) 324-6704, www.sistercreekvineyards.com

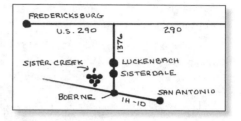

If you have any interest in antique buildings, this winery is a required stop. Housed in an 1885 cotton gin, the Sister Creek Vineyards tasting room is like falling back a hundred years. Low ceilings and incandescent lights make you feel like you're walking into a grotto. Still, it's easy to imagine the bustling gin that prospered for forty years until the boll weevil put an end to cotton in the Sisterdale Valley. The place sat empty until its hundredth birthday, when San Antonio stockbroker Vernon Friesenhahn bought it, intending to use the surrounding land to raise cattle.

At the same time, Danny Hernandez was looking for work. After a hitch in the service and moves all over the world, Danny was anxious to come home to San Antonio. He wanted an agriculture job in the Hill Country. Danny went to work for Vernon and has been with him for more than twenty years. They've forged a good working relationship. Vernon is the idea man and Danny is the implementer.

Winemaker Danny Hernandez, a 20-year veteran at Sister Creek.

Early on the two discovered that they shared an interest in wine. Danny had fallen for wine while stationed in Germany and Washington. Vernon loved the ultra-expensive and suave wines of the French Burgundy. Vernon made the decision to plant some grapes, insisting on Chardonnay and Pinot Noir, his two favorites from France. What started as a 1.5-acre vineyard soon grew to five acres with the addition of Cabernet Sauvignon, Merlot and Cabernet Franc.

They finished planting in 1988. By 1991 they were rejoicing over a beautiful crop. Just one year later, they lost 80 percent of their vines to

Pierce's disease. They rallied and decided to move away from farming and just make wine. After lining up suppliers, they started buying 98 percent of their grapes. Most came from the Hill Country and the High Plains, but they found a Cabernet Sauvignon in Arizona they like.

As the wines became more popular, the winery expanded. It's an intriguing attachment; you won't even see the expansion from the tasting room. (Ask someone to show you the back; you'll be amazed.) Things were humming along smartly until the rains of 1996. Sister Creek burst its banks and flooded both vineyard and winery. It seemed unbelievable that Danny and Vernon would pick themselves up and start again, but they did. "Yeah, it's tough," Danny tells me. "We just try to stay optimistic and not rush things."

Now they are adding better equipment and storage facilities, and they have planted four acres of Black Spanish. Their ongoing goal is to make a consistent wine, one that fans of Sister Creek Vineyards will come back for repeatedly. Given what they've been through, that could be a tall order. The place reminds me of a fighter who's been knocked down a few times but bravely keeps coming back for more.

The Wines

Sister Creek Vineyards aims at a French style of winemaking, using sixty-gallon French oak barrels (from Allier, Trocais and Nevers) and trying to avoid or to minimize filtration. All of the grapes used, with the exception of Muscat Canelli, are French grapes. The wines of Burgundy and Bordeaux are touchstones. Recently Sister Creek wines have been better than ever before, showing Danny's continuing growth as a winemaker.

The big winner here is what they call the **3 Cab.** It is a Meritage blend using one-third new oak, one-third that's one year old and one-third that's two years old. The result is an aroma with a nice hint of vanilla and toast to go along with the blackberries and plums. This is the best red wine I've ever had at Sister Creek.

The best white I've had is the **Muscat Canelli** (the regular, not Reserve). Robert Mondavi used to make a wine called Moscato d'Oro which had a similar profile: room-filling aromas of narcissus, peaches and pears, bright acidity and just a little spritz for palate cleansing. The wine is simple in the most positive sense; even people who know nothing of wine can enjoy its seductions. But making the wine is complicated. "We use an Italian approach which takes more work," Danny explains. "We keep the temperatures low, around forty-five to fifty degrees, then do a very long fermentation. Then we cool it down to twenty-eight degrees and inject it—v-e-r-y slowly—with CO_2. When we bottle it, some of the CO_2 stays in, so we get these little microscopic bubbles."

I'm glad they make the effort, and I'm not alone. The Muscat Canelli is their number one selling wine.

🍁 Singing Water Vineyards

316 Mill Dam Rd., Comfort, TX 78013. Sat. 11 am–5 pm and by appointment. On Wine Trail Weekends, Fri.–Sun. noon–5 pm. (830) 995-2246, www.shopcomfort.com/singingwater

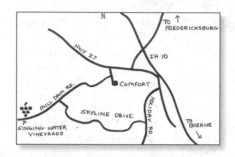

Like a lot of Houstonians, Richard and Julie Holmberg dreamed of having a getaway in the Hill Country. After roving the corporate world with Exxon, Richard landed a permanent place in the human resources hierarchy in Houston in 1988. For five years Richard and Julie looked everywhere from Lampasas to Utopia looking for that perfect plot of land.

In 1993, they got an excited call from a realtor who had found the precise place. They drove over and walked the land four times in three days. (Are these folks careful before they jump?) On the fourth day they bought the land. It was paradise. That was the heaven part. The hell was over one issue: Richard was stuck in a job in Houston.

What to do with all that land? In the oft-heard story, they went to California (Napa in their case), fell in love with the lifestyle and decided to plant some Merlot grapes to make a little wine. They sold their crop to Sister Creek, made a little wine and had some fun. The "careful before they jump" factor shows up in the progression from vineyard to winery.

Singing Water Winery has started out small.

"We took this thing real slow," Richard tells me. We're sitting in a room off the tasting room. An elder Lab is trying to live through harassment by a young Lab puppy. ("Hey! Play!!" "Hey! Play!!" If you're a dog person you know what I'm talking about.) Richard continues. "We started with a small vision and have grown incrementally. Our theory is to let the business grow itself and, if we do things right, that will work."

In general terms, Julie's proud of what they've accomplished. But she positively beams when she says, "I'm most proud of the fact that he hasn't retired to a wheelchair." He smiles back at her. This has to be a long-term marriage. "We try to make little improvements every year in both the winery and the vineyard," Richard says. "We're really small," Julie interjects drolly. "It would be fun to make money."

"Yeah, but we really want to stay around 2,000 cases," he finishes.

As if their affect didn't spell it out, they both make sure I understand. "We love this whole thing," he says. Julie agrees: "We've never been happier."

The Best Wines

The vines are young, and the Holmbergs use Enrique Ferro as their wine consultant. Ferro has specific ideas on how a wine should taste and what methods should be used. As Richard blooms and starts developing his own style, and as the vines gather a little more maturity, things should get better every year. Currently, the best wines are **Sauvignon Blanc,** a lovely, light wine, partially oaked to give it a Fumé Blanc characteristic, with nice perfumed aromas; and the **Reserve**, a combo of 55 percent their Merlot and 45 percent Newsom Vineyard Cabernet. It's a solid offering with a little red fruit flavor to go with the vanilla and tobacco nose.

leaf icon *Poteet Country Winery*

400 Tank Hollow Rd., Poteet, TX 78065. Fri.–Sun. noon–6 pm. (830) 276-8085, www.poteetwine.com

Jim Collums's real passion is pre-1900 windmills. He has a lot of them, and people from all over the United States hire him to come restore their old windmills. We're sitting there one Sunday afternoon

Jim Collums has a passion for early windmills.

sipping his excellent Strawberry Wine as he explains the subtle differences between "Monday oilers" and "annual oilers." Again, I find myself in the presence of a true Texas wine maverick.

As he leans back in his chair, he points over his shoulder and tells me that his grandma's land, over there, has been in his family since 1882. Then he explains how the building site of the winery has been in his family since 1952. "This place was originally a chicken barn with 3,000 laying hens. Then we changed over to milk cows. I was raised up milking cows here."

Jim was president of the Poteet Strawberry Festival, an annual early April bash that draws over 150,000 folks each year. In 1982 the farmers were looking for an outlet for their strawberries, and they came to Jim for help. He went to a couple of Texas wineries, and finally Dean Valentine offered to make up a batch of strawberry wine. It sold well, but Dean didn't want to do it anymore, so they tried Piney Woods. They would make 500 gallons a year. People loved it so much that it would sell out by the second day of the festival.

A few years later, the dairy business went south and Jim started raising strawberries. He found right away that he could sell all his early-season sweet strawberries during the festival. Poteet strawberries are famous for their sweetness (15 percent sugar versus 5 to 6 percent for California versions), so when harvest happens customers rush to get the first fruits. Late-season strawberries were harder to sell, but he set up a deal with H-E-B and Promised Land Dairy to buy his frozen strawberries for ice cream and milk. Then NAFTA came along.

Suddenly his old buyers could get Mexican strawberries for 40 percent less than Poteet strawberries. Jim had to come up with a use for the late-season strawberries. His buddy Bob Denson had been making homemade fruit wines for years. The festival needed more wine. And he had strawberries to spare. Why not open a winery?

Their first batch of strawberry wine sold out fast. But customers wanted something else, so they started making Mustang Wine from the local wild grapes.

Poteet Country Winery specializes in wines made from strawberries grown in the area.

"If the grapes are good and we have a wet spring, we can usually get all we need from folks around here just out picking them," he says. "You have to cut them off of the vine with scissors, 'cause they wrap all around the fences. That's why no one grows them commercially." Later, they added several other wines. They are proud that everything they make comes solely from local fruit.

They are also proud to serve customers who love fruit wines and don't intend to move into the dry Vinifera marketplace. As Jim explains, "Neither Bob or I are connoisseurs; we just like a little home brew."

The Best Wines

Emily and I once lived in Oregon, before it became a big Pinot Noir state. There were several wineries making Chardonnays and a few other white wines. But the big market was for fruit wines, especially the berry wines. I was too snooty to pay much attention to them. After tasting the Poteet wines, I wish I'd been a little more respectful. These are not replacements for Cabernets and Merlots, and they don't try to be. Instead, they are delicious drinks with delightful fruit flavors.

If these strawberry wines came from some small European country and had highly limited distribution, wine snobs like me would be tripping over their preconceived notions to buy them. Instead, this is from Poteet, Texas, and like Rodney Daingerfield, it don't get no respect, at least from the wine police. Don't be like I was. Drop your prejudices and enjoy them.

Strawberry Wine is a perfect place to start. If you like strawberries, this will surprise and charm you. Don't even think of comparing it with Boone's Farm Strawberry Hill. This stuff is good. It's their number one seller, and I understand why.

But the tête du cuvée (Jim will choke when he reads that term applied to his wines, but it is appropriate) is **Poteet Strawberry Reserve Wine.** Jim uses only the late harvest, over-ripe fruit to give you a huge flavor-packed wine. Just to make sure the aroma overpowers you, they add a little concentrated strawberry juice. This is very sweet and very thick wine, absolutely delicious for dessert. My favorite Poteet wine and one of the best fruit wines anywhere.

TRIP NINE

🍃 Dry Comal Creek Vineyards

1741 Herbelin Rd., New Braunfels, TX
78132. Wed.–Sun. noon–5 pm.
(830) 885-4121, www.drycomalcreek.com

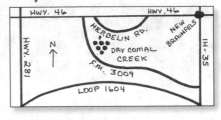

In the 1950s, Franklin D.
Houser was a soldier in Germany,
where he fell in love with the local
Riesling wines. When he got back,
after graduating from UT Law he set up a plaintiff's practice litigating for personal
injury clients and founded the law firm of Tinsman and Houser in San Antonio.

He loved Texas, but it always bothered him that, try as he may, he couldn't
find any American wines that he liked. By the 1960s Napa was starting to build a
reputation, so he went, hoping to find wines that would strike his fancy. He fell in
love with the wines of Peju Province and started to have some hope for American
wines. As his patience with the practice of law was diminishing, his belief grew
that the 103 acres he'd bought outside New Braunfels in 1975 might just be the
place he could grow grapes.

During the mid-1990s he decided to move forward with his dream and leave
law. He conscripted Dr. Enrique Ferro to consult and in 1996 planted an acre of
grapes. They did so well that he planted another 4,000 vines. Remember, grapes
should take three or four years to really bear fruit. His produced after a year and a
half. Not only did they produce, but Dr. Ferro proclaimed them high quality. They
bottled 900 cases and eventually won multiple medals for both their Cabernet
Sauvignon and Chardonnay. Then a series of catastrophes struck.

First he discovered the Dry Comal Creek isn't always dry. A big rain in
1998 left the winery two and a half inches deep in Dry Comal Creek water. The

*Franklin Houser left his
plaintiff's practice to start a
winery.*

Dry Comal defines Texas wines as "about taste and ways you make it."

winery was in a flood plain. The next set of tribulations was worse. Houser had determined to release unfiltered wines, their upside being more grip and depth. Unfortunately, he discovered the downside of unfiltered wines.

"In 1999 we had an unbelievable Cabernet Sauvignon with no filtering. But because we didn't filter it, the Cab went through secondary fermentation. It was lousy. I refused to sell it and so we lost 7,000 bottles." He shakes his head. "We didn't have any product, so we had to release our 2000 Cab early. Then one day while we were out in the vineyard we noticed the Chardonnay was looking bad. It was. Pierce's disease hit us hard. That year we only got a 10 percent crop." You can tell he's still not over his loss. An aerial photo of his vineyard tells the tale, nearly total destruction and $150,000 down the drain.

Houser wasn't thwarted. "My philosophy was that the only way you get anywhere is get up and stay in and don't give up," he explained. So, in 2000, he ripped out his vines and replaced them with Norton and Black Spanish.

He's ecstatic that his daughter has come on board, taking over the day-to-day hassles and leaving Franklin time to enjoy whatever strikes his fancy. In the meantime, no matter where he buys his grapes, he's calling what he makes Texas wine. "When I say Texas wines, I'm talking about taste and ways you make it," he explains. "I like to take grapes and reduce the tannins, get the fruit forward and make them smooth from beginning to end. The wines closest to the way I think Texas should be are Australian, but even then I think we should be different."

What has Franklin learned through his travails and successes? "Two things." He gives me that straight-in-the-eye look he probably reserves for imparting wisdom to juries and his children. "First, life is a lot shorter than you think. And when it comes to wine, well, I've been wiped out twice and I don't want to learn any more anytime soon."

The Wines

Franklin Houser cares more about the finished product in the wine bottle than where the grapes come from. Accordingly, he buys grapes from West Texas, New Mexico, Arizona, California, Washington and anywhere else he can get top grade grapes.

He is one of the true masters at coaxing every possible pleasant nuance from a grape most people gave up on in the 1960s: French Colombard. His **Bone Dry French Colombard** is a miracle of winemaking. It is pleasingly aromatic (who knew the grape had it in it?) and has a wonderful crisp acidity that makes it totally yummy.

Whether or not you like pink wines, **Franklin's White Black Spanish** is a winner. Here again Franklin takes two grapes that make a lot of bad wine and cajoles them into something delicious. In this case, the wine is made from Black Spanish grapes and French Colombard. Wine aficionados will love its shocking complexity. If you didn't know what it was, you'd guess for days. People who are normally blush wine drinkers may find the wine a little dry (it's only semisweet), but try it with an Antler's burger (see the food listings at the end of this section) and you'll be convinced.

I think the best wine Franklin makes is something he calls simply **White Port**. It's an unfortunate choice for a name, since it neither resembles a white port nor is from Portugal. But once you taste it, you'll stop worrying about labels. It's as rich as honey and incredibly complex, both in aromas and flavors. If you have a taste for the French dessert wines of Languedoc and Roussillon—Frontignan, Rivesaltes, Banyuls—this will be right up your alley. The bad news is Franklin sells out right after he releases it. And at $75 a bottle, it may very well be the most expensive French Colombard on earth. Don't miss it.

❧ La Cruz de Comal

Startzville, TX 78133. Not open to the public (see note below). (830) 899-2723, www.lacruzdecomalwines.com

Legal pundits will tell you that if you've had criminal charges brought against you and have to get off, and you have the $100,000 or so it will cost, the only firm to call is DeGuerin and Dickson. They've managed cases from Senator Kay Bailey Hutchison and Tom DeLay to Branch Davidian David Koresh (who didn't actually get off; blame our government there).

Despite the big bucks and notoriety, Lewis Dickson wants more out of life than the trappings of a big-time attorney. He wants something that money can only help with: a sense of oneness with the land that manifests itself in a nice glass of wine. Make that Texas wine.

Longtime Houston attorney Lewis Dickson runs his winery without a tasting room.

His place is down a windy road, past some barking dogs, through a couple of low water crossings, back against a limestone cliff. My poor Chrysler bottoms out about four times during the drive. When I arrive, Lewis is working in a shed. Old blue jeans, a ripped flannel shirt, dirty Redwing boots, an eight-day-old beard and incongruously, a pair of Zylo Windsor eyeglasses. (You know the look if not the name. Think Groucho Marx, Theodore Roosevelt, Mahatma Gandhi.)

When Lewis sees me drive up, he immediately sets a couple of wineglasses on a homemade bar. I purposely did not use the term handmade, because that denotes something that was carefully designed and created by hand. That would describe Lewis's wines, but not his outdoor bar. It looked like someone took some scrap, cobbled it together and had a drink.

He's already in full "go" mode. Lewis has a kind of nervous energy that can look like he's finding his way through a maze headed for a nice big piece of cheese. "This is my home," he says, and points over to small log cabin. "Come on. I want you to see it." We walk through the door and I'm surprised to see a cluttered house, stuff strewn here and there, books, magazines, guitars, CDs. It looks just like my office. I immediately feel at home. But it's definitely not what you think when you conjure a Houston lawyer.

In the kitchen, he with some embarrassment opens a book on great country homes and points at a chapter. "See, that's my house." It looks much more Ralph Lauren than Davy Crockett in the book. Personally, I like the Davy Crockett look more.

We walk back to the shed while he tells his wine philosophy. "I make unfiltered, unfined wines from Texas grapes. I ferment with natural yeasts only and don't add acid or any other of the crap you see winemakers use. I don't add grape concentrates or powdered tannins or oak chips or artificial colors. I don't add sugar or water, I don't do reverse osmosis or micro-oxygenation. You won't ever find a warning on my back label saying "Not for Sale Outside of Texas" because I tell the truth about what's in my wines and, the truth is, I don't use grapes from California or New Mexico or Arizona or anywhere else on earth other then Texas." Lewis is on a roll, arguing to a jury of one, and I'm already convinced.

In order to make wine a pure playground for commercial yeasts, you have to first kill all the naturally occurring wild yeasts. But, Lewis thinks, "When you kill off the natural yeasts and use commercial yeast it's like cutting the umbilical cord. We have fundamentally changed what the baby is. Then when you add all those acids and sugars and tannins, you end up with a Frankenstein monster." He pauses for a second. "Let me show you my cave."

We walk over to his handmade cave and stop at massive, lovingly handcrafted doors. He carefully explains how they made every part of it. When he opens the doors, there's a table with a fancy spread: Riedel glasses, linen napkins, and a centerpiece platter filled with handmade sausage, lamb ribs, grilled peppers and various cheeses. A loaf of crusty bread sits on the side. Most important, every wine Lewis makes is lined up and ready for tasting.

He's obviously a thoughtful person, and I mean both considerate and contemplative. As he opens the first wine, I ask him to share what he's learned so far.

"Three things," he says. It's obvious he's anticipated the question. "First, find out what will work on your property. Don't grow Syrah because you love Syrah. Plant what will work. Second, be prepared for the 'international school of wine' mentality. There's lots of Yellow Tail in a tuxedo out there for $100 a bottle. Why should we try to emulate that? We should make wines that honestly demonstrate how the grape tastes when it's grown in the Hill Country of Texas. But I still get people saying that since it doesn't taste like California Merlot, it can't be any good." He mutters a few off-color invectives about narrow-mindedness. "Finally, hire someone who knows what they are doing." He has the legendary California winemaker Tony Coturri on board.

Finally we settle down to the wine tasting. Lewis is a gracious host, affable and intelligent, just the kind of person you'd enjoy having a leisurely lunch with. He tells me that the main reason he doesn't—and won't—have a tasting room is because he believes his wines deserve the type of attention he's giving to them while he and I are tasting. Thoughtful consideration.

Is there any way he would ever open his winery to outsiders? He ponders the question. "You know, this is my home. Under what circumstances would you invite someone into your home? I guess if someone who sells my wine called me and told me that they had a really good customer who is serious about wine— and I mean smart enough to come in with an open mind instead of prejudging what we do—and is really wanting to learn something, maybe. Don't put that in your book."

"Please," I say. He pauses, takes a bite of cheese and a sip of wine.

"Just say it's not open to the public, but maybe it is if they catch me at the right time and I know they're really right with one of the restaurants or stores that sell the wine." What he's trying to say is that, normally, the answer is no. But if the stars should align just perfectly, if he has the time and he feels like he wants to, he might let someone see his operation. But probably not.

After years of working with juries and doing the Houston scene, I think he just wants to be careful with his little slice of heaven. I can't blame him. I'm just glad I got to share it for a few hours.

The Best Wines

This is difficult, because all of Lewis's wines have something to say. If it's not good, he'll pour it out before he puts his name on it. There's something to be said for having a successful career to help finance a perfectionist's other business. Plus, Lewis works too hard on each bottle of wine to let a mistake sully his reputation. "This morning, I was out putting organic fertilizer on the vines, one vine at a time. Who else does that? Look at the indentations at the top of the cork. You know why that's there, it's there because I hand cork every bottle. I put the label on every bottle. I glue every case. When you buy one of my wines, you're buying a part of my life."

The fact that Lewis makes less than 500 cases of wine per year allows all that attention, but it also means that he never has enough wine, and he has to charge more than most just to recoup his higher-than-average fixed expenses.

All of his wines have nice, natural acidity. Don't come looking for overly opulent jam bombs. But since everything is natural and occurring in the order God intended, the wines have a cohesiveness that is as welcome as it is uncommon. Wine lovers often talk about a wine's beginning, middle and finish. Here there are no distinctions.

But I need to pick the best wines, so here goes. I have a soft spot for his **Petard Blanc**, a near perfect rendition of Blanc du Bois, one that's better than 98.7 percent of the rest of Texas's version. When you get a whiff of his you can tell the grape has Muscat in its heritage. Plus he has found a way to bring out some complexity in this notoriously bland wine. Lewis describes it correctly as "a cross between a fine Pinot Blanc from Alsace and a Rhone-like blend of Marsanne and Rousanne."

Pinot Noir lovers should try **La Rosa**, which, despite its name, is not a rosé. It is a light-colored red wine with strawberry, raspberry and cherry aromas similar to Pinot. It goes great with the venison sausage. And a nice sideline for Texas summers—it tastes great just slightly chilled, say, at the European version of cellar temperature (57 degrees).

His best red is **Cohete Rojo** (Spanish for Red Rocket). It's a blend of Merlot, Cabernet Sauvignon, Syrah, Tannat and Alicante Bouchet. The last two grapes give intense color and the first two lend elegance, structure and some good tannic grip, while the Syrah offers a big red fruit and pepper profile. In some years Lewis will add some Norton or Black Spanish like a chef adds herbs.

All of his wines are expensive and mostly available only at really adventurous restaurants. His Website lists where you can look them up. And, who knows, maybe once you're a good customer, they'll make a call on your behalf to see if you can experience La Cruz de Comal.

🍂 Fawn Crest Vineyard

1370 West Side Cir., Canyon Lake, TX 78130. Sat. noon–6 pm or by appointment. (830) 935-2407, www.fawncrest.com

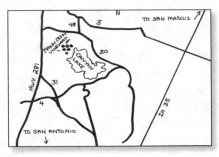

"My wife is from Berkeley, California, and she thinks red wines goes good on her Post Toasties," Wayne McNeil says about his wife, Patty. This winery is really their house and a little vineyard. Their "tasting room" is a tiny porch overlooking Canyon Lake. When they broke ground for the vineyard in November 1998, their first idea was a variation on the Blue Bell mantra, "Drink all you can and sell the rest."

That may not have been the best business plan. As Wayne says, "Like most novices, we grow the varietals we like instead of what grows best." So they planted Chardonnay, Cabernet and Merlot. As close as they are to the lake, and with all the vegetation they have around their vineyard, they should be getting killed by Pierce's disease. Instead, it's been even tougher forces of nature that have gotten their attention.

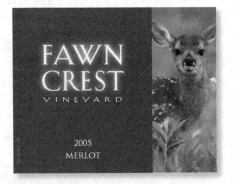

"We planted our first vines in April 1999. We had a nice small harvest in 2001. Then we got hit hard by late rains in 2002. A late freeze in 2003 killed all our fruit. Then in 2004 we got hit by late rains again." Wayne shakes his head and gives a gentle laugh. You can almost see a cartoon bubble over his head reading, "What are you gonna do?"

What they have done is buy additional grapes to make their wine. Then, tired of being rained out, Wayne and Patty installed some serious French drains in 2005 and have had better results since. Hopefully, they are in for a run of good luck.

Three Dudes Winery

125 Old Martindale Rd., San Marcos, TX
78666. Tue.–Sun. noon–6 pm.
(512) 392-5634,
www.threedudeswinery.com

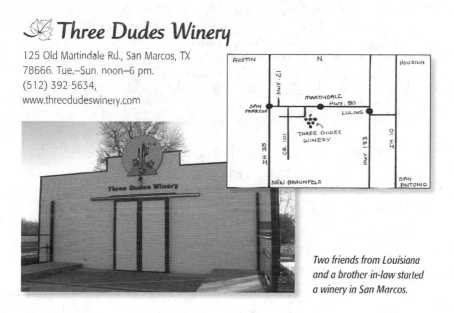

Two friends from Louisiana and a brother-in-law started a winery in San Marcos.

The three dudes are Terry Alford, Jeff Felderhoff and Ron Poitiff. Terry and Ron grew up together in Southwestern Louisiana, and Jeff is Terry's brother-in-law. The three enjoyed a regular dominoes game accompanied by the national beverage of Texas—beer. "One night we were sitting around playing dominoes and drinking a few beers," Terry explains. "We started talking about some of the wines we had made together. Everyone always said it was good, so we decided to open a winery."

Just that simple. Of course, it helps that all three are otherwise gainfully employed. Terry operates an RV park and ranch and the other two are engineers. It also helps that they've hired Bénédicte Rhyne, one of Texas's winemaking stars, to make their wine.

All three dudes are food lovers; Ron even has a degree in culinary arts, so they aim their wine at being food-friendly. They'll even take that love of food out on the back patio, where customers will be able to see cooking demonstrations and take classes in Cajun culinary arts.

Sixty percent of their wines—a fancy way to say three out of five—are dry offerings aimed at steak and seafoods. But Bénédicte warned that they needed a version of Chateau Cash Flow, so they also have a sweet wine called Texas White that outsells all their other wines combined by eight to one.

I sense that the winery is mostly a fun sideline so these buddies can spend more time together and occasionally get a little tipped. "Right now, we're having a blast," Terry tells me. "We don't mind being small. In fact, we want to stay small for the next four or five years, and if it stops being fun we'll stop doing it."

Things may grow a little faster than they expect. I ask Terry what the future holds and he says, "Follow me." We walk down two hundred yards to a high bank overlooking a gorgeous bend in the San Marcos River. "We're going to build a deck here and serve wine," he says. Isn't he worried about his business dying in the hot summertime? "Oh, I think once word gets out that this is a prime spot to watch the Texas State girls float by naked, we'll get plenty of business."

He may just have something there.

The Best Wines

The more opportunity I have to taste good **Chenin Blanc,** either dry or just off-dry, the more impressed I am with the grape. Three Dudes' Chenin Blanc is a light style, very refreshing as an aperitif, but with enough acid to make it a good food wine with raw oysters or steamed mussels. Of course, with the heavy Louisiana accent at Three Dudes, they'll tell you it's perfect for mud bugs (sorry, I want a cold Lone Star). Their red wines are light in color and body, but I liked the **Merlot's** peppery flavors and complex aromas.

¶◎ FOOD

Fredericksburg

August E's, 6258 Hwy 290 East. about five miles east. (830) 997-1585. Dinner Tue.–Thu., lunch and dinner Fri.–Sun. If you're not up for the drive to Café 909 in Marble Falls, this is the best food you'll find in the Hill Country wine region. You'll notice a decided Asian bent to the high-end cooking. Check first to make sure there's no 'skeeters, then choose outdoor dining. Are we really in Texas?

Hill Top Café, 12 miles north on Hwy 87 North. Lunch and dinner Wed.–Sun. Moderate to expensive. (830) 997-8922. This Greek boogie-woogie blues joint is way better than you would believe for a place in an old gas station in the middle of nowhere. Food's a little pricey, but the quality is there. There is also have a very nice wine list. Order from the blackboard;it's almost always the best stuff.

Lincoln Street Café, 111 South Lincoln St. (830) 997-8463. Tue.–Sun., 10 am–late. Limited food, inexpensive and wine-friendly. One of the top three or four wine bars in Texas. Imagine a wine store where you could go in and ask for any wine in the place, but by the glass. LSC offers a one-fourth bottle of any wine in the shop for one-fourth of its retail cost. That's right. No penalty for sampling the wares. I love it.

Plateau Café, 312 West Main St. (830)-997-1853. Lunch and dinner Mon.–Sat. Moderate. Great chicken fried steaks, plus Tex and Tex-Mex with a few surprises. Nice outdoor dining available.

Rather Sweet, 249 East Main St. (830) 990-0498. Breakfast and lunch Thu.–Sun., dinner on weekends. Inexpensive to moderate. Rebecca Rather has become rather famous for her high-quality home cooking. Don't expect haute cuisine, but do expect everything to be perfect.

Austin

Austin has some of the best restaurants in the state. People in this business lead unpredictable and complicated lives, so restaurants come and go, chefs come and go. The most reliable and up-to-the-minute resource is the *Austin Chronicle*, www.austinchronicle. com. The restaurants below have been in business long enough so they should ride out any economic storm and are known for having good, fairly priced wine lists. There are many more wonderful places. This is just a start.

Aquarelle, 606 Rio Grande St. Dinner Tue.–Sat. (512) 479-8117. A culinary delight. I never cease to be amazed at the amazing and consistent creativity. This is the place in Austin if you like French food.

Asti Trattoria. 408 E. 43rd St. (512) 451-1218. Lunch Mon.–Fri., dinner Mon.–Sat. Moderate. There's a list of sixty wines, offered with delicious contemporary Italian cuisine. The food is both simple and sophisticated. Owners Emmet and Lisa Fox sweat the details.

Eastside Café, 2113 Manor Rd. (512) 476-5858. Lunch and dinner daily. Moderate. A smaller wine list, thirty-five wines, twenty-three by the glass, but maybe the most perfect small list I've ever seen. Prudently picked by owner Dorsey Barger, and each bottle is a treasure. The food is garden fresh, light and always delicious.

Mirabelle, 8127 Mesa Dr. (512) 346-7900. Lunch and dinner Mon.–Fri., dinner Sat. Moderate. Owner Michael Vilim knows wine. The food, a New American style, is made to go with his wines. Mark-ups on wine are the lowest in town, with more Texas wine than most places. If Michael's in residence, tell him you're a friend of mine and get him to pick your wine. You won't be disappointed.

Vespaio, 1610 S. Congress Ave. Dinner Tue.–Sun. (512) 441-6100. Restaurant reviewers usually get paid to go to restaurants, so we can be a pretty picky group of people when we have to pay our own money. The *Chronicle* food staff's vote, by acclamation, is consistently won by Vespaio. I don't know whether to point you to the nonpareil service, to the best bartender in the city or to the ever-changing, seasonal Italian menu. You'll love it. One warning: if you're hard of hearing, this place is loud.

Johnson City

Silver K Café, 209 East Main St. Lunch and dinner daily. Moderate. (830) 868-2911. Foremost to our needs, the Silver K carries one of the best selections of Texas wines in the state. Rustic but elegant, and that describes both the food and the atmosphere. Weekends bring first-rate music, too.

Llano

Cooper's Barbecue, 604 W. Young St. Lunch and dinner daily. (325) 247-5713. Locals put their hand over their heart before uttering the name of this landmark. I'm not going to try to describe it; you have to go. If you care anything at all about barbecue, this is heaven. Plus, you get to share tables and paper towels with a hundred of your newest friends. The pork chops are to die for; at least that's what a doctor eating one told me. Open for lunch and dinner seven days a week.

Marble Falls

Blue Bonnet Café, 211 Hwy 281. (830) 693-2344. All meals daily. The old-timer of Marble Falls restaurants and one of the few more than seventy-five years old anywhere that can still keep customers standing in line, seven days a week, waiting for food. Don't worry about waiting; you'll love watching the acrobatics as the wait staff zooms around. Be sure to try as many baked goods as possible; all are made in the restaurant. Try to save room for the peanut butter pie!

Café 909, at 909 Second St. Dinner Tue.–Sat. (830) 693-2126. The owners call their cuisine "rustic gourmet." I don't know how rustic it is, but I can vouch for the gourmet. Café 909 is one of the best restaurants in Texas, with dishes like seared sweetbreads with lobster, haricot vert and white corn or seared diver scallops on an English pea griddlecake, with teardrop tomatoes and watermelon vinaigrette. How about Belly of Berkshire Pork with braised fennel, sweet potato spaetzle and curried apple butter? Also, pay attention to the music; one night we heard Blossom Dearie, Dinah Washington, Carmen McRae and Billie Holiday, a triumph of good taste—and a good iPod. Dinner only, but worth driving out of your way.

Janie's Mexican Food, 710 Ave North. Lunch and dinner Mon.–Sat., lunch Sun. Inexpensive. (830) 693-7204. Janie started almost thirty-five years ago with a simple taco shack. She was badly undercapitalized, so she got her daughter to run the shack while she cleaned people's houses. Today dining at her restaurant is a tradition, with its homemade salsas and tortillas and ultra-fresh food.

Patton's on Main. Lunch and dinner Tue.–Sat., brunch Sun. (830) 693-8664. Classy without being stuffy, owner Patton Robertson earned his spurs working with Wolfgang Puck, then brought his young family home to raise the kids with a proper Marble Falls education, just like the one he got. His restaurant is elegant yet comfortable, the wait staff is friendly and the food is good haute southwestern. be sure to try the chicken fried pork loin, the mustard crusted catfish, and, best of all, the shrimp and grits.

Spicewood

Poodie's Hilltop Bar, 22308 Hwy 71 West. Lunch and dinner daily. (512) 264-0318. When friends ask me what Austin was like during the reign of cosmic cowboy music, I just take them to Poodie's. Poodie Locke has been Willie Nelson's stage manager and right-hand man for more than three decades. More important to the rest of us, he owns a restaurant that makes the best damn hamburger on the planet. The Poodieburger has some secret ingredients, but one stands out—jalapeños. It's a yummer when washed down with an ice-cold Lone Star. And the nighttime music, well, let's just say Poodie calls in a few favors—Pat Green, Leon Russell, Billy Joe Shaver, Willie Nelson, all in a club that might hold a hundred people. Don't miss it.

RO's Outpost, 22112 Hwy 71 West. Lunch and dinner Mon.–Sat. (512) 264-1169. You say you've got a jones for barbecue, the real pit-smoked, mesquite-laden, juicy, multi-napkin stuff? How about one of the two best BBQ sauces in Central Texas (along with the Salt Lick)? Now add an absolute master/mistress of the art of pies, a funky, down-home feel and service as friendly as your sweet auntie Em could offer.

⌂ SHELTER

Fredericksburg
Bed and Breakfasts

This is where the action is in Fredericksburg accommodations; more than 250 B&B's compete for your attention. There is no way you could see all of them, so why not have a local expert book it for you? Fredericksburg has a number of booking services, but the most trusted by the folks I talked to is Gastehaus Schmidt, which books more than 150 B&B's at prices ranging from $80 up. (866) 427-8374, www.fbglodging.com.

If you would like to stay at a winery, **Becker Vineyards,** (830) 644-2681 has its own nineteenth-century one-room cabin right next to the tasting room. It's a dream of a place, small and cute with a comfortable sitting area, a working fireplace, a good bed and a bottle of the Beckers' excellent wine waiting for you.

Rose Hill Manor, 2614 Upper Albert Rd. in Stonewall, (877) ROSEHIL, is a southern mansion-style building with spacious suite accommodations and fantastic food. Wednesday through Sunday nights they offer a dynamite prix fixe ($40) five-course dinner. Rooms go for $150 and up. www.rose-hill.com.

Hotels

Holiday Inn Express, 120 N. Main St. (800) HOLIDAY. The newest econo-box, which means it should be in the best shape. Rates run about $100, depending on how full they are.

Sunday House Inn and Suites, 501 E. Main St. (800) 274-3762. A large hotel that still maintains a homey feel. This is a kid-friendly place, and the upper-priced rooms are great for families. Pets allowed. Moderate price.

Austin

Austin Motel, 1220 S. Congress Ave. (512) 441-1157. A funky 1930s hotel, renovated with the traveling rock-and-roller in mind. Small rooms for low prices, but the high-priced spread is nearly palatial. The *New York Times* picked it number one in Austin in the affordable category. www.austinmotel.com.

Four Seasons Hotel, 98 San Jacinto Blvd. (512) 478-4500. The best Four Seasons in the United States. My opinion, of course. The rooms are spacious and well furnished. The bar overlooks the Congress Street bridge, which allows you, in season, to watch the earth's largest urban concentration of Mexican free tail bats as they take off at dusk on the hunt for juicy mosquitoes. Add one of the best restaurants in Austin and you can almost forgive the prices, which start at $280 and go up to $1,400 a night.

Hotel San José, 1316 S. Congress Ave. (512) 444-7322. Renovated by one of Texas's top architectural firms and decorated like a minimalist show house. Comfortable, cool and oh-so-chic. Just a block from the Austin Motel and right across the street from Austin's coolest music venue, the Continental Club. Moderate prices. www.sanjosehotel.com.

Marble Falls

Marble Falls is largely a retirement community. Not much trendy going on, but the hotels are clean and relatively cheap. The three main choices are the **Best Western** (830) 693-5122, **Hampton Inn on the Lake,** (830) 798-1895, and the **Holiday Inn Express,** (800) 465-4329. All are similarly priced. You can also go to the **Marriott Resort at Horseshoe Bay,** about 15 minutes from Marble Falls. Room rates there are quite high.

Bandera

Bandera calls itself the Cowboy Capital of the World, which probably makes it the Dude Ranch capitol of the world. Go ahead and try something new. Be a dude at the **Twin Elm Guest Ranch,** (888) 567-3049. For $135 a night per person they feed, shelter and entertain you. www.twinelmranch.com.

☼ FUN

Austin area

Hamilton Pool Preserve. There's a lot to do at Hamilton Pool, but the real deal is swimming. For decades people used to sneak onto the Reimer Ranch, go to this swimming hole and stand under the sixty foot waterfall to cool off. The Reimers finally sold it to the county. While we never worried about it when the Reimers owned it, now the government is worried about the cleanliness of the water. So be sure to call (512) 264-2740 to make sure you can swim. If you can't, then nearby is Westcave, for hiking to a waterfall, or Krause Springs, where their view of swimming is a little more enlightened. From Hwy. 71, take FM 3238 (aka Hamilton Pool Road) and drive thirteen miles. The preserve is on your right and open from 9 am to 6 pm daily, weather permitting.

Krause Springs. Privately owned and formed by natural springs. Native Americans were swimming here while Europeans were debating whether the world was flat. Seventy gallons a minute of 70-degree water flows in. No matter how hot it is outside, this is a cool paradise. You can camp year-round, but swimming is only in the summer. From Hwy. 71 in Spicewood, take Spur 191 by the Exxon station, then turn right on County Road 404 and look for the sign on your left. (830) 693-4181.

Westcave Preserve. Back in the 1960s, student referred to this place as Dinosaur Swamps. No swamps, no dinosaurs, but it was the sixties, so there were plenty of seeds and stems. Today it is a preserve offering gorgeous rare and endangered plants in their natural habitat. The cave itself is considered very spiritual. Part of it collapsed many million years ago. Now the sunken part is shaded by cypress trees, which, along with the gently flowing stream, keep the place about fifteen degrees cooler than the rest of Central Texas. The only way you can get in is with a guide, and then only on tours on Saturday and Sunday afternoons. Once a tour fills up you have to wait two hours for the next one. No reservations. Same directions as Hamilton Pool, but keep on going on FM 3238 until you cross the Pedernales River on a low bridge, then start looking to your right for the signs. (830) 825-3442.

Bend area

Canyon of the Eagles. That's bald eagles; this is where they spend their winters. Take a lake cruise to see their nesting grounds up close. One warning: this looks like it's close to Fall Creek Vineyards, but that's as the eagle flies. For those of us confined to cars, the trip takes almost ninety minutes. There is also a lodge. I haven't seen it, but Ed Auler, owner of Fall Creek Vineyards, says it is nice, and the lodge apparently has a boat that will transport you to Fall Creek Vineyards. From Hwy. 29, take Ranch Road 2341. (800) 977-0081, www.canyonoftheeagles.com.

Fredericksburg area

Comfort. Comfort was founded by German settlers in the 1850s. They loved the area so much they called it Camp Comfort. Trees for shade, plenty of water, so they stayed and built a town. Comfort is on the National Register of Historic Places and jammed to the gills with art galleries and antique shops. Comfort sits right on Hwy. 10, due south of Fredericksburg.

Devil's Backbone. A beautiful drive across the Hill Country with some nice vistas, also a convenient way to get back to Fredericksburg from Driftwood. The Devil's Backbone is the nickname for FM 32. Pick up the road from Hwy. 12 just south of Wimberley, drive west until you hit Hwy. 281. That's the end of the Backbone, but there's more fun to come. Turn north on 281, then west on FM 1623 in Blanco. When the road makes a Y take FM 1888. That dead-ends into FM 1376. A right turn will take you to Luckenbach and then to Fredericksburg. A left will take you down to Sister Creek Vineyards. You'll also see a lot of beautiful Texas country.

Enchanted Rock State Park. A 1,650-acre park with a huge granite outcrop for hiking, climbing or rappelling. Picnic and camping available. Eighteen miles north of Fredericksburg on Ranch Road 965N.

LBJ State and National Historical Parks. Seven hundred acres that includes a good visitor center, lots of info on our thirty-sixth president and opportunities to photograph buffalo and longhorns. Sixteen miles east of Fredericksburg on Hwy. 290 East. (830) 644-2252.

Lavender Garden at Becker Vineyards. The Beckers wanted both the looks and aromas of southern France, some of which looks very much like the Texas Hill Country, so they planted a three-acre lavender garden. The aromas are so powerful they had to stop doing tastings outside, since no one could smell the wine. A paradise for your nose.

Luckenbach. Let's go along with Waylon, Willie and the boys (actually, Waylon has passed this mortal coil), enjoy the free-spirited cosmic cowboy crowd, drink some ice cold beer and listen to the various troubadours who just bring their guitars and sing. A delightful place to wile away an afternoon. Eight miles southeast of Fredericksburg on Ranch Road 1376.

National Museum of the Pacific War. Dedicated to those who served in the Pacific during World War II. If you have even a remote interest in the war, you can't miss this. Newly refurbished and one of the best small museums in the nation. 340 E. Main St. (830) 997-4379.

Shopping in Fredericksburg. Shopping's fun (if touristy) in this sweet old German town, where road names are bilingual. Join one of the other 250,000 annual visitors and just stroll Main Street. Delightful.

Wildseed Farms. The nation's largest wildflower seed farm, open daily with self-guided tours. The best time to go is from spring through the first frost. Seeds for sale. Seven miles east of Fredericksburg on Hwy. 290 East. (830) 990-1393.

Willow City Loop. One of the most beautiful drives in Texas, but it is not easy to find. Mostly on private roads, where the residents tolerate, but not always with a smile, the fact that everyone wants to see the sights. Do it anyway. If you think Texas looks like a John Ford western, this will change your mind. Keep your eyes out for bald eagles. From Fredericksburg, head north on Hwy. 16 toward Llano. Turn right on 1323 and drive two miles until you get to Willow City (take the term "city" loosely). In Willow City, 1323 makes a sudden hard right, but you want to turn left. Stay on that road and follow it until you get back to Hwy. 16. Turn left and head back to Fredericksburg. If you need directions, stop at Harry's, a little store that has been in Willow City since 1870. They also have good beer and barbecue.

New Braunfels area and south

Poteet. See the world's largest strawberry! Okay, it's a model. But who doesn't want to have their picture taken with a seven-foot-tall, 1,600-pound fruit?

Schlitterbahn Waterpark. Schlitterbahn is German for "slippery road." This place outside New Braunfels is filled with water rides and kids. Open 10 am to 8 pm during the summer. From IH 35 take exit 189, turn right onto Loop 337; follow Loop 337 to Common Street; turn left and go straight to Liberty Street; turn right and drive through the entrance.

CHAPTER 4

The Wine Roads of the
Prairies and Lakes

I n this huge region of Texas, two clusters of wineries are at opposite ends, 170 miles apart. The northern section around Dallas/Fort Worth has twenty-three wineries and takes five days to cover. The southern section around Bryan/College Station has eight wineries and takes two days.

NORTH

Here you choose between an urban and a rural setting for your lodging. Grapevine makes a handy central home base, especially with the Las Vegas–size Gaylord Opryland Hotel. But if you're averse to spending a couple of long driving days, stay in Grapevine for Trips 1 through 4 and stay near the gorgeous quarter horse country surrounding Tioga for Trip 5.

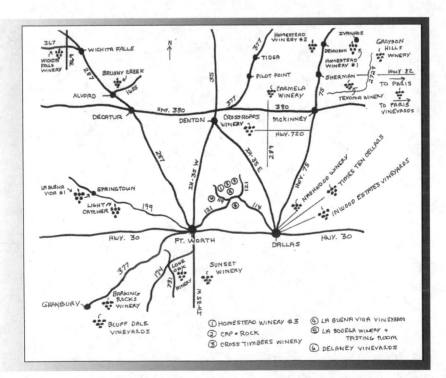

Here's the layout for the trips:

TRIP 1: Lightcatcher Winery, La Buena Vida Vineyards–Springtown, Brushy Creek Vineyards, Wichita Falls Vineyards and Winery.

TRIP 2: La Buena Vida Vineyards–Grapevine, Delaney Vineyards, Homestead Winery Grapevine and, if you can figure out a post-9/11 strategy to get into an airport, La Bodega Winery.

TRIP 3: Nashwood Winery, Times Ten Cellars, CrossRoads Winery, Carmela Winery and, finally, Inwood, in the unlikely event he will let you in.

TRIP 4: Sunset Winery, Barking Rocks Winery and Vineyard, Bluff Dale Vineyards and Lone Oak Winery.

TRIP 5: Homestead Winery–Denison, Grayson Hills Winery, Texoma Winery, Paris Vineyards.

TRIP ONE

🍂 Lightcatcher Winery

6925 Confederate Park Rd., Fort Worth, TX 76108. Thu.–Sun. noon–6 pm. (817) 237-2626.

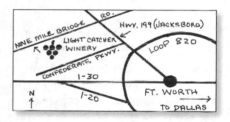

My wife and I are sitting outside on a pleasant October afternoon with winemaker Caris Palm Turpin and her husband, Terry. We're enjoying a spectacular glass of Caris's Orange Muscat and talking about how she became a winemaker.

Terry came from a long line of Texans and Caris is from a Texan house in San Francisco. Caris worked in her chosen field as a cinematographer for Industrial Light and Magic on films like *The Witches of Eastwick*. But they longed for a little Texas in their life and moved from San Francisco to Texas in 1989. Caris made films for the Boy Scouts and then got a call from PBS producer Betty Buckley about handling visual effects for a new kid's show about a dog named *Wishbone*. That show required sixteen-hour days and a pledge to avoid any personal life. Her grandmother had made wine for the family. Caris thought making a little of her own juice might relieve some stress.

As in most things Caris gets interested in, she became driven to figure out how to make great wine. She started using five-gallon car-boys and grape concentrate but describes the results as vile. She decided her problem was the concentrate. So the next year she bought fruit from Napa and ended up winning Silver Medals in the Best of Texas competition. Caris was hooked.

But she still didn't understand the process, so she started looking for a place to learn. Two years at Davis was financially out of the question, but then someone told her about the enology program at Grayson County College. She set a simple goal: "I want to make better wine than Opus One using Texas fruit." Shouldn't be a problem, right?

"So many people were tasting my wine and telling me I should go professional," she says. "Terry and I decided to go out to California and check out the smaller wineries and see how they make a living."

"We went out to California and visited micro-wineries," Terry cuts in. "We found two types. There were the retired rich guys who only had to break even. We also met folks like us who really want to make great wines but also need to make a living. Now, I'm not crazy. We would never have committed to the time, energy and money involved if Caris hadn't been such a good winemaker. But I knew how good she was. That was the determining point about whether to go ahead."

They took their wine to Grape Camp, the annual gathering put on by the Texas Wine and Grape Growers Association. While there, Neal Newsom, owner of one of Texas's premiere vineyards, decided that Caris's work was good enough for him. Her first wine from Newsom's Vineyard grapes won another award.

"Neal's confidence in our ability came from his tasting my amateur wine," Caris explains. "We won all those awards and now we have a permanent contract with Newsom. I believe in serendipity: when a door opens, I need to be aware of it and walk through it."

Terry sums it up: "We took a leap, mortgaged everything we owned and jumped into the wine business."

Caris and Terry have become very popular among other winemakers. They both share a nice cross between perfectionist and laid-back, relaxed, affable bohemians. They've built a gorgeous winery just outside Fort Worth. It's nothing like the places on Highway 29 in Napa, but instead is cozy, comfortable and inviting. A true reflection of the owners.

Caris and Terry Turpin at Lightcatcher's tasting bar.

Carris says, "Everything we believe in is in our wines. We've tried to tie in everything we love: music, art, wine. Expressions of a lifestyle I like to call the culture of the table."

They are succeeding.

The Best Wines

Picking Caris's best wines is a tough assignment. Everything she makes displays a strong personality, as Caris does. However, I can say that one of my favorite wines in all of Texas is her **Dry Orange Muscat.** The highest compliment I can give it is that the flavors and aromas are reminiscent of the world-famous Zind-Humbrecht Muscat Herrenweg de Turckheim from Alsace. On the palate, it is a bit lighter, but all the Muscat aromas that bloom when the wine is fermented to dryness—tropical fruits, narcissus, orange blossoms—are there in a huge bouquet. Wow!

I also am a big fan of what Caris accomplishes with Merlot. Both her **Lightcatcher Merlot** and her **Newsom Vineyard Merlot** have flavors like chocolate, mint, dark berries and more chocolate. She judiciously gets just the right amount of oak into the wine and provides a welcome density of fruit, providing a substantial wine.

Try everything.

La Buena Vida Vineyards–Springtown

650 Vineyard Ln., Springtown, TX 76082.
Open by appointment only. See the section on La Bodega.

Brushy Creek Vineyards

572 County Road 2798, Alvord, TX 76225. Daily 10 am–6 pm and by appointment.
(940) 427-4747, www.brushycreekvineyards.com

Les Constable is a man with the intellect of a nuclear engineer and the soul of a dreamer. His father was a research botanist, so Les grew up around research in the family garden. He is a nuclear engineer by trade and has the personality of an inveterate tinkerer

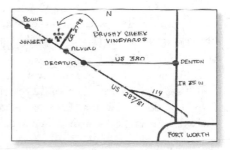

Les Constable does a wintertime check of his vines.

and experimenter. Les sees his movement from nuclear-powered submarines to wine as just part of a continuum.

"The sun is a nuclear reactor," he says, "and the sunshine that grows the grapes is just another form of nuclear radiation, so owning a vineyard is just a continuation of my earlier career."

We're riding a golf cart around his vineyard. As rows whiz by, I see odd varietals next to obscure clones. Les is trying to suss the secrets of Mother Nature to figure out which grapes grow best in his corner of the world.

"I've been making wine here for fifteen years, and there's still a whole lot I don't know," he says. "I originally planted the Bordeaux varietals because I love Bordeaux. But they were the wrong grapes." He sighs, as if all the work he put into those inappropriate grapes has just hit him again. "So now I grow the Tablas Creek Clone of Mouvedre, Tempranillo, Grenache, Carignan and Carnelian." He starts watching me for my reaction. When I look at him quizzically—I've never heard of Carnelian—he starts giggling like a happy Santa Claus. Les loves to surprise people.

Carnelian is a cross between Cabernet Sauvignon and Carignan, which is then crossed with Grenache. It was developed by the University of California for hot weather growing, and what little is left in California goes into jug wines. Now you know more than I did.

My favorite Les Constable story is about growing Rkatsiteli (ri-cats-a-TELL-ee), a grape from Eastern Europe that is hugely popular in the Georgian Republic and in Bulgaria. Some estimate that it is the second most highly planted white grape on earth, although few knew it in the United States.

Les wanted an expert, so he hired a Greek Orthodox monk living near the Black Sea who was also a botanist. That's classic Leo.

"What you'll find is that if everyone else is doing something, I'm doing it different." How true.

Back in the petite but comfortable tasting room, Les gets a phone call. My wife, Emily, leans in and whispers, "He's like an artist. This is incredible." Now my wife should be suffering from winery burnout, given all the places I've dragged her to over the years. When she gets genuinely excited, something special is going on. Les Constable is someone special. Don't miss him.

The Best Wines

Les doesn't make a bad wine. The big problem is he doesn't make enough. "I am selling every wine out as soon as I can make it," he says wistfully. "I can't put my wines in contests because I already can't keep up with the demand." The longer I talk with Les, the more I get the feeling he is one of the winemakers in the game purely out of love. Oh, I think he'd like to make a profit, but the key for him is the quest, not the conquest. Luckily, those of us who can get to his winery can enjoy the fruits of Les's expedition.

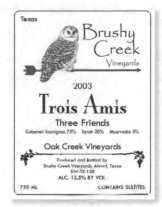

Since Brushy Creek wines sell out shortly after release, if you find one you like, buy it. Despite the fact that Les loves big, assertive red wines more than anything, he makes the most delicate and delightful white wine: **Heritage White Table Wine,** one of the few dry Muscats in the state. Bone dry and intensely aromatic, the wine is cold fermented and babied until it hits the bottle. Great stuff.

Big red wines are where Les really shines. **Trois Amis** is Cabernet Sauvignon, Shiraz and Mouvedre. There's lots of smoky richness with intense Mouvedre and Syrah-style pepper and earthiness. And what deep color! While you're at the winery, ask Les if he has any Mouvedre from his own vineyard. It's supremely jammy, dark colored and as delicious as any Rhone version. **Syrah's Shiraz** is another intense, rich and delicious wine, gussied up with all-new American oak.

If you really want some wine fun (designated driver required), buy a bottle of the **Mouvedre** and one of **Syrah's Shiraz** and try blending the two in your glass. Start with 80/20 Mouvedre/Syrah and work your way by tens to 20/80 Mouvedre/Syrah. When you wake up, you'll have had one of the best wine experiences Texas has to offer.

Wichita Falls Vineyard and Winery

3399 Peterson Rd. South, Iowa Park, TX 76367. Mon.–Sat. 10 am–6 pm, Sun. 2 –6 pm.
(940) 855-2093, www.wichitafallsvineyardsandwinery.com

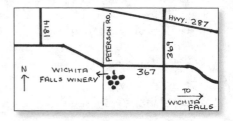

After traveling in Napa, Sonoma and in the Finger Lakes region of New York, Alton and Lana Gates got the winemaking bug. They took some classes at Grayson County College, found some help from Les Constable at Brushy Creek and set about making their dream into a reality. They planted their vineyard in 1997 and opened their winery in 2003.

Just one problem: There's not enough high-quality Texas grapes to go around. So they started another label using out-of-state grapes and call it Gates Vineyards. For wines made from Texas grapes, they continue to use the Wichita Falls Winery label.

I applaud this truth in packaging. Too many wineries in Texas aren't straightforward about where they get their grapes. Wines made from out-of-state grapes can still have an appellation, either where they're from or an American appellation. If the wine says Texas on it, it's supposed to be from Texas. If it says Hill Country or Texoma or High Plains—then that's where the grapes are from. But the oddball laws allow wineries to make wines without being completely candid. Look on the back label, in small print, for the words "Not for sale outside the state of Texas." That means the wine isn't following the federal standards but meets the state's.

So kudos to the Gateses for being totally up front.

The Gateses have had one of the fastest growth trajectories I've seen in Texas wine. In the space of three years they went from a production of zero cases to 18,000, and their wines are available at more than 150 outlets throughout the state. That's phenomenal progress. Walking through the winery, I could see that they have room and equipment for making even more wine. Alton really planned ahead on this.

Another kudo for being the first winery in Texas to put in a full-time screw-top bottling line. Alton uses the best there is: Stelvin Plus seals. I'm a big fan of screw tops. Most wine is consumed within six hours of being purchased, so why put a cork, meant to help a bottle age well, in a wine that will be drunk tonight? Plus, corks have a 2 to 10 percent failure rate, when a pesky microbe gets in and makes the wine smell like a wet cardboard box. No such problems with the screw top. Plus, nothing beats a screw top for an impromptu picnic.

Alton feels he's learned a few important lessons in his years of business. Here's a good list for someone thinking about opening a winery:

1. Be aware that this is a very capital and labor intensive business. In the best of all possible worlds, it will be sixteen months to three years before you make any money at all.

2. You have to get a good idea of how many bottles you can really sell. Our original goal was to make wine enough for selling on weekends. When I decided to try to make a living at wine, I had to buy all new equipment to make sure I could cover the increased numbers. If I'd known then what I know now, I would have made a bigger winery and bought better equipment.

Wichita Falls Vineyard and Winery owners Lana and Alton Gates have built one of the fastest growing wineries in the state.

3. When you are just starting, make lighter and sweeter wines. They sell the best and you can at least build up a little capital.

4. Most important: Remember, you can't make only the wines you like—for instance, I like big dry red wines. You also have to make wines for the casual wine drinker.

5. Find a mentor. I only took two enology classes and one viticulture course at Grayson. But I learned more from Kim McPherson than anyone.

The Best Wines

Gates Vineyards wines are mostly from Amador County in California. Amador is known for its hot days and ripe fruits, and Gates Vineyards wines reflect that profile. The best of the lot is the **Zinfandel Reserve Port**, an unbelievably dense and rich wine with the flavor of a real Port, as in the stuff that comes from Portugal.

Alton's Texas wines show a keen sense of getting strong fruit flavors and deep colors. His **Wichita Falls Winery Sangiovese** shows the influence of mentor Kim McPherson, and that's a good thing, since Kim makes one of the best Sangioveses in the state. Alton's version has a little more depth and darker color than Kim's. It is a real winner. I also like his **Wichita Falls Winery Viognier**. While it could use just a little more acid, Alton's version really pumps up the white peach and apricot aromas and finishes clean and tasty.

TRIP TWO

🍁 La Bodega Winery and Tasting Room

Terminal A Gate A-15 and Terminal D Gate 14, DFW International Airport.
Daily 11 am–8 pm. (972) 574-1440 or (972) 973-9463.

La Bodega's place in an airport makes it difficult to visit in a post-9/11 world. For a full description, see the section below on its co-owned La Buena Vida Vineyards.

🍁 La Buena Vida Vineyards — Grapevine

Tasting Room, 416 E. College St., Grapevine, TX 76051. Mon.–Sat. 10 am–5 pm, Sun. noon–5 pm. (817) 481-9463, www.labuenavida.com

Vineyards, 650 Vineyard Ln., Springtown, TX 76082. Open by appointment.

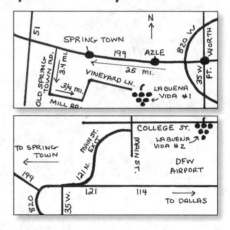

Gina Puente-Brancato is a fascinating jumble of contradictions. She's got the energy of a small stick of dynamite yet has the political savvy to enjoy widespread respect from growers and winemakers. She has a quick mind and an entrepreneurial spirit yet pays attention to the details. And she looks so sweet and nice, but I wouldn't want to be across the negotiating table from her.

In 1988 Gina's father, then 6si, decided to buy some news dealerships at DFW Airport. Things were going well, except for one location in the American Airlines terminal. Gina had a killer idea. Thousands of people walk through the American Airlines terminal each day. What would happen if she put a winery there?

Travelers are always hassled and either scrambling for a plane or sitting, bored. It's almost impossible to find good wine in an airport. Why not open a place with the stylish relaxation of a winery and take care of the traveler searching for some good wines at the same time? Like most good ideas, you wonder why someone else didn't think of it first.

They applied for the winery license, then renovated and transformed a 430-square-foot area into an operating winery. The manufacturing part had to be small.

Gina Puente-
Brancato at her
DFW Airport winery.

Since they sell a lot more wine than they have space to make, Gina uses facilities of other Texas wineries to make her wines. Something is going right, because she's winning a bunch of awards.

But La Bodega answers an even higher calling: representing Texas. Many travelers who come through have no idea about Texas wines. So rather than hog the space exclusively for La Bodega Wines, Gina offers thirty-plus wines from other Texas wineries, both by the glass and by the bottle. No telling how many wine enthusiasts have their first taste of Texas wine in Gina's winery.

"You know what I love about the wine business—it's not cutthroat, everyone wants to help," she says. "A rising tide raises all ships." Gina is an optimist and a true entrepreneur, something she inherited from her father.

The most exciting recent occurrence for Gina is their purchase of La Buena Vida Winery in Grapevine. "After 9/11, it's been tough to get our wines to consumers other than the folks running through the airport," she explains. "I'm so excited about finally having a land-based winery. Our wines always do well in contests, but it was always so much trouble to buy our wines for people not traveling."

Dr. Bobby Smith, founder of La Buena Vida, will continue to make wines from his own vineyard in Springtown. The wines will go by La Buena Vida—

La Buena Vida's Camille
McBee was the first female
president of the Texas
Wine and Grape Growers
Association.

Springtown. Dr. Smith is an institution in Texas wine, personally responsible for changing a few key laws that helped pave the way for the modern Texas wine industry. He's also learned a lot in his years of winemaking, knowledge Gina hopes to tap. She's also happy that Camille McBee is staying on at La Buena Vida's tasting room. Besides having managed the place for an eternity, Camille shares something in common with Gina: they've both been president of the Texas Wine and Grape Growers Association. Camille was its first female president, Gina its second.

The Best Wines

La Bodega Private Reserve Merlot is a big prize winner. This wine has chocolate and tobacco flavors with intense vanilla and black cherry aromas. Okay, there may be just a little too much vanilla. It's my favorite La Bodega wine. I also enjoy **La Bodega Private Reserve Chardonnay**. It has a nice balance of new oak to fruit and a nice mouth feel.

Over in the La Buena Vida tasting room, I really like **La Buena Vida Pinot Blanc,** a light and refreshing wine in the style of Alsace. But their most famous wine is in shorter and shorter supply. The **1984 Walnut Creek Cellars Port** has won twenty-two medals in international competitions. Its $150 for a .375, a price range most folks think is beyond Texas wine. If they have a bottle open, buy a taste. You'll be amazed.

⚜ *Delaney Vineyards*

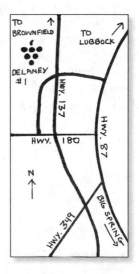

Tasting room, 2000 Champagne Blvd., Grapevine, TX 76051. Retail store open daily. Tours and tastings Saturdays. Call ahead for times. (817) 481-5668, www.delaneyvineyards.com

Vineyard and Winery, County Rd. J-16, north side, 1 mile north on Hwy. 137 N., Lamesa, TX 79331. (806) 872-3177. By appointment.

Jerry Delaney is a successful businessman with a taste for French wine. A native of West Texas, he studied engineering at Texas Tech and formed several companies in the aeronautics and electroplating fields. He always loved the area he grew up in. He eventually bought 240 acres near his hometown of Lamesa and planted it in cotton. But after traveling to France he was bitten by the wine bug and wanted to try his hand at growing grapes and making wine. His goal is to produce the highest-quality French varietal wine in the state

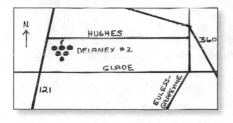

and be able to charge proportionate prices for it.

He also wants a chance to spend more time farming. "I'm getting more heavily involved with the wine business, because of all my businesses this is where my heart is," he says. "I love tilling the soil, watching the sun coming up, seeing all these clusters of grapes. And I love driving my tractor."

Delaney started in Lamesa with Cabernet Sauvignon, Merlot, Cabernet Franc, Chardonnay, Zinfandel and Riesling. In 1996 he decided to build a showcase winery in Grapevine. He planted Merlot and Cabernet Sauvignon but lost his entire vineyard to Pierce's disease. Since then he's planted Cynthiana, aka Norton, which is less susceptible to disease but not currently up to snuff in the world of fancy French wines. He also had to redo the entire site, adding loamy soil to the hard clay soil. These new grapes should adapt much better to the tough soils around Grapevine.

When you drive up, you'll see that Delaney not only loves French grapes but loves French architecture. The imposing French Baroque 14,000-square-foot, $6 million winery is a massive building, opened in 1996, one of the most beautiful wineries in the state.

The Lamesa site is almost the polar opposite. Down a dusty county road, this winery looks more like a warehouse—which is appropriate, for it's set up for work, not touring. They don't mind people coming out to see the place, but there's no tasting room or on-premises sales. This is also where Delaney has the most fun. "I love agriculture," he says. "I don't expect to ever make a lot of money, but I just love it." In fact, if he had it to do all over, he'd focus more on being a vineyard owner than a winemaker. "The retail business is tougher than I thought. In all my businesses, I have always been in the manufacturing side, so I'd focus a little more on the agriculture side. Like I said, I love driving my tractor."

The Delaney Vineyards winery building is one of the finest in Texas.

The Best Wines

Over the years **Sauvignon Blanc** has won a lot of awards for Jerry Delaney. It is a smoky, oaky style with plenty of tropical fruit coming through. This won a Best of Show award at the Best of Texas tasting. The award is based on double-blind tasting by a knowledgeable crew (this writer included), and this wine blew everyone away. He also does well with his **Reserve Chardonnay**. This wine uses new oak, well integrated with the fruit. Delaney's Chardonnay has good weight and is rich. On a recent visit it was good enough to drink at room temperature.

The best wine, now sadly in short supply, is the **1996 Lamesa Cabernet Sauvignon**. Jerry Delaney still has a tiny bit of this long-lived wine. Aromas of pencil lead and dark berries lead to a nicely acidic and somewhat tannic mouth feel. Let it sit open for a while and the wine turns chocolaty and rich. Fascinating wine.

Homestead Winery–Grapevine

211 East Worth St., Grapevine, TX 76051. Wed.–Sat. 11 am–5:30 pm, Sun. 1–5:30 pm. (817) 251-9463, www.homesteadwinery.com

This location is mostly a tasting room and knick-knack shop. Its main benefit to you is its proximity to other wineries in downtown Grapevine. If you need the time, this is a good introduction to Homestead Winery. If you have an hour or so to kill, go to the Denison outpost. You'll find a complete description of the three facility operation under **Homestead Winery–Denison**.

TRIP THREE

Nashwood Winery

11661 Preston Rd. #240, Dallas, TX 75230. Wed.–Fri. 11 am–6 pm, Sat. 10:30 am–5 pm. (214) 346-9932, www.nashwoodwinery.com

Karen and Steve Eubanks have the only commercial vineyard within Dallas city limits. It's small, but it's there. They also have a winery in the dry section of Dallas.

For those not used to the arcane, post-Prohibition rules of Texas, each area of the state can decide whether

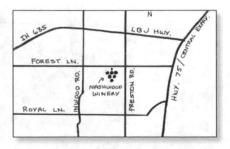

Nashwood is the only winery open to the public within the city limits of Dallas.

to allow demon alcohol on its streets. For some unfathomable reason, Dallas, one of the largest and most sophisticated cities in the United States, is a crazy patchwork of wet and dry areas. Imagine the surprise of visiting business road warriors finding out they can't buy wine in the posh area bordered longitudinally by Central Expressway and Inwood Lane, and extending from Northwest Highway all the way north to Addison.

Karen and Steve thought they'd have a gold mine on the ground when they opened in dead center in that wine-parched, well-heeled part of Dallas. But as financial professionals, they probably knew that most business plans don't end up coming true and that a real problem is perception. Wine shops with world-class collections exist a few miles away at Inwood and Belt Line, and they'd have had trouble competing simply as a wine shop. So they've worked hard to get the word out that they are also a winery. "People are always surprised we actually make the wine here," Karen says. "They think we are just a wine shop."

Indeed, though it's one of Texas's smallest-scale operations, this is a fully functioning winery. The wine is fermented and aged in their little shop across Preston Road from Whole Foods. Most of the grapes come from Lamesa, south of Lubbock. Each year Nashwood makes different wines but generally keeps about six in production.

Since opening in mid-2004, Karen and Steve have had to work hard, and neither is quitting their day job. If they knew then what they know now, they say they'd probably spend their money on buying and drinking wine instead of making and selling it. Of course, they are not alone in reaching such a conclusion; wine's siren song has sunk a lot of financial ships. But in the meantime, they're taking it one day at a time, savoring the moments when customers really like their wines.

The Best Wines

Karen and Steve grow small amounts of Pinot Grigio and Zinfandel in their Dallas vineyard. Otherwise they buy everything from West Texas. Karen's favorite wine is also mine, their **Chenin Blanc**. Fermented slightly sweet, the wine is a perfect match for Asian food. Their biggest seller is their **Meritage** ("probably because it has the medal around the neck," Karen quips). It's also Steve's preferred drink.

🍁 Times Ten Cellars

324 Prospect Ave., Dallas, TX 75214.
Tue.–Wed. 1–10 pm, Thu.–Sat. 1–11 pm,
Sun. -7 pm. (214) 824-9463,
www.timestencellars.com

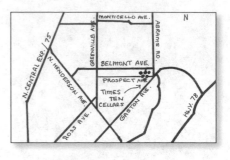

A truly trendy and cool location almost guarantees Times Ten Cellars success. Right in the dead center of Lakewood, ensconced in an old bank building and featuring a comfortable, conversation-encouraging interior, this place could hardly be topped for a Dallas winery.

Apparently a lot of women in the area agree. When we first walk in, there are two rooms filled with about twenty women each, chatting happily and drinking the house wines. One room contains birthday revelers while the other has a wedding shower, both groups seemingly delighted with being beautiful (dress is casual but Dallas-fancy) and being at Times Ten.

This place is as much a wine bar as a winery. Kert Platner and Chris Lawler are the original partners. Kert is the creative spirit and Chris is the winemaker. After about a year they added a business person and Rob Wilson joined.

The Times Ten vineyard is just south of Alpine, where days are bright and warm and nights cool and dry. If everything goes right, this could be a scenario similar to the western hills outside Paso Robles—ideal for Rhone and Spanish wines like Syrah and Tempranillo. But based on current demand, Ten Times production has to be more than the West Texas vineyard can provide, so grapes are bought from California.

It's a good strategy. California is experiencing a glut of grapes, so Chris can buy them dirt cheap. Rob would like to be a little more Texas-centric: "Somewhere

Ten Times Cellars is headquartered in a former bank building in Lakewood.

down the road we'd like to go to all Texas wines, but we'll probably always have to use some grapes from outside the state." They hope the Texas wines will eventually account for 2,000 cases. Add to that the 7,000 cases they are currently making from California juice, and you have a sizable operation.

I'm not sure that's where they'll stop. Chris is making some very good wine, and Times Ten is selling most of it at the winery. If they expand distribution at all—which I think is likely given Rob's low-key but savvy marketing ideas—they may be looking for a lot more fruit. In the meantime, the three seem to enjoy each other and naturally gravitate to their roles. Rob comes from the pharmaceutical business and loves to keep order around the place. Chris is the earthy guy, willing to do the dirty work. Kert loves to chat up the customers and think of new ways to make the place more comfortable and inviting.

Which brings up the most important things you will find at Times Ten Cellars: a relaxing environment for a civilized glass of wine, just enough buzz to keep you interested, great music in the background and decent wine in your glass. It's a terrific way to get out of the Dallas commotion and unwind.

The Best Wines

Times Ten makes about a dozen wines, depending on what's in the vats and what they can buy. When the vineyard reaches full capacity, they'll have a few more. As of 2007, most of their wines come from California. Chris provides some cellaring and the final blend. Since the wines are from California, they should be judged against other Californian wines, and some are quite competitive. Their best wine is their **Napa Cabernet Sauvignon**. It's a big wine, full of interesting aromas like mint and olives and chocolate. You can spend a good ten minutes or so just analyzing what's there. I also highly recommend their **Rosé**, made in a bone-dry, Provence style, from Sonoma County Zinfandel grapes.

CrossRoads Winery

15222 King Rd. #301, Frisco, TX 75034. Sat. and Sun. 1–6 pm or by appointment.
(972) 294-4144, www.crwinery.com

I was in Austin at the Texas Wine and Grape Growers Association shindig, an annual event aimed at getting the legislature more interested in helping the Texas wine industry. Milling around with politicos is always difficult work. There were about twenty tables

Monica Otis pours her husband, John, a taste of the CrossRoads Ryan's Choice Syrah.

arranged in a horseshoe, another few in the middle. Each table had one or two wineries pouring their best in hopes of getting some legislative attention. I tried to get to all the tables to taste what each winery had brought.

As I went around, the normal favorites popped up. Then I came to a table for CrossRoads Winery in Frisco. I'd never heard of it. There had been a Cross Roads in Aubrey a few years ago, but this one was a new deal. I waited patiently to try the wine. Generally, new wineries are in the learning stage, and what you hope to find is the seeds of talent. My first sip of their Syrah changed everything. This was spectacular wine. Next I tried their CSM (a play on the Aussie GSM), made from Cabernet, Syrah and Merlot. I wrote one word on my tasting note: "Wow!" I tried to get a chance to talk to the winemaker but could only get the attention of his nephew. The table was so busy no one really had much time to say anything, so I filed the name away and vowed to look into this winery.

Flash forward. My wife and I are driving into the CrossRoads parking lot. This is a true garigista operation. That refers to the fact that, in France, many of the best wines are made in cheap warehouse space, or even in people's garages. CrossRoads is in an out-of-the-way industrial park. When we walked through the door, everything changed. The place is comfortable, clean, warm and inviting.

So how on earth did they figure this wine thing out so fast?

John Otis is the winemaker. He explains: "My best friend was working at Erath [a first-rate winery in Oregon] and he said, 'Hey, John why don't you come up and volunteer?' Now I've been up there twelve years in a row. I've been enough that the winemaker often allows me to do some of the more important things, because he knows I'll do them right."

Both John and his wife, Monica, are in unique positions to be able to keep a winery afloat. John is a flight attendant for Delta and Monica a realtor in North Dallas. Both have schedule flexibility that allows them to pay attention to their budding business. They had the idea of waiting to create a winery until after John retired, but when Delta closed its Dallas hub, they decided to get the winery moving a little faster. About the same time they heard that the original Cross Roads was going out of business and selling its equipment. John and Monica felt that the stars had aligned in their favor and that it was time to build their dream.

So now John flies twelve days a month and has the other eighteen to make wine at CrossRoads. Monica is learning the paperwork side of a winery as she goes, and she's selling real estate.

What's the best lesson John has learned? Without hesitation he says, "If you want to do this, do what I did. Volunteer or apprentice at a winery for two to three weeks a year. Get dirty, work hard and learn what the unromantic side is. You have to feel the work and feel the hurt, work the twelve-hour days and wake up with a backache. This isn't all just fun. But I love it more than anything I've ever done."

Based on what's in his bottles, I'd say that's good advice.

The Best Wines

CrossRoads makes a dozen wines, not a dud in the bunch. The best white is **Sunfusion**, a blend of 22 percent Chardonnay and 78 percent Sauvignon Blanc. The name is a good clue because you taste sunny, tropical flavors. The Chardonnay richens the Sancerre like Sauvignon Blanc, leaving a complex, fascinating wine.

John has really figured out the art of red wine making. **Ryan's Choice Syrah** is named for his nephew, the one I met in Austin. The reason he gets his name on the bottle is because he found a barrel he really liked, went to John and said, "Uncle John, this is the kind of wine my age group is looking for, a big, intense red wine." Ryan is right. This wine has it all. Very dark colors, peppery aromas, good grip and bright acids.

My favorite is the **CSM**. A blend of Cabernet, Syrah and Merlot, it shows off John's abilities as a blender of wines. "I like blends and these are my favorite grapes," he says. "I try to make wines to please our customers, but this one I make for me." And me. This is delicious wine with lots of wonderful, deep color, good tannins and loads of dark berry aromas.

I can't wait to see what else John comes up with.

🍁 Carmela Winery

210 W. Broadway, Prosper, TX 75078.
Open by appointment. (972) 346-2894,
www.carmelawinery.net

120 N. Preston Rd. #10, Prosper, TX
75078. Mon.–Sat. 11 am–9 pm.
(972) 346-2894.

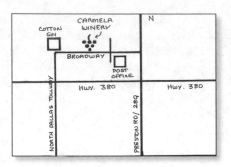

"I make wines the way I like them. If you like them, fine. If not, there's another winery down the road." Joseph Anselmo is a jocular guy, happy and straightforward. "I like fruit-forward wines; I like to know what I'm drinking. And no one should tell you whether a wine is good or bad. If you like the taste of the wine, it is a good wine. If you do not like the taste of a wine, it is a bad wine. It's as simple as that."

He has strong feelings about a lot of things, like fruit. "I make wine from concentrate. I started with concentrates because I couldn't get Texas grapes. Now I like the way they taste. Today, I have no Texas wines."

Joseph started life as a commercial banker. When he saw some numbers for a famous winery, he thought it might be a good business for him. He left banking and did well putting ATM's in convenience stores. He sold that business and moved north of Dallas out to Prosper, a sleepy farming community. Suddenly it's a suburb. As he says, "I moved to Propser to get away from everyone else, and now they're following me."

Joseph got bit by the wine bug when Jerry Delaney of Delaney Vineyards gave him some Cabernet Sauvignon grapes. "I made the best Cab I've ever made," he tells me. "Now it's a hobby that got completely out of control."

Don't let the gruff talk fool you. He loves what he's doing. "It's my passion," he says. "I'd rather make wine, talk about wine, drink wine. I mean it's just something I love to do." Then he gets a little sentimental. Is that the beginning of a tear in his eye? "Hey, would you put in your book that my dad, my daughter Tina and I all work on the winery, and my dad and Tina both are such a huge help to me?"

Sure I would.

Carmela's Joseph Anselmo started out as a commercial banker.

The Best Wines

Since Joseph is making these wines specifically for his palate, you'll either like what he makes or, as he says, there's another winery down the road. The two most conventionally straightforward wines, and his best, are a **Pinot Grigio**, almost golden in color and extremely rich with a very dense, almost too dense, mouth feel; and his **Sauvignon Blanc**, in a California style with opulent pineapple aromas and a similar density.

Inwood Estates Vineyards

1350 Manufacturing St. #209, Dallas, TX 75207. Open by appointment.
(214) 902-9452, www.inwoodwines.com

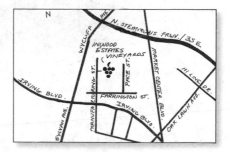

Dan Gatlin is filled with nervous energy. A little over six feet tall, he paces a lot. He's not sure that he wants to be in the book. "I want to distance myself from Texas," he says. "Texas wines are mostly bad, and I don't want to be lumped in with them. I just want people to taste them and not think Texas."

He's also reticent about talking to me because his production is small and he's trying to build a brand by using restaurants. At a restaurant, from two to eight people will taste a wine. A single buyer will likely drink all the wine at home. If people start calling him up and asking for tours, they might want to buy more wine than he wants to sell, creating a public relations problem.

So when we meet, there is a little tension at first. "Look, I hope you understand," he says. "I have so many friends in the business that I could sell all my wine out in local stores too quick. I have to hold my allocation back and put them in high-end restaurants so I can build a brand. I'm angling for a much larger market."

Gatlin has the background for it. His father, Vernon, started the Hasty chain of liquor and convenience stores in the Dallas area. It grew to twenty-six stores, and Dan rose to vice president.

When the company was sold, Dan decided to try his lot as a winemaker. He started with an experimental vineyard in Denton County, raising nearly every type of vinifera to see what would work. He didn't deem the wines worth public sale. Over the years he planted five vineyards, never achieving wines up to his standard —which is to say, good enough to stand on the table next to the best of California, France, Spain and Italy.

Dan Gatlin uncorks a bottle in Inwood's lab.

"I am not brilliant," he says. " I stood in hot vineyards for twenty-five years and kept moving and changing and trying until I got something I was proud of." He's proud now, and it revolves around two grapes: Tempranillo and Palomino.

The Palomino grape was one of his early discoveries, circa 1984. This is the grape widely grown in southern Spain around Jerez de la Frontera, home to the world's great Sherry makers. That area is West Texas–style barren and water-deprived, yet the Palomino grape thrives. Tempranillo is best known as a Spanish grape from the northern and central parts of Spain, where the weather is cooler and where pests and diseases are minimized. Dan has found ideal areas for both grapes in an area east of Dallas for the Palomino and in the High Plains outside of Lubbock for the Tempranillo.

Dan crushes his grapes in the vineyard in the cool of the night to preserve as much flavor as possible, then lets them spend a good long time in oak— thirty months for his red wine—so the flavors coalesce. He adds Cabernet to his Tempranillo and Chardonnay to his Palomino to give both a little more structure, but his main grapes provide the dominant flavors. He's confident he's discovered the future of Texas wines.

"I'm 51 years old and I'm tired," he says. "I've done more experimentation than anyone except the UT experiment station, and, I'm telling you, these grapes are the only grapes capable of making premium wines." Obviously a big statement, but how does he define premium? "We can make a good $15 Cabernet in Texas, but can Texas make a $50 Cab? No way. But these wines I'm making are selling for those kind of prices." Even more, actually. His white wine generally runs about $75 and his red runs about $90. In restaurants, of course.

The final impression you walk away with about Dan Garlin is that he is passionate, dedicated, opinionated, intense, hyper and more than just a little eccentric. He is one of Texas wine's true characters. Even though he doesn't want visitors, I hope you get a chance to meet him. He's worth a side trip.

The Best Wines

My experience with the Palomino grape comes from running around southern Spain trying wines at every stage from still to Sherry. In Spain the grape is rather bland and susceptible to oxidation. It also yields large crops, in the vicinity of 7,500 pounds of fruit per acre. For his **Palomino-Chardonnay** Dan cuts his production back to 1,000 pounds per acre, which makes the wine denser, and he handles it with kid gloves from picking to bottling. The result is an intense wine loaded with honey and honeydew melon aromas. Dan adds Chardonnay to thin the wine out a little (!) and add some flavor complexity. This wine was really an eye-opener.

Tempranillo-Cabernet. These grapes come from the closest thing Texas has to a first-growth vineyard, Neal Newsom's vineyard in Yoakum County near Plains, Texas. He sells grapes to a lot of Texas winemakers, and each product is a worthy wine. Dan Garlin goes to a little more trouble than most buyers, spending time overseeing his plots and custom-crushing right at the vineyard in the dark of night to make sure he gets every possible flavor trapped and ready to put in your bottle. The wine has nice red fruit flavors, a silky mouth feel and enough structure from the Cabernet to offer a nice long life. This is not an old-style Rioja wine—brick-colored and smelling of leather and cigar boxes—but a modern wine, pointing a fascinating direction for Texas Tempranillos.

If you'd like to try the wines you can find a list of restaurants pouring Inwood Estates wines on Inwood's Website.

TRIP FOUR

🍇 Sunset Winery

1535 S. Burleson Blvd., Burleson, TX 76028. Tue.–Thur. noon–5 pm, Fri.–Sun. noon–6 pm and by appointment. (817) 426-1141, www.sunsetwinery.com

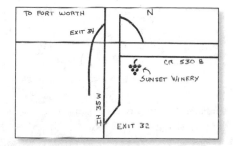

Bruce Anderson is an educator by trade. He trained in sociology, psychology and statistics at Stanford, Northwestern and Duke, then taught at universities in Canada and the United States. After twenty-six years at UT–Arlington he

Sunset Winery is housed in Bruce and Birgit Andersons' pre-dancing home.

took early retirement to pursue other interests. Wine has become his overriding passion, but it didn't come naturally.

"It's all Birgit's fault," he says. Birgit is his wife, a Danish woman who, despite having spent decades in America, retains the lilting accent of her homeland. When Bruce makes his comments, her eyes go up to the ceiling and she sighs. I think she may have heard that before. "We bought this house in 1973," she explains. "When our children flew the nest, we took ballroom lessons. But we needed a larger house to practice dancing. On a business trip to Napa we fell in love with the whole thing, and I thought I wanted to use some of our original land to grow vines. We planted Cabernet, and that got Pierce's disease, so we ripped it up and planted Black Spanish."

That's the Cliff Notes version. Actually, things have been much more complicated. The idea of buying a house for dancing is only part of the story. Their youngest daughter, Bodil, died in a car accident in 1989. For four years the home reminded them daily of their lost daughter. So they moved to Fort Worth. One of their criteria was finding a place where they could dance.

Their daughter Belinda bought the original house. When Bruce and Birgit really did catch winemaker fever, they bought the house back with an eye on turning it into a winery/tasting room. Then the government weighed in. I could fill a chapter on how Bruce and Birgit had to fight, cajole and, finally, romance the legal system. If you'd like to alternately laugh and wince for about fifteen minutes, ask Bruce to tell you the story about getting his TABC approval. It involves grapes on a truck and a truculent bureaucrat, with a holiday backdrop. That's all I'll say. Ask him.

While both Bruce and Birgit hold the title of winemaker, it seems neither is anxious for the title of marketing director. Bruce gives that "what are you gonna do?" shrug and says, "I've enjoyed the winemaking a lot, but now I have a lot of wine. Now I'll have to spend more time marketing it."

The Best Wines

Sunset Winery hasn't been open all that long, so they're still deciding which wines will be their cornerstones. Both Bruce and Birgit have trained at Grayson, and they're getting good advice from pros like Les Constable at Brushy Creek.

Bruce says his best wine is the Proprietor's Reserve, a blend of Cabernet Sauvignon, Merlot and Malbec. Since none was available when we visited, I can't give you an opinion. Of the wines I did taste, my favorite was the **Newsom Vineyards Merlot**, a wine with dark colors and plum and bell pepper aromas. The **Newsom Vineyards Cabernet Sauvignon**, Birgit's favorite, is a bit light in color but has the characteristically first-rate Newsom Vineyards taste.

🍂 Barking Rocks Winery

1919 Allen Ct., Granbury, TX 76048. Sat. 1–6 pm and by appointment. (817) 579-0007, www.barkingrockswine.com

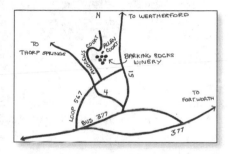

Like Sting and Seal and the Artist Formerly Known as Prince, Barking Rocks Winery's owner prefers the singular sobriquet: call him Tiberia. Like many Texas winemakers, he is something of a renegade. His parents emigrated from Italy to upstate New York, where Tiberia was born. This heritage is important: "I'm Italian. I've been around winemaking all my life and I just wanted to create a small-scale winery."

Tiberia worked for in Human Resources at TXU for twenty-five years, and the drive to downtown Dallas bugged him. "It was funny," he says and laughs gently. "My wife and I looked all over Hood County for a place to put a winery when the land across the street from our house came up for sale." Today he walks across the street to the winery.

He's constantly moving yet seems unhurried. This lifestyle suits him, one of the reasons he's popular with other winemakers. And he has a good idea of what his ideal life would be: "I never want to get big; I'm not looking for a profit machine. My ideal would be to have 600 customers and make each of them a case of wine."

Tiberia started his winemaking career after attending wine symposia and deciding he liked the people in the business. The ride hasn't been all that easy. "Yeah, I lost my first three acres of wines at Glen Rose to Pierce's disease." You can see the anguish on his face; his shoulders slump when he talks about all his work

The Artist Still Known as Tiberia.

going down the drain. But his spirit carried him through. Like many others, once hit by Pierce's he started looking on the at-least-for-now Pierce's-resistant High Plains. In 2002 he formed an agreement with Quail Ridge Vineyard on the High Plains and has been purchasing their entire production.

What drives him is trying to get a just representation of the grapes he's working with: "I'm all about trying to figure out what the grape's true nature is, then trying to get it into the bottle." His winemaking area is modest but clean. He really spends time trying to make sure he honors the original flavor profile of the grape.

Since the birth of Barking Rocks Winery in 2004, Tiberia's gone over his goal of 600 cases, even hitting 1,000 at one point. But he's intent on keeping production low. That means if you taste something and like it, buy it now. Two of his best wines—the 2002 Cabernet from Newsom Vineyards and his Bordeaux blend, named Casena after his wife's grandmother—sold out quickly, and his best wines will continue to be snapped up by a growing group of Barking Rocks aficionados.

The Best Wines

Tiberia makes five wines, all worth trying. He has shown particular talent with Cabernets, and we can look forward to a long and productive partnership with Quail Ridge Vineyard. The **Cabernet Quail Ridge Vineyard** is a really nice version of Texas Cab, brimming with bright cherry aromas and mouth-cleansing acids. Tiberia never makes more than about 250 cases, so if you like it don't wait to get your allocation.

Tiberia says **Casena** will be a one-shot wine, 2003 vintage only. It likely will be gone by the time you get there, but maybe we can all put some pressure on him to make it again. It's a combo of Cabernet Sauvignon and Cabernet Franc. The Cabernet Franc gives the Cabernet Sauvignon a little more tannic grip and produces a delicious wine with aging potential.

I could only taste barrel samples of his **Viognier**, but I think Tiberia is on to something with this delicious, understated wine. The peach and apricot aromas insinuate rather than overwhelm. Nice stuff.

🍁 Bluff Dale Vineyards

5222 County Rd. 148, Bluff Dale, TX
76433. Daily 11 am–6 pm.
(254) 728-3540,
www.bluffdalevineyards.com

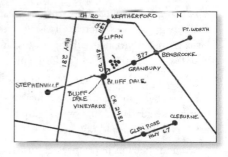

David and Theresa Hayes have lived and worked all over the world while David marketed ultra high-end currency sorters to governments and large banks. I don't know why I never thought of that as a business, but imagine the complexity of machines that can handle different sizes, denominations and languages. I can't imagine how you would engineer such a beast.

Anyway, David's company was first sold to a German company, so he had to travel there a lot. Then it was sold to an Italian company, and he traveled there. In between, they lived in Japan three times. Their marriage is even cross-cultural. David is originally from Chattanooga, Theresa from China. Even after years of American residence, Theresa speaks with a distinctly Chinese accent.

While traveling around Italy, David and Theresa noticed that some of the best wines they tasted came from home winemakers who just happened to have made a little too much. To get rid of the excess they make a sale to a local restaurant or put a little sign on the road saying "vino da vendere." That struck them as a romantic way to live.

"I used to work for my grandfather, who made wine and whiskey, so this is full circle for me," David tells me. "We've also made wine as a hobby, mostly Cabernet. But when I got transferred to Dallas I started going up to Grayson and taking classes. Then, about ten years ago, we started looking for a place." Bluff

Theresa and David Hayes lived all over the world before settling in Bluff Dale.

Dale won the prize. Now David and Theresa have four acres of Black Spanish and Blanc du Bois grapes.

Sitting on the porch of their pretty tasting room, you look down over a valley with leafy grape vines. Pierce's disease limits the vineyard to resistant hybrids, and David is a Cabernet man all the way, so he is committed to buying grapes from West Texas and other places to keep vinifera wines on his menu.

I can tell David likes talk. I suppose all marketing people do. But there's something more interesting about hearing his story. It boils down to enthusiasm. "I really like farming. I like brewing up a little something that tastes good. And I love to meet people and talk."

Sounds like he's in the perfect business.

The Best Wines

David is trying to make dry wines he likes so he can drink them himself, but he's also trying to make high-quality wines for the sweet wine lover. **Dulcet**

is a perfect example of a well-made semisweet wine with character and interesting flavors. It's made from Chenin Blanc grapes and features good acids that balance the sugar.

The best wine of his collection is the **2004 Cabernet Reserve**. It has good color and very intense fruit flavors, along with gentle tannins. His 2002 Cabernet isn't near the wine the 2004 is, so he may be learning how to get it right. Based on the 2004, I'd say he's well on his way.

🍃 Lone Oak Winery

2116 FM 731, Burleson, TX 76028. Sat. and Sun. noon–6 pm. (817) 426-6625, www.loneoakwinery.com

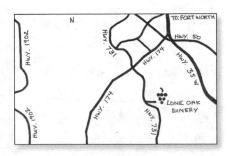

Here's something new. In my travels around Texas, other winemakers took time from describing their own wines to single out the Lone Oak Vineyards Texas Merlot as a wonderful wine. Loan Oak's original owners, Jamey and Robert Wolf, wanted to get into the wine business so they hired some of the best people in Texas: Dr. Roy Renfro from the Munson School of Viticulture and Enology at Grayson County College and Jim Evans, who'd been running the UT Experimental Vineyard. The team planted a top-rate vineyard— Bordeaux varietals only, if you please— and packed their three-acre vineyard so densely that everything had to be done by hand. The theory is that all those vines competing with each other for water and nutrients will stress the wines, naturally lowering the yield but boosting the flavor and aroma.

Lone Oak's wines were unequivocal successes from the first vintage in 1999. But Robert was having to spend more time on his chain of Rudy's Barbecues, and the location in Valley View was a bit isolated, so in 2006 they made the painful decision to sell the winery.

Enter retired pharmaceutical executive Gene Estes. Gene has been making wine on an amateur level since the mid-1980s. "I've been interested in wines for a long time," he says. "I worked in Alsace and fell

Gene and Judy Estes bought Lone Oak Winery in 2006.

in love with the wines, and it just became a dream of mine to have a winery." He was trying to learn all he could when he met Robert and Jamey at a seminar in 1995. They became friends. Gene watched as the Wolfs garnered rave reviews and multiple awards.

Gene started his vineyard a year after Lone Oak, planting Shiraz. After a lot of success in amateur competitions, he was ready to make a stab at commercial wine. In 2004, Gene planted three more acres, using Tempranillo, Shiraz, Malvasia Bianco, Blanc de Bois, Ruby Cabernet and Chardonelle. As his winery was coming to fruition, the Wolfs were feeling the need to slow their involvement. That's when Gene offered to buy the winery from Robert and Jamey. Gene showed wisdom in signing a long-term contract to continue getting the fruit from the original Lone Oak vineyard. He also wisely retained the winemaking services of Jim Evans.

The new facility outside Burleson is a strikingly pretty place. Gene and his wife, Judy, live on the vineyard. The vines are neatly kept by a full-time worker, and there are nice little picnic areas around the property. What does Gene think will make his operation stand out among the other wineries in the state? "It's an internal belief that I can be more successful partly because of my knowledge, plus my belief that I can exceed the expectations of my customers and myself," he says with confidence. "This is something I've always wanted to do. I have chosen a very scenic and nice place for having a winery, and I think people will just love it."

The Best Wines

With the services of Jim Evans, the future bodes well for Lone Oak wines. The first wines from the Burleson vineyard will come in 2007. Until then, Gene and Judy will be selling the wines made by the prior owners. Try to get a taste of the **Reserve Merlot,** a spectacular wine, one of the best in Texas. It's intense, opulent, filled with ripe dark fruit flavors and so well balanced that you don't even notice the wine is 14.6 percent alcohol. This is where Lone Oak made its name, and it promises to be the new winery's flagship for some time to come.

TRIP FIVE

Homestead Winery — Denison

220 W. Main St., Denison, TX 75020. Wed.–Sat. 11 am–5:30 pm. (903) 464-0030.

Production Facility: P.O. Box 35, Ivanhoe, TX 75447. By appointment. (903) 583-4281.

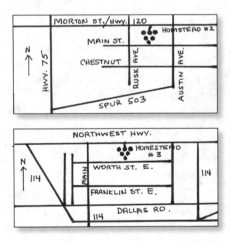

There are a lot of ways I could start this section. I could say how well respected Gabe Parker is among his peers. I could talk about how his discovery of the marketability of a sweet red wine has kept a lot of small wineries afloat. I could go on about the years he spent as a consultant.

What I will start with is what he's learned. Gabe made a good living selling his advice for big bucks; this is free. So if you are a budding winemaker, pay close attention. If you are a wine lover looking for a place to visit, this will tell you a lot about the operation and the man.

Here's what Gabe calls the Parker Principle: "No matter how much you know about wines, the only way to do it in the Texas wine industry is to do it in reverse. Start with a tasting room. When that's successful, add a bottling line and a place to blend. When that's successful, add a de-stemmer and crusher and some barrels. When that's successful, add a vineyard."

He finishes: "The reason to do it this way is, I don't care how extensive your background is, until you work in a Texas tasting room you really don't know the consumer."

Gabe Parker believes the way to succeed in the wine business in Texas is to start in reverse.

Gabe is a big believer in giving consumers what they want. He thinks you have to be willing to really listen. He says his professional life can be summarized by the Parker Principle and the Rose of Ivanhoe story. (Rose of Ivanhoe is not a rosé. It's a red wine with about 6 percent residual sugar and accounts for more than half of Gabe's business.)

Here's the story: "We moved back to Ivanhoe in the mid-1990s. I went to the little Church of Christ congregation my grandmother founded, and they looked at me funny because I was a winemaker. So I switched to the Presbyterian Church. We had this dinner and the minister asked us to bring the wine, since we made wine. A lady told me I should bring red wine, 'but don't bring any of that sour stuff.' So Roy Mitchell, our winemaker, made a wine up. It was Cabernet Sauvignon with enough sugar added to bring it up to 6 percent sugar.

"And, would you believe it, the little old ladies of the congregation loved it. Roy made four gallons of it. We didn't know what to do with the rest. So we sent it to Cord Switzer at Fredericksburg Winery. He sold through it so fast that he called back and ordered two hundred cases. It blew off the shelves; it's still blowing off the shelves. People love it."

It's now the most imitated wine in Texas.

Only you know if you are a sweet wine person or a dry wine person. Personally, I like to think of wines as either good or bad. I've had great sweet wines and lousy dry wines and vice versa. When I'm drinking wine I generally like dry wines. Gabe, too. But the fact remains that traveling tasters usually prefer sweet wines. That's true in Texas, it's true in Virginia, it's true cruising Highway 29 in Napa. The number one Chardonnay in the world is Kendall Jackson. That appears to be a dry wine, but it's not. There's enough sugar there to qualify for semisweet.

The point I'm trying to make is that dry wine lovers shouldn't look at sweet wine lovers as rubes, and sweet wine lovers shouldn't look at dry wine fans as snobs. Instead, everyone should try to shut off their biases and try as many different wines as possible. Who knows what you might like?

Gabe recommends starting a winery slowly. He started v-e-r-y slowly and patiently. It took him ten years after planting vines—until 1993—before he was able to leave Anderson and become a full-time grape and wine man. During that time he found that almost all the grapes they had tried wouldn't work. In fact, the only big winner was Cabernet Sauvignon. So he had to make a decision. He headed out to West Texas to find some High Plains high-quality grapes. Now most of Homestead's production comes from West Texas. Gabe now buys from vineyards and growers he knows personally and has worked with for years.

Gabe was smart enough to hire Dr. Roy Mitchell as his winemaker. Dr. Mitchell, one of the founding partners of Llano Estacado, has deep roots in the Texas wine industry. While a chemistry professor at Texas Tech he started working with Teysha Winery (now Cap*Rock) and then switched to Tech's horticulture department. After retiring from Tech he brought his knowledge and his Sherry solera to Homestead. Now Gabe offers the broad ideas and Roy implements them. In his spare time, Roy teaches about wine at Grayson County College.

The Ivanhoe location is now where production and fermentation of the sweet wines and white wines are done. There is also a ten-acre vineyard and lots of cattle. The Denison location has a tasting room, a huge entertainment area and a Sherry bodega. Denison is also where they produce dry red wines. The Grapevine location operates as a tasting room, with wine accessories and knick-knacks for sale.

All are worth visiting, but the Denison location has one compelling benefit: Frank DeVolli's restaurant is at the back of the shop, serving delicious Italian food. If you ask real nice, he'll sometimes make recipes from his family home in Albania.

A bottle of wine is always happier around good food. After a fun couple of hours listening to Gabe gush truisms, I ask where he got the name Rose of Ivanhoe. "I named it Ivanhoe for our hometown. But the wine is named for my grandmother. She raised roses and had gorgeous red hair. But she was strict Church of Christ. If I named it after her, she might come back from the grave to get me. So instead of calling it by her name, Ruby, I called it 'Rose' for her flowers and her hair."

The Best Wines

Gabe aims at making wines you can enjoy any time without having to check with your banker first. So all his wines are fairly priced. But the bargain of the bunch is the wonderful **Desert Rose**. It's made from 100 percent Muscat Canelli from Texas's premier vineyard for the grape, Young Vineyards south of Lubbock.

This is a dry Muscat with enormous fruit and aromas of roses and paperwhites and tropical fruits, and I could just go on. Do yourself a favor. Buy a bottle, sit somewhere quiet and count all the different flavors and aromas you get from this wine. And it's less than $10.

The best red wine is the **Cabernet Sauvignon**. Half the fruit comes from Gabe's own vineyard in Ivanhoe, and the other half comes from Young Vineyard. He lets his dry reds rest at least three years before he releases them. In the case of the Cab, that extra time gives the wine a roundness and ease on the palate that's seductive. Try it with some of DeVolli's Italian food.

The last recommendation is for a wine that's only partly Gabe's. Dr. Roy Mitchell, mentioned above, is one of the pioneers of Texas wine. For the last thirty years he's been feeding his **Sherry** solera (for a description of how a solera works, go to www.madaboutsherry.com/aging.html). Dr. Mitchell placed his solera in Gabe's Dennison facility, and it's now big enough that he can make almost a hundred cases a year. It will never get any bigger, and the wine sells out within six months of bottling. It's the single most-awarded wine in Texas, and for good reason. It is decadently rich, nutty, properly sweet and, oh, so fragrant. The $39 tag might seem like a lot, but once you taste it that will seem like pennies.

Grayson Hills Winery

2815 Ball Rd., Whitewright, TX 75491. Sat. and Sun. noon–5 pm or by appointment. (903) 627-0832, www.graysonhillswinery.com

As a wine writer, I get the opportunity to kiss a lot of frogs while looking for a few pretty princesses (please excuse the gender bend). We live for those few that bust through the bell curve of mediocrity and land out on the skinny parts of the curve.

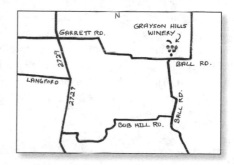

Grayson Hills is way out there on right side of the skinny part. And what a surprise.

To get to Grayson Hills, you drive through some of the prettiest country in all of north Texas. Hilly, bending roads drop down into a tree-covered gravel road. After a lifetime in Texas, I had no idea any place in the area looked so beautiful. When you arrive you'll see a perfectly maintained vineyard and a little road up to the winery.

The winery is small but functional. Owner Rick Magers describes it: "I'm proud of this place. It started off as a dirt-floor tractor barn. Then I built it by

Rick Magers started out drinking beer but liked the camaraderie of the wine business.

hand. I had to be resourceful, too. The windows came from Goodwill and a lot of the materials are scavenged." You wouldn't be able to tell. It just looks like a well-loved and well-used winery.

Rick is an interesting guy. He's quiet, and it takes a few minutes to get him comfortable, but when he is, he's got a hearty laugh. It's also clear he is very perceptive and still learning how to deal with customers' reactions to his babies. Before wine he worked for years at Xerox, then started a little network business. While taking courses at Grayson, Dr. George Ray McEachern took some students on a trip to Europe and Rick was hooked. All he wanted to do was start his own winery.

"I grew up drinking beer," Rick says. "But I love the camaraderie in the wine business, and everyone's so friendly. I guess it isn't the wine so much as how much I love the people. Being involved in the Texas wine scene is more than a lifestyle. I'm not trying to make a million bucks, I just want to be a part of the industry. I'm just a regular Joe wanting to find something to do, and this really makes me happy."

Connie Magers comes in about this time. She's more outgoing, more verbal. Rick perks up when she enters the room. Maybe the interview process feels better with two. I love seeing happy couples, and this one qualifies. Connie works at J.C. Penney's in the corporate office, a busy job that requires a lot of attention. So at least for the near future, the winery is going to end up being mostly Rick's job. He's already showing he can handle it. If he can build on what he's already started, he could be one of our best. This is a winery I'll be watching very closely.

The Best Wines

I don't really know where to start on Rick's best wines. He only has three, and all are top-notch offerings. He's made one available to the public. Called **Celebration**, it's a blend of Cabernet Sauvignon, Ruby Cabernet and Cabernet Franc—all Texas fruit. This is a wine for folks who love the big Zinfandels of Sonoma County. Like his California cohorts, Rick leaves a little sugar in the wine. Under 1 percent is considered dry, and Rick leaves just a hair over 1 percent. Some of the Sonomas have up to 3 percent, so let's say that Celebration has some honest sugar left in it. But it's still drier than a lot of California "dry" wines.

The jewel in the Grayson Hills portfolio is the estate **Cabernet Sauvignon.** That word *estate* is an important one. You won't find it on many Texas wines. It means the grapes have to be grown there and the wine has to be made, bottled and stored there. The Grayson Hills Cabernet is the first in the Texoma appellation to be an estate wine. Of course, none of this would be important if it wasn't so good. It's great. The color is deep and dark, zooming past the normal bugaboo of Texas Cabs. The flavors are almost explosive, yet the wine goes down smoothly. For a first effort, this is just short of miraculous.

Rick also makes a first-rate dessert wine called **Moscato Dolce.** It is done in a Sherry style, slightly oxidized with a rich and nutty aroma followed by a creamy mouth feel and an endless finish.

What a start!

Texoma Winery

9 Judge Carr Rd., Whitewright, TX 75491. Sat and Sun. 11 am–5 pm or by appointment. (903) 364-5242, www. texomawinery.com

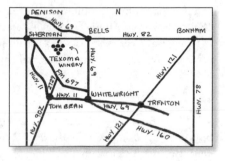

Owner Bob White is a happy, open man with a kind smile and a readiness to give credit for his successes to others. That's why the grape growers get some credit on his labels. He loves to teach people about wine, tasting, evaluating, picking the right foods. He enjoys teaching and wine so much that he teaches a couple of courses at Grayson. Budding winemakers should be on the phone to Bob as soon as the fever hits. He has a great checklist he's willing to share.

He came to the whole business recently. In the summer of 2004, he and his wife took a vacation to California. Not for wine, but to take a driving trip along the Pacific Coast Highway. On the way over they stopped at a winery in Sonoma and then another in Paso Robles. While they were sitting on a patio at a winery in Paso, Bob decided he could do this for a living. He got my book (thank you very much) and went through the Grayson program lickety-split. He interned at Spicewood and Homestead and decided he really did like the life.

Bob took a gamble and decided to enter a couple of his first wines, a Pinot Grigio and a Merlot, at the Texas Wine and Grape Growers Association Amateur Competition. He won both a silver and a bronze metal. Then he entered the wines in the Thirty-First Annual U.S. Amateur Winemaking Competition, and got two medals. "I had tears rolling down my cheek when I heard the news," he tells me. "So then I got cocky and entered the Winemaker International Amateur Wine

Bob White won silver and bronze medals in the first wine competition he entered.

Competition and won another medal. I figured I must be doing something right, so I decided to open a winery. I was licensed in twelve months and open in thirteen."

Ask any other winery owner and they'll tell you that qualifies for some sort of a land-speed record.

Here's what excites me. This land has been in his family since 1880s, and they have other land in the area that his family has been farming since the 1850s. With more family farms dying every day, I'm so happy that every time one of us visits a winery that uses Texas fruit we're helping to save a family farm. Bob is just opening, and has many good winemaking years ahead of him.

The Best Wines

It's hard to say what Bob's best wine will be. He makes small quantities, so his wines sell out quickly. On the day we visited, a number of his best were already gone. But we had one that qualifies for another award—**Whispering Willow Chenin Blanc**. Bob let the wine sit on Muscat lees, then let it rest in oak barrels. The combo of floral Muscat and vanilla oak, and the depth and complexity of old vine Chenin Blanc add up to a scrumptious wine.

Paris Vineyards

545 County Rd. 43500, Paris, TX 75462. Fri.–Sun. noon–6 pm. (903) 982-7216, www.parisvineyards.com

Hometown boy does good. That's the story in Paris, Texas, as Larry Dority gets his new vineyard open. Of course, the truth is, as usual, that it's the woman behind the man who's having the influence.

"Oh yeah, it's her fault we're in this. Blame it all on her." Larry

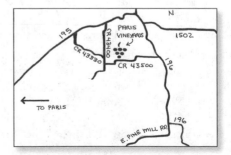

is actually laughing, though his wife, Denise, looks like she's heard these statements before. She's anxious to make sure the writer in the group doesn't misunderstand and end up writing half the story.

"We've always been wine enthusiasts," she says. "We had just come back from a trip to Branson, where we visited some vineyards. We already had some land so …" Like most long married couples, they finish each other's sentences. As soon as "so . . ." comes out of her mouth, he adds, "I put pencil to paper and figured out you can't make any money growing grapes. At least not where we are. So we decided to open a winery."

Denise Dority started out as a wine lover, and Larry followed.

Larry is a good pencil-and-paper guy, being a CPA by trade. Denise writes grant proposals for huge entities like cities and counties, so she's fully aware of what a budget looks like as well. As befits their trades, neither was up for jumping into a new business without taking a few baby steps first.

"We decided to take some classes at Grayson and learn something before we started," Denise explains. Both earned associates degrees in viticulture and enology. "Then we started by planting one and a half acres," he says. Eventually, we'll get up to eight and a half acres." She started out a wine lover, but Larry came along a little later. "I've always liked wine," says Denise. "He had to acquire a taste." Larry interjects, "We always had beer. I started off liking sweet wines, but now I like the robust, dry wines."

There's already a division of labor. Larry loves planting. "I've tried to grow vegetables like tomatoes and everything. But planting the vineyard and watching it bud and produce— I just love the whole part of growing grapes." Denise is big on making a comfortable respite. "I'm so proud of all we've had to do getting the place built and making it beautiful." He throws in: "The neat thing is we don't owe anything on it." Careful as they were, Larry thinks they still made a few costly mistakes trying to hurry the process. Would they take the leap again? "Sure, why not?" Larry says. "It's been great fun."

The Best Wines

The Doritys grow two grapes, Black Spanish and Blanc du Bois. Their goal is to make the highest-quality wine with Texas grapes, so they will usually have to buy some grapes from West Texas or other spots around the state.

I tried all three of their wines. **Tex Red** is my favorite, a dry Ruby Cabernet from Texas High Plains with robust flavor and body reminiscent of the glory days of Gallo Hearty Burgundy. Their **Blanc du Bois** is semisweet with acids that are getting good play at the end. It's a really nice, Haak-style wine (that's a high compliment for Blanc du Bois) with even more density.

℉◎ FOOD

Dallas

Dallas is chock-full of great restaurants. The best place to find out about the new ones is either in the *Dallas Morning News* or the *Dallas Observer*. I have a few favorites that I think are especially worth a trip.

Arc-en-Ciel, 3555 W. Walnut St. (972) 272-2188. Daily, dim-sum until 3 pm and great Vietnamese food all day long.

Lola, 2917 Fairmount St. Dinner Tue.–Sat. (214) 855-0700. Fancy European food in a quiet, sophisticated environment and the largest list of white Burgundies I've seen outside of New York's Le Montrachet.

The Burger House, 6913 Hillcrest Ave. Lunch and dinner daily. (214) 361-0370. Simply the greatest cheeseburger on earth, no hyperbole. Ask for a double-double and watch the griddle-master work his magic. The only thing better than the burgers is the fries, ultra-crispy with a salty-garlicky-peppery flavor. The only thing better than the fries is the milkshakes. Don't miss it.

Fort Worth

Bonnells, 4259 Bryant Irvin Rd. Lunch Tue.–Fri., dinner Tue.–Sat. Moderate to high. (817) 738-5489. Fine Texas cuisine is what they call it. If the idea of elk tacos or wild boar chops appeals, you'll find it here. But don't miss the grilled axis venison.

Joe T Garcia's, 2201 N. Commerce St. Daily all day. (817) 626-4356. Some people don't get it. Since 1935, there's always been a line to get into Joe T's. Tortillas? Maybe. Fajitas? They're great. I think it's the enchiladas. Yummy.

Silver Fox Steak House, 1651 S. University St. Dinner Mon.–Sat. (817) 332-9060. Rib eye, rib eye, rib eye.

Grapevine area

Main Street Blues Room, 814 S. Main St. Grapevine. Lunch and dinner Tue.–Sat. Moderate to high. (817) 310-3211. What would you rather have: Upscale southwestern restaurant? Cool bar? Blues and jazz club? How about all three at once? The Main Street Blues Room is a cool place.

Railhead Smokehouse, 5220 Hwy. 121, Colleyville. Lunch and dinner daily. (817) 571-2525. Melt-in-your-mouth tender brisket, perfectly cooked ribs and cheap schooners of beer. What else could you ask for? Be sure to order the fries.

Ravioli Ristorante,120 E. Worth St., Grapevine. Lunch Mon.–Fri., dinner Mon.–Sat. Moderate and higher. (817) 488-1181. An Italian place with white tablecloths and candlelight at dinner. Ask—plead—for seafood crepes, a dish not on the menu but that, if you're nice, they'll make for you.

Silver Fox Steakhouse, 1235 William D. Tate Ave., Grapevine. Dinner Mon.–Sat. High prices. (817) 329-6995. The best steak house in the area. Try the rib eye. By the way, ask them why they don't carry more Texas wine.

⌂ SHELTER

Grapevine

Garden Manor Bed & Breakfast Inn, (877) 424-9177 is the new name for Allen's Liberty House, long the best in Grapevine. Antique furnishings and nice bathrooms are a plus. The best room is the Classic Cottage Room.

You simply have to experience the **Gaylord Texan Resort,** (817) 778-1000. Expensive. You'll think it's either garish and gaudy or lavish and lush. If you have a soft spot in your heart for the high-end Las Vegas hotels, this will be right up your alley. Intimate it ain't, but there's enough stuff to do that you never have to leave. Plus a couple of very good restaurants.

Tioga

The Spirit of the West, (940) 437-5000, a fancy guest ranch in Tioga, right on the lake with a good restaurant (Diverso) and surprisingly good values. Some of their rooms are as low as $50 a night.

☼ FUN

Grapevine

Grapefest is the largest wine festival in the southwestern United States. It happens every year on the second weekend in September and includes tastings, auctions, dinners, music and over 100,000 of your fellow wine lovers. Hotel rooms evaporate, so book early. This is probably the single best festival for learning about Texas wine. (800) 457-6338.

For shoppers, the **Grapevine Mill Outlet Mall,** (888) 645-5748 is a huge destination. Power shoppers head straight for Neiman Marcus's Last Call or Saks Fifth Avenue's Off Fifth. If those don't appeal to you, there are about 200 other stores.

The Tarantula Excursion Train, (817) 410-3459 is pulled by a ten-wheel Cooke Steam Locomotive. It leaves from the old Cotton Belt Railway Depot downtown and takes you to one of the biggest tourist attractions in the area, the Fort Worth Stockyards National Historic District. The trip takes about six hours and runs daily from Wednesday through Sunday.

Fort Worth

My favorite Fort Worth attraction is the **Cultural District**, home of the Kimball Art Museum, (817) 332-8451, the Modern Art Museum of Fort Worth (817) 738-9215, and the National Cowgirl Museum and Hall of Fame, (800) 476-3263. For anyone remotely interested in museum architecture, a visit to the Kimball is a must. Even after thirty years it's one of the most flawlessly designed museums ever built.

Movie fans who remember the, uh, classic film, *Logan's Run* will want to go to the **Fort Worth Water Gardens** (next to the Convention Center) at night.

Don't miss **The Grape Escape,** (817) 336-9463 at 500 Commerce St. Lots of great Texas wines, light food and the option to try wines in flights of four at a great price.

The Stockyards National Historic District, (817) 624-4741, is like a little Disneyland for buckaroos. Old West themes everywhere you look, plus lots of shops.

Tioga

Lake Ray Roberts is the big attraction around here, especially for bass fishers. The lake is home to two delightful state parks. **Johnson Branch State Park,** (940) 637-2294, is a great place to put your boat in. For picnics and camping, the **Isle Du Bois State Park,** (940) 686-2148 is perfect. It also has equestrian trails.

SOUTH

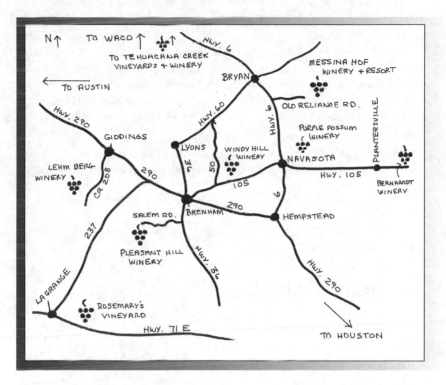

For Texans, Bryan/College Station is synonymous with Texas A&M, now the third largest university in the United States. Despite A&M's size and fame (or infamy, depending on where you went to college), Bryan/College Station is smaller than most people guess, with hardly 130,000 people. The large school and small town merge to make an area that is both sophisticated and homey.

The area around Bryan/College Station is rich in outdoor activities, with great places for hunting, fishing and camping. It's also equidistant from Dallas, Houston, Austin and San Antonio, making it an easy destination from the state's largest population centers.

One warning. Few schools in the country are as nuts about football as A&M, and alumni travel from everywhere to see the games. Remember, this is the school where the students and alums are so football-crazed that they stand during the entire game, ready to leap on the field if the need arises. When the game is in town, hotels double their prices. Restaurants run extravagant specials. None of this really matters, because if you didn't make your reservations last year you won't find a room or a meal. Forewarned is forearmed.

This southern end of the Prairies and Lakes region has eight wineries and requires a good bit of driving. You could easily see all of them in two days, but then you'd miss the fun of spending some leisure time at the fancy B&B at Messina Hof.

If you decide to hit all eight in two days, start with the delightful Cottle family at Pleasant Hill, then stop at the Blue Bell factory on your way to Windy Hill. Then hit Lehm Berg and Rosemary's Vineyard. Spend the night at Messina Hof and have dinner at their restaurant. The next morning, filled with a delicious breakfast, stroll the grounds of the winery and take an early tour. Head off to the Purple Possum, then Bernhardt, and finish with a longish drive up Highway 6 to Tehuacana.

But consider making it a three-day, two-night trip, adding some more leisure time at Messina Hof and maybe a tour of the George Bush library at Texas A&M.

TRIP ONE

🍁 *Pleasant Hill Winery*

1441 Salem Rd., Brenham, TX 77833. Sat. 11 am–6 pm, Sun. noon–5 pm. (979) 830-8463, www.pleasanthillwinery.com

Bob and Jeanne Cottle are two of the nicest people in the Texas wine business—a big statement, since a lot of very nice folks make wine. The Cottles treat guests entering their tasting room as if the visitors have come into their own home. When they accomplish something great—

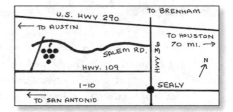

and I believe Bob helped change the face of Texas wine—they don't act like, "Look at me, I'm important." It's more an enthusiastic, "Wow! Isn't this cool!"

We meet a lot at Texas wine events. I first learned about their generosity while standing in their tasting room watching a busload of retirees get tastes. About twenty elderly men and women ambled in while Jeanne set up tasting glasses. The first pour was a Cabernet Sauvignon. I love having the opportunity to melt into a crowd of wine tasters and listen to the comments. One old gentleman took a sip, scrunched his face and turned to the woman next to him. "Why, it's bitter," he said, shaking his head. Some people were having trouble getting up to the bar, so Bob came out and poured for people. When Bob appeared in front of him, the man asked why the wine was bitter.

Bob and Jeanne Cottle have vineyards in two locations.

The truth was that the wine wasn't bitter; it was excellent Cabernet, but the man was obviously used to sweet wines. Bob patiently explained the role of expectation and experience in tasting wine. By the time he was through, the man understood that the Cab was well-made wine. It just didn't happen to appeal to him. At the end of the talk, people bought wines and sauntered back to their tour bus—except for the old man who'd complained about the Cabernet. He hung around till the end, then slowly walked up to the counter and bought a bottle of Cabernet. "I think my daughter will like it," he said. Bob gave the man a kindly smile. I wanted to give Bob a high-five.

Jeanne has Sicilian heritage. Both of her grandfathers made wine. She and Bob started making Cherry wine in the 1970s in Wisconsin. They came to Texas in the late 1970s and settled in Spring, near Houston. Bob worked as a mechanical engineer and Jeanne taught high school Spanish. Wine was already on their mind. They were making homebrew and giving it to friends. Everyone loved it and finally, as Jeanne said, "It got out of hand, so we decided we had to try to do it commercially."

Bob was the second graduate of the Grayson County College School of Enology and Viticulture. As Jeanne likes to say, "We figured that if we were going to risk our retirement, we should know what we were doing." She says it with such understatement you might think she is kidding. She isn't.

Has Bob learned anything that would help budding winemakers?" Yes. Join TWGGA and go to classes at Grayson. *The Wrath of Grapes* by Lewis

Perdue is a great book to read before you start. He helps you realize that if you invest this money anywhere else, you could make much more money. But if I had followed his advice I wouldn't have had as much fun. People do ask me if I enjoy owning a winery, and I always tell them the same thing. If you enjoy getting up in the morning and banging your head on the bedpost, having a winery is a great job."

He looks me in the eye to make sure I understand that he's being more ironic than honest. Then the old optimism pops back. "But, really, if you think you can stick to it, go for it."

The Best Wines

The Cottles have vineyards in two locations. The first is next to the winery outside Brenham and features Blanc du Bois, Lake Emerald, Favorite, Black Spanish, Cynthiana, Herbemont and Champanel. All resist Piece's disease. Their other grapes come from Fort Davis, where they grow Cabernet Sauvignon and Sauvignon Blanc.

Their wines are made in limited quantities, and the Cottles don't play games like hiding wine or artificially raising prices to quell demand. If it's available you can have it. The downside is that they sell out of all wines every year. So if you like something, snag it; it may be gone tomorrow.

How Bob helped change the face of Texas wine is a complicated story and you should get him to explain, but the net result is that Bob was the first man in the state to make a drinkable, desirable **Blanc du Bois**. Since then, Raymond Haak, and more recently Lewis Dickson, have matched Bob's accomplishment. But Bob was the first to make a really great wine from the grape that had defied so many other winemakers before. His version is still one of the best you can find. Apples, flowers, smooth mouth feel and a long finish. It's worth a side trip.

That's not all that's good. Bob is making a delicious un-oaked **Chardonnay**. It's crisp, clean and delicious and makes a great aperitif. He's also making two Cabernets from the Fort Davis fruit. The regular **Cabernet Sauvignon** is a classic Texas-style Cab with impressive fruit, a hint of oak and a winemaker's good sense to not mess with Mother Nature. The **Cabernet Barrel Reserve** is very limited and is basically the best barrel of the other Cab. All the same pluses apply; it's just a smidge better integrated.

Port lovers should try the **Tawny Rosso Forte**. Most Texas Ports are simply sweet wines. Some rise above the standard with so much richness and density that you forget about Portugal. Why wineries continue to call their wines "Port" is beyond me, but kudos to the Cottles for calling it something else. Isn't it ironic that the Pleasant Hill Tawny Rosso Forte offers a glimpse of the real thing? That's a very high compliment. They offer tastes along with a couple of chocolates for $5. Take them out on the porch and wind down your day.

Windy Hill Winery

4232 Clover Rd., Brenham, TX 77833. Fri and Sat. 11 am–5 pm, Sun. 1–5 pm. (979) 836-3252, www.windyhillwinery.com

"Texas Wines From Texas Grapes ©." That's right, it's copyrighted. Augie and Linda Meitzen apparently feel it's a wise marketing move to copyright the phrase. They also make some bodacious remarks on their Web site, like the claim that Windy Hill Winery is one of the few Texas wineries using Texas grapes exclusively and bottling 100 percent of the product on site. "We know exactly what goes into our wine."

Visiting with them, you'd never know they were so, well, assertive. They seem like a nice, happily married couple. Augie tells me he was a pencil pusher by trade, the president of Great Western Financial. Linda, a sweet person, is obviously devoted to Augie and really likes being in the wine business: "Everyone in this business is so nice."

The Meitzens started to grow grapes in the Hill Country but didn't like having to use a jackhammer to dig in the dense, hard caliche, so they moved to Blue Bell country and set up a winery in Brenham. In 2007 a frame on their Website sought an "angel" investor to help them create a franchise operation.

The Best Wines

All Windy Hills wines are made from grapes grown in Washington County. The Meitzens grow Blanc du Bois, Black Spanish, Champanel, Cynthiana (aka Norton) and Muscadine grapes. All are resistant to Pierce's disease, a real problem

Bob Meitzen outside his Windy Hill Winery.

TEXAN
Semi-Sweet Red Wine

Produced and Bottled By
Windy Hill Winery
Brenham, TX USA
Alcohol 18% By Volume

in the Brenham area. They are from all the *Vitis* available in the United States—*Vitis labrusca, Vitis rotundifolia* and American Hybrids—except the *Vitis vinifera*, easily killed by Pierce's, so the Meitzens don't grow Cabernet Sauvignon, Chardonnay, Merlot or any of the normal grapes that you hear about from the West Coast.

The best wine they make is a *Vitis vinifera*—**Shiraz**. It's not barrel aged, so everything you are tasting is from the fruit the Meitzens buy. Bright strawberry aromas predominate, but there's also a little wet hay aroma.

If you have come for sweet wine, the best is their **Tejas Port**. It's made from 100 percent Black Spanish grapes and has an attractive acidity to help balance the sweetness.

Lehm Berg Winery

1266 County Rd. 208, Giddings, TX 78942.
Sat. 11 am–5 pm, Sun. noon–5 pm. Call
ahead. (979) 542-2726,
www.lehmbergwinery.com

Carl Droemer feels like he's just about ready to retire. He'll be eighty-five in 2009. He's picked a doozy of a way to relax—creating a winery.

His family settled in 1928 in the house that now serves as the winery. They started making Wild Mustang grape wine in Giddings sixty years ago, but the wine was just for the family. They used hand-me-down German recipes predating

his people's original settlement in Giddings in the 1860s. Carl is a big fan of Wild Mustang grapes. "People in this area growed up liking it, but not everyone likes it. I growed up drinking it. It's my favorite."

While he's knowledgeable about modern winemaking techniques, Carl is a traditionalist. "Well, the problem is that the old ways of

Carl Droemer makes wine from Wild Mustang grapes using the traditional methods of his German pioneer forebears.

winemaking are disappearing 'cause the young people are reading the books and the books don't cover the old ways. I'm afraid the whole thing will be lost. I want to help the industry so I can leave something behind for the wine people. Then maybe they'll remember the old ways." The community is solidly behind him, because they want the tourism. Carl is proud of that support. He's also pleased that the house he grew up in is being restored.

Why has he taken on such a big job at an age when most folks are lounging around? He smiles. "The hobby just got out of hand."

The Best Wines

Carl makes more than a dozen different wines, but the best place to start is with **Von Droemer Red** (also his best seller). It's a history lesson in a bottle. These recipes and flavors are a century or more old. If you want to find out what the Texas pioneers were tasting back in the days of six-shooters and warring with the natives, here's your place. The wine is made from sweet Mustang grapes, with a little bit of the acids removed. As Carl says, "This is the way we made it in the old days."

🍂 Rosemary's Vineyard and Winery

5521 Hwy. 71 E., La Grange, TX 78945.
Daily 10 am–dusk. Call ahead. (979) 249-
2109, www.wines-made-in-texas.com

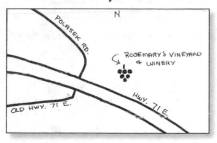

Rosemary's Vineyard and Winery sits on a hill overlooking Highway 71 just east of La Grange. For owner Emmett Schulze, living in La Grange is a full circle. He grew up in the tiny town of Rutersville just four miles away. Over the years he's had various careers—he owned a bait shop, did house remodeling, had a restaurant. His wife, Beatrice, had a very successful Mexican restaurant (and oh, my God, does she make good tamales) outside Houston.

Beatrice went to Italy with her sister and fell in love with the lifestyle. She loved the vineyards in everyone's backyard and how they all made a little wine. So how did they get from a little homemade wine to a winery? "My wife wanted to have hobby, but it got way beyond a hobby," Emmett tells me. "So we decided we'd better make a few nickels from it." Beatrice adds, "There is a romanticism to owning an vineyard, but you have to do a lot more work than most people realize, until you get to sip your first glass of wine under the oak tree."

Emmett Schulze at Rosemary's, the first licensed winery in Fayette County.

I sense a little stress, so I ask if they would do it all again. Emmett gives me a look like he's not sure he wants to answer. Beatrice is up to the challenge. "No," she says. "I wouldn't do it again."

The reason appears to be what the Marines call Overcome By Events (OBE). They had a nice, quiet retirement with a few vines to make grapes and it was fun. So they added more. And more. The next thing they knew, they no longer owned the vineyard. The vineyard owned them.

Emmett and Beatrice are fine people—considerate, open and as sweet to each other as they are to their customers. But right now they are clinging to the successes like mana. They're proud they were able to work through the governmental systems and get the first winery license in Fayette County. Beatrice is pleased that she was able to name something after her sister, Rosemary, who died of breast cancer. She hopes that the winery can be a small beacon to victims' families and to survivors. And, most of all, they love it when people like their wines.

The Best Wines

The Schulzes produce mostly sweet wines from Muscadine or Blanc du Bois grapes. The best of these is their **Blanc du Bois**, a semisweet wine with nice varietal flavors and aromas. They also make two dry wines. Their **Chardonnay** is in a Kendall Jackson style, with about 1.5 percent sugar (below 1 percent is considered dry, though most people can taste it at that level). It has vanilla aromas and butterscotch flavors. Their **Cabernet Sauvignon** is bone dry with soft tannins and a quaffable style.

I wish Beatrice would hire someone to help her and start making those scrumptious tamales—she currently only makes them for family once per year— and sell them at the winery. Yummy!

TRIP TWO

🍂 Messina Hof Winery

4545 Old Reliance Rd., Bryan, TX 77808.
Mon.–Sat. 10 am–9 pm. (800) 736-9463.

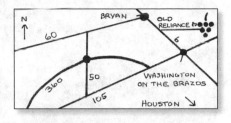

Paul and Merrill Bonarrigo just keep looking forward, reinvesting profits, adding to capacity and increasing their Texas market share. If you are from the Gulf Coast area, it's likely that Messina Hof is second only to Ste. Genevieve in terms of shelf space at your local H-E-B or Spec's. They make fifty-eight different wines, all credible and some outstanding.

The big news is the awards they're getting from the Houston Livestock show and Rodeo. In 2006, Messina Hof was the only Texas winery to win a Double Gold. It was for a wine called Angel, a late harvest ice wine made from Johannesburg Riesling. The award for being the top Texas wine is a gorgeous handmade saddle. Messina Hof won the saddle in 2006. And in 2005. And in 2004. And in 2003.

Winning one might be luck. Winning four in a row is an amazing recognition of Paul's winemaking, especially given the fact that the judges, all one hundred of them, are knowledgeable wine experts from the restaurant and retail world. When the wines have been drunk, they have a monster auction that's now raising more money—for scholarships to Texas universities—than the steer auction. In 2006, Messina Hof wines raised $110,000, or 10 percent of the total.

Angel, the award-winning wine from Messina Hof, costs $15. Paul and Merrill understand that to compete on the shelves, they have to offer bargains.

They also have some specific thoughts on the future of the Texas wine industry. Both are tireless champions of Texas wine. Paul served as president of the Texas Wine and Grape Growers Association three times and was also on the Department of Agriculture's Texas Wine Program Advisory Committee. While the figures are confusing for mere mortals, Messina Hof—with Fall Creek and Becker—has claim to being the third largest winery in Texas, after Ste. Genevieve and Llano Estacado.

Paul and Merrill travel to every possible Texas wine event. You're bound to run into them. With all this accomplishment, you'd think all people would want to know about them is how they've achieved the growth and the awards. But what everyone always wants to know about is the clothes.

Start with the red hat. It's not a quiet red. In fact, it looks like someone plopped a big maraschino cherry on Paul's head. And the handmade clothes are

Paul Bonnarigo on the grounds of Messina Hof Winery, one of the largest in Texas.

zany. He usually looks like a cross between an Indian maharaja and a New Jersey rock-and-roller, with the cherry hat. Paul loves the notoriety. When he walks into a room, everyone stops to see what sense-assaulting clothes he's picked. He never disappoints. Paul comes by this showmanship honestly. His father was a showbiz comedian and boxing coach. Paul really was a New Jersey rock-and-roller and lead singer for the Fabulous Brookwoods. The hat is a sixth-generation family tradition given to the first-born male on his sixteenth birthday.

Underneath the plumage is a smart businessman committed to making Texas a great wine state. Paul says we can eventually outdo the West Coast wineries. "If you ever look at it from a business standpoint," he said, "we are in a much better position for distribution, land is cheaper and we can grow great grapes. We're kind of like the Northwest was ten to fifteen years ago. When Oregon and Washington got together to market their wines, everything changed for them." He wants to be in the forefront as Texas moves closer to the top.

Paul fears that some new winemakers will get into the business for the wrong reasons. "I always ask potential winemakers why they want to do it and what expertise they have. Usually, the answer to the first or second question is illogical, so the real reason is usually a very emotional response. I'm always worried when I hear they like swirling wine on the patio.

"You have to have more than passion. Any honest individual in this business wakes up every morning scared. We have 40,000 choices in the state of Texas for wine. That means your product has to be worthy to stand up to that. Brands come and go. Big brands like Almaden and Christian Brothers are gone. It takes both passion and business savvy to keep going." He pauses for a second, probably for emphasis. "By the time a winery thinks they have a leg up, they're halfway dead."

He tells aspiring winemakers to keep their day job. His father knew showbiz was a roller-coaster ride, so he kept up his coaching career. Paul knows wine goes through its ups and downs. That's why he keeps his sports and back clinic going and continues to practice as a physical therapist.

Messina Hof has been open for more than a quarter century. What changes in Texas wine most impress him? "I'm really proud of the Texas wine industry," he says. "In the last twenty years it has gone from every man for himself to a group that comes together, especially under the leadership of Susan Combs." He calls the former Secretary of Agriculture "the best thing that ever happened to Texas wine."

What is Paul most proud of? "I'm proud that we love what we're doing so much that we feel like we're on perpetual vacation. But both Merrill and I think the thing we are most proud of is the strength of our marriage. The winery has strengthened and made ours a soulful relationship through adversity." He laughed, kind of a wise, knowing laugh. "When you close your eyes for the last time on earth, you're not going to think, 'Wow. I made a great Cabernet.' Merrill and I have each other. That's what I'm proud of."

The Best Wines

Messina Hof makes a lot of wines, fifty-eight at last count. Just like Honda will take a single chassis and make three Accords, an SUV and two Acuras, Paul takes raw ingredients and blends them in numerous ways to come up with different products. For example, several of his wines come in four levels: **Traditions**, a non-vintage blend of three previous years; **Barrel Reserve**, barrel aged in one- to five-year-old barrels; the **Private Reserve** line, barrel aged in both new French and new American oak; and **Paulo**, their showcase for the best red wines they're capable of producing. Besides the oak, Paul also tinkers with the blends just enough to allot it a unique label.

The Bonnarigos' original vineyard was planted in a Pierce's disease Petri dish. They wisely decided to plant the whole vineyard in Lenoir, a grape that resists the disease, and started buying good grape land in non-Pierce's areas of the state. Messina Hof is now one of the largest vineyard owners in West Texas, where Pierce's is less of a problem.

Picking the best from a roster of fifty-eight is impossible. You and I will have different choices for a best wine. But one thing impresses me when Paul and I sit down in his wine bar to try wines. I expected his Paulo wines so he could show off his best. Instead, he wanted to show me how good his least expensive wines are. His standard **Johannesburg Riesling** is anything but standard, something like biting into a green apple with a light grind of white pepper. Paul ferments and bottles this wine under refrigeration. That leads to the lightest little *frizzante* character, something that wakes up your taste buds. I'm generally not a big fan of this grape, but this is spectacular wine. Apparently I'm not alone in my appreciation of this wine. Paul sells 8,500 cases a year. That means this wine alone has larger sales than 90 percent of Texas wineries.

In the Private Reserve line, the **Chardonnay** takes square aim at a California style. It's buttery and rich and easy to drink as an aperitif. The **Merlot** has deep, dark color and resembles a Saint-Emilion more than a Napa version.

The tête de cuvee of Messina Hof is the **Paulo Port**, a masterful blend of fruit and oak flavors that hits 16 to 18 percent alcohol without any fortification from spirits. The **Paulo Meritage** offers similar quality in a dry, Bordeaux-style wine.

The best way to taste Messina Hof wines is to check into the winery's lovely B&B (a must for grand antique lovers) and while away an afternoon in the wine bar overlooking a little pond, tasting whatever strikes your fancy. Since you won't have to drive, you don't have to worry about tasting a couple more wines than usual. When you need some reinforcement from food, the restaurant is just across the parking lot, and you'll find a good repast.

🍁 Purple Possum Winery

5492 Rabun Rd., Navasota, TX 77868.
Sat and Sun. 10 am–6 pm "or just come by
and ring our bell." (936) 825-2830,
www.purplepossumwinery.com

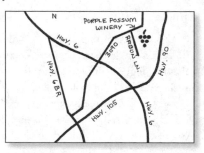

"Just come by and ring our bell" tells the whole story about the owner, Monty Galloway. Casual, friendly, gregarious, fun-loving, open. It's all in that one little statement.

Though Purple Possum is now a meadery, Monty started by growing a little Muscadine. One night, after picking a bucketful, he set the container down on the porch and went inside, and got sidetracked by some deviled eggs. A few minutes later he heard a loud crash; he got outside just in time to catch a chagrined marsupial that had just come to know the dyeing power of the Muscadine grape. Not one to cry over spilt grapes, Monty decided to get creative. "I know. I'll name a winery Purple Possum!"

That's only partly apocryphal (you'll have to ask Monty which part), but what they needed then was some wine so they could have a winery. Well, Monty had been selling his soap and balms at the Renaissance Festival, which attracts 250,000 folks every year. He also took along for his friends some homebrew mead, the alcoholic brew, popular in Medieval times, of fermented honey and water, with spices and fruit often added. Everyone kept telling him he should make it commercially, so he dipped his toe into the regulatory abyss. Finding it only burned instead of bitten off, he decided to proceed. Buying that first fifty-gallon barrel of honey was a little frightening, but he knew he was on to something.

Monty
Galloway's
Purple Possum
is more
meadery than
winery.

Monty
Galloway's
Purple Possum
is more
meadery than
winery.

Since then, Monty sells all he can make, and with good reason. I never realized this, but there's a whole underground of folks who like to pretend they are Medieval characters, ready to joust or sword-fight or slap wenches on the behind. They like nothing more at the end of a hard day than to have a feast and drink lots of mead. Honest.

Another thing that never occurred to me is that there is such a thing as dry mead. Water the honey down and ferment it until it's about 14 percent alcohol, and viola! Dry mead.

As much fun as Monty is, don't miss the fact that he is a serious mead-maker who works just as hard as many of his winemaking cousins. He is diligent about his blends, uses top-notch ingredients and tries to keep the prices reasonable.

Visiting the Purple Possum is one of those experiences that wine snobs would love if it were a place called Le Pourpre Kangourou in a little town outside Beaume-de-Venice in southern France. Open your mind and give it a try.

The Best Wines, er, Meads

None of Monty's wines are overly sweet. That was a big surprise to me. His **Vanillous Mead** is downright tart. My favorite, by a good distance, is the **Habanero Mead**. Sounds weird, but the habanero flavor presents as a slight kick at the finish. Delicious stuff. For cold winter nights, in place of the Lipton's mulled wine try the **Purple Possum Spiced Mead**, a delicious alternative.

Bernhardt Winery

9043 County Rd. 204, Plantersville, TX
77363. Sat and Sun. noon–6 pm. Or by
appointment. (936) 520-8684,
www.bernhardtwinery.com

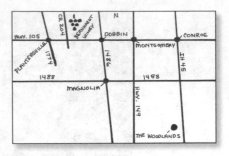

There seems to be an odd trend in the Texas wine world: Teachers are starting wineries. We're used to seeing hobby wineries started by lawyers, doctors, hedge fund owners and other well-paid workers whom we used to call gentlemen farmers before the de-genderization of pronouns and adjectives.

But on the ratio of pay to benefit to society, teachers have to be near the bottom rung. Maybe it's because they're tired of banging their heads against the wall of underfunded classrooms. Maybe it's the idea of being outside instead of inside. Whatever, I have a lot of respect for someone who rolls the dice when the stakes are high. It's one thing to invest $1 million in a winery when it's 10 percent of your net worth, but still quite another to create a business when failure would be devastating.

I'm not sure any of this applies to Jerry and Jerri Bernhardt. In general, I never inquire about people's financial status. Call me old-fashioned; I just think it's impolite, unless the person is parading wealth. Even then, I just make a wild guess.

Jerry and Jerri are both teachers. He grew up on the southern coast of Alabama in a family that enjoyed wild fruits and berries. "My mother was always making jelly and candy from the fruit," Jerry says. "I was in charge of running around and selling the stuff to the neighbors." He had a change of opinion when he read Sugar Busters. "I decided that using sugar was bad for you. But I still wanted to do something with fruit, so I thought it would be great to make fruit wines."

Jerry Bernhardt in his Plantersville winery's tasting room.

They planted an orchard with peaches, apricots, plums, persimmons, pears and figs. Jerry ended a thirty-two-year run as an engineering and architectural design teacher and set out to be a winemaker. With his training, a helpful brother, several high school students and a supportive wife, they built an elegant tasting room and functional winery. Even better, "We built it ourselves and did it all out-of-pocket," Jerry tells me, quiet pride evident. "We see this as a journey more than a destination, and we're taking our time doing the journey right. We want to spend the second part of our lifetime doing this. I guess I'm proud of the fact that we are still enjoying the journey."

One of the special moments I get the opportunity to witness is when winemakers have a moment to tap into whatever it was that originally filled them with passion about wine. I see a lot of choked-back tears of genuine happiness. Most people get embarrassed. I feel like I've just been given a gift. I'm a counselor by training and used to asking concrete questions, and I'm never afraid to show some empathy. I've been around a lot of crying, but the majority was from people crying sad tears. When I see a winemaker tearing up over something joyful, I never fail to be touched.

Jerry tells about one of those joyful moments. A policeman had his retirement party at Bernhardt Winery. As his family members and friends took turns giving tribute, everyone was crying happy tears, hugging each other, sharing affection and respect. "There was just so much love," he remembers. I can see Jerry being transported to the moment, almost like lovers trying to conjure when they first met their loved one. He dabs a tear with a Kleenex. "To think that Jerri and my dream is now a part of other people's lives . . . it's just very humbling."

The Best Wines

Jerry is quick to credit other Texas winemakers who have generously shared time and experience. He got big help from Ed and Madeline Manigold (Spicewood Vineyards), Mac and Maureen Reynolds (McReynolds Wines) and most especially Brian Wilgus, prior owner of Woodrose Winery. "When I was trying to decide what to do about this winery idea, I went visiting Hill Country wineries," he tells me. "When I walked into Woodrose, I had the weirdest déjà vu. I had gone to the three wineries and it hit me: I had a teacher—the Manigolds, a builder—Wilgus—and a person with five acres and limited resources—McReynolds. It seemed like destiny. So for three years I went out one weekend a month and a couple of weeks in the summer and worked with Brian, and learned everything I could." Wigus fell ill and Bernhardt and ace winemaker Bénédicte Rhyne had to make the Woodrose wine from Brian's grapes. They produced one of the greatest Cabernets ever made in Texas.

So I had big hopes for Jerry and Jerri's wines. The first that catches my attention is the **Pinot Grigio**. It's very soft and easy to drink, crisp acids and an appealing bit of grapefruit aroma. The **Sarah** (named for Sarah Bernhardt, no relation) is a meritage blend with well-integrated new American oak and strong fruit flavors. This wine profits from spending some time open before you drink it. Straight from the bottle you get a tiny bit of sulphur, but it blows off quickly and then you are left with a very good wine.

The best of the lot is the **Port**, made from 100 percent Cabernet Sauvignon. They use a proprietary barrel system and finish it off with twenty-year-old brandy. A whiff starts with butterscotch, then dark fruit like plums, then blackberries. In a state where about half the wineries make some version of Port-like wines, this stands out as one of the best. They only make about twenty-five cases a year of this wine, so buy it while you can.

Tehuacana Creek Vineyards & Winery

6826 E. Hwy. 6, Waco, TX 76705. Fri. noon–6 pm, Sat. 11 am–6 pm. (254) 875-2375, www.wacowinery.com

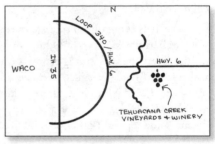

Ulf and Inga-Lill Westblom emigrated from Sweden in 1981, but not without some difficulty. Ulf had already attended the most distinguished medical school in Sweden, but as far as the American Medical Association and state governments were concerned he'd have to do his internship and residency all over again. That meant years of sleepless nights, working for doctors who knew less than he knew, and all for slave wages. Why'd he do it?

"America is a land of opportunity, and I felt as a doctor I would have so much more available to me," he says. "The medical system over there is a victim of decades of socialism. Plus, I wanted my children to grow up here." Ulf is an internist with a specialty in infectious disease. He ended up in Missouri, where he and Inga-Lill developed a taste for wines made from the Norton grape. They delved into the wine world with gusto. "My wife and I were semiprofessional wine tasters for the last thirty years," he says. "We were wine judgers and critics and also taught about wine."

While working peripherally in the wine trade they made some decisions. They believe that it is very hard, if not impossible, to make a perfect wine from a single vineyard or even from a single grape, and that blending is the only correct way to make wine.

They were bitten by the winemaking bug. They knew they wanted to own a winery, but where? California prices were too high, even by doctors' standards. In 1993 they were on vacation in Texas. In Galveston a friend said they should visit Messina Hof. "One night when we were sipping a little wine we suddenly fell in love with wine and Texas and everything," he says. "We went back to St. Louis and I immediately started looking for a job in Texas." That job came from the VA Hospital in Temple.

Then they went looking for land appropriate for a vineyard. They found the place they liked and planted Norton, not only because they liked it but because it is resistant to Pierce's disease. They also started looking for some other grape sources so they could experiment with blending.

By blending the wines they believe they can produce wines closer to what they consider correct. "We spend days and days comparing different blends," Ulf says. "I think that since all our wines are blends, plus our background as wine tasters, we end up with new and more interesting wines than you get anywhere else. I know I have the right formula. I don't want to gloat or boast, but 90 percent of our customers tell us that they love all our wines, and 90 percent tell us we have the best Port they've ever tasted."

The Best Wines

There are currently seven Tehuacana Creek Wines (pronounced, as Ulf says, "To-Walk-In-A Creek"). Since Ulf and Inga-Lill are such strong proponents of blending, you know you'll be seeing multiple grape names on each bottle. Blanc de Bois and Norton provide the backbone for everything, but they also add Syrah, Malbec, Black Spanish, Favorite, Cabernet Sauvignon and Nebbiolo.

Norton is of the big and bold school. The Norton vegetal and animal aromas are muted, partly because the wine is only 75 percent Norton. The rest of the wine is from Syrah and Malbec, both offering some interesting dark fruit flavors. This is a wine for folks who love 'em big. Ulf's pick for his best wine is the **Port**, and I can understand his affection. It tends more to the Ruby style than Tawny, but the sweetness and acids balance nicely, with the added alcohol coming to the fore.

As to the label: there really are cougars on the property—seven or so. "The mother came up to our land recently," Ulf says. "I took my .357 magnum and told her to go away. She growled a few times and left."

⭑◎ FOOD

Bryan/College Station

Café Eccell, 101 Church Ave., College Station. Lunch and dinner daily. (979) 846-7908). Inventive American food, probably the best place in town for seafood. They also have the only wood-burning oven in town and use it to make great pizzas. My favorite is pizza margherita, the soul of simplicity. Just dough, Roma tomatoes, fresh mozzarella and fresh basil.

Christopher's World Grill, 5001 Boonville Road, Bryan. Lunch and dinner daily. (979) 776-2181. Owned by Christopher Lampo, a CIA grad. The restaurant is in a stylishly decorated 100-year-old house and serves recipes Christopher picked up while chef-ing on private yachts in Europe and the South Pacific. When an owner names a dish after himself, you can be sure it's his choice for best dish. Christopher's House Filet is a grilled beef tenderloin on a bed of creamed spinach and roasted potatoes. To make sure you don't starve with just the beef, spinach and potatoes, he tops the whole thing with crispy fried crawfish tails, béarnaise sauce and a Port wine demi glace. Wow! Off the menu, but worth asking for, is a plate of grilled vegetables. Christopher's has a nice wine list, but the prices are a little steep and it needs more it Texas wines.

Vintage House Restaurant, 4545 Old Reliance Rd. at Messina Hof Winery. Lunch and dinner Wed.–Sun. Closes at 6 pm Sundays. (979) 778-9463 #31. Moderate to expensive, unless there's a football game. Hard to top. I can't recommend a specific dish because the chef changes the menu based on what's fresh. Ask for the chef's recommendation.

Brenham

Capital Grill, 107 W. Commerce St. Hours vary. (800) 481-1951. Part of the Ant Street Inn, a gorgeous old B&B. The attraction here is beef; good steaks are the order of the day. Owner Domenic Catalano has put together a comfortably stylish place that ten years ago no one would have imagined could be in Brenham, Texas. There's something nice about being able to roll out of your chair and into your bedroom.

Volare Italian Restaurant, 205 S. Baylor St. Lunch and dinner Wed.–Sun. (979) 836-1514. Good, homemade Italian food. Ask for the pork bolognaise and eggplant.

⌂ SHELTER

Ant Street Inn, 107 W. Commerce Street, Brenham. (800) 481-1951. A gorgeous old B&B filled with nice antiques and overlooking a breezy garden. Just the kind of place to enjoy a book and a glass of wine.

Hilton College Station, 801 E. University St., College Station. Prices start at moderate levels but rise quickly if football is in the air. (979) 260-1931. A 300-plus-room business and convention hotel. Its greatest benefit is the location, just minutes from attractions in town. www.hiltoncs.com.

Villa Bed and Breakfast at Messina Hof, 4545 Old Reliance Rd at Messina Hof Winery. Moderate to expensive. (979) 778-9463, #22. My first choice. Rooms are furnished with antiques, there's an on-premise manager to make sure you stay happy and you're across the parking lot from the best restaurant in town. What could be better? www.mesinahof.com.

Vineyard Court Executive Suites, 1500 E. George Bush Dr. College Station. Not too expensive, unless the Aggies are playing football. (888) 846-2678. A modern suite-style hotel with local ownership, which I think makes the service better. All suites have complete kitchens. www.vineyardcourt.com.

FUN

Bryan/College Station

There are two must-see attractions in the area, also the area's two largest tourist draws. First is the **George Bush Presidential Library and Museum,** 1000 George Bush Dr., Mon.–Sat. 9:30 am–5pm, Sun. noon–5 pm. (979) 260-9552. This place isn't just filled with papers; someone put thought into how to keep a restless crowd interested. For instance, did you ever wonder what the Camp David office looks like? Or the president's cubicle on Air Force One? They're both recreated here. I love dogs, so I was happy to see that Millie gets some space, too.

The second biggest draw in the area is **Messina Hof Winery.** A winery? Yes, the second biggest attraction is a winery, but not just any winery, as Merrill and Paul Bonarrigo have turned theirs into a place that functions with the meticulousness and fascination of an adult Disneyland. The professional staff operates the tours and tasting rooms with military precision and good humor.

Brenham

Brenham is worth a day by itself. Besides the creamery and winery, there is something for horse lovers, gardeners and antique devotees. Antique lovers can while away a morning walking through the old part of downtown Brenham with its restored buildings and cute shops.

Antique Rose Emporium, 9300 Lueckemeyer Rd. (979) 836-9051. Famous among gardeners across the nation. More than twenty years ago the owners decided to start collecting abandoned roses from cemeteries. These roses are hearty enough to live without watering or pesticides. www.antiqueroseemporium.com.

Blue Bell Creamery, FM 566 on the east side of Brenham. (800) 327-8135. Home to some of the best ice cream in the United States. Tours tell you everything you'd ever want to know about ice cream and end with a scoop of your favorite flavor. They only offer tours during the week, and you should call ahead to see how crowded it is. If you happen to be there on the weekend, you can still go to the ice cream parlor for a scoop.

Monastery of St. Claire Miniature Horse Ranch, 9300 Hwy 105, nine miles outside Brenham. (979) 836-9652. The Franciscan Poor Clare Nuns operate this horse farm to fund their monastery, aimed at the "contemplative life of prayer, penance and union with God." The horses are sweet-tempered and very smart. Prices range from $3,000 to $30,000. Self-guided tours are free and available daily from 2 to 4 pm. They ask that you respect their privacy at other times.

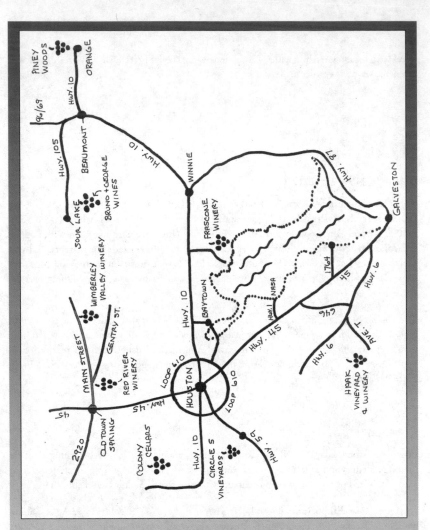

TRIP ONE
Piney Woods Country Wines
Bruno and George Wines
Frascone Winery
Circle S Vineyards

TRIP TWO
Colony Cellars
Wimberley Valley Winery
Red River Winery
Haak Vineyards and Winery

CHAPTER 5

The Wine Roads of the
Gulf Coast

T his section has eight wineries from the outskirts of Houston to the Louisiana border.

The city of Houston is a perfect central location from which to start. There are great museums, a vibrant music scene and the best restaurants in the state. Add to that one of the greatest wine stores on the planet—Spec's at 2410 Smith Street. The downside is that Houston, the fourth largest city in the United States, is teeming with traffic, and the air is thick with humidity and gunk from the refineries. Galveston has a beautiful coastline with picturesque Victorian neighborhoods. It puts you a little out of the way, and you'll still have to drive through Houston, but there's something relaxing about looking out over the gulf and listening to the waves break on the sand. Either way you'll have plenty of places to eat, sleep and recreate. You could also cover these places from Bryan/College Station, if you want to add on some Prairies and Lakes wineries and make a week of it.

My strategy would be to hit all eight Gulf Coast wineries in a weekend. I'd stay at the Lovett Inn in Houston, but Houston has every type of place to stay from cheap to stratospheric. Get on the road Saturday morning early and head for Piney Woods Winery—be sure to call the day before and make sure he'll be there—then work your way back, stopping at Bruno and George, Frascone and Circle S.

On Sunday have an early brunch at the Backstreet Café or Ruggles, then start at Colony, followed by Wimberley Valley, Red River—both within walking distance in Old Town Spring—and end with Haak. Spend a little time in Old Town Spring, only twenty miles north of Houston but in a different century, shaded by sycamores and pecans and with boutiques, galleries and antique shops crowding the streets.

The hour-long trip to Santa Fe for Haak Vineyards will be worth it. Not only are there great wines; there's usually something special doing on Sunday afternoons. After you leave, take an out-of-the-way nighttime drive back to Houston via the Fred Hartmann Bridge. You'll catch a phenomenal view of the working guts of big oil with a million lights as a backdrop. *Blade Runner* fans will feel at home.

If you've got an extra day, take Circle S from the first day and Haak from the second and spend a little more time at both, then meander through Galveston and end with a ride across Galveston Bay on the picturesque Port Bolivar Ferry.

TRIP ONE

🍃 Piney Woods Country Wines

3408 Willow Dr., Orange, TX 77632.
Usually Mon.–Sat. 9 am–5 pm, but call
ahead to make sure. (409) 883-5408,
www.pineywoodswines.com

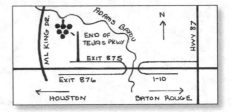

Alfred Flies, owner of Piney Woods Country Winery, has been in Texas since 1949. He spent ten years working for other people and for the next twenty-nine operated an interior design and decoration business. Around 1975 he started making fruit wines as a hobby. He loved it. "I just got involved and tried to make wine out of everything I could find," he said. "I read a lot of 'how to' books but never took any courses except seminars with the grape growers association. I never really intended to make a business out of it."

He started a little home brew winery and set about making wines to his taste. When friends raved about his wines, he decided to apply for a license. He jumped through all the hoops and finally received his winery license, the fourteenth in Texas. He planted more vineyards in 1984 and 1985 but ran into a problem. He liked Muscadine and fruit wines, but distributors didn't think they could sell it. "Most of my business, because of the type of wine I have, doesn't sell from grocery stores," he explained. "They're always pushing beer or Strawberry Hill in front of it. But once I could get it to places where they could taste it, people liked it, and it grew up really quick. Every year since we've been going we've increased our sales."

Hurricane Rita destroyed two-thirds of Alfred's producing vines. He planted a trial run of Black Spanish and Blanc De Bois and tried some plum trees but decided to go for all Muscadine, other than a few orange trees he uses for sparkling wine.

Alfred enjoys making wines for a certain type of drinker. "Not everyone wants Vinifera," he explains. "They're not all

Piney Woods Country Winery specializes in sweet Muscadine wines.

'educated,' so to speak. Some people like fruity wines and light wines and semi-sweet Champagnes. Within the last six or seven years, my Muscadine has gotten so popular that it's all we want to grow."

The Best Wine

Alfred is unabashed in preferring fruity sweet Muscadine wines. How you feel about them depends on how you feel about the grape. I'm not a fan, but there are millions of Americans, mostly from the Southeast, to whom Muscadine means memories of wild grapes and Grandma's jelly. If you are one, then I can tell you that Alfred makes a quality product in enough different styles so anyone should be able to find what they are looking for. If you know nothing of the grape, this is a good place to start.

My favorite wine from Piney Woods Country Wines is the **Blueberry Wine**. Like the Poteet Strawberry wine, I'm certain that if you placed this wine in a French bottle and labeled it L'Amour de Myrtille, people would gladly pay $30 a bottle. So taste with an open mind and you'll find something special.

Bruno and George Wines

400 Messina Rd., Sour Lake, TX 77659. Sat. 9 am–3 pm and by appointment. (409) 898-2829, www.brunoandgeorge.com

This is a saga of a man with vision and a passion who wouldn't give up until he found a way to share it with the world. Shawn Bruno wanted to make raisin wine. He has an almost mystical connection to it, one that causes him on more than one occasion to reach for the Kleenex to dab away a few tears.

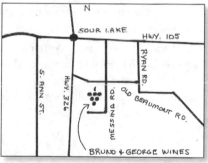

It all started with his grandfather. In 1902, Rocco Bruno left his home in Salaparuta, Sicily, and took his two sons—Joseph, fourteen, and Salvatore, twelve—to try to find a living in the US. Rocco worked hard in coal mines and on the railroad, raising his sons and following the traditions of his homeland in making raisin wine. When he finally had enough money he went home to pick up his wife. She refused to come. So Rocco stayed and left his sons in America. They worked in sawmills until they heard about black gold on the gulf bay in Texas.

Salvatore went to work for what became Texaco and became a citizen in 1944 at the age of fifty four. He and his wife, Mary, had three sons and six daughters.

Shawn Bruno got laws changed so he could make his ancestral raisin wine.

He kept up his father's tradition of making raisin wine, which he passed on to his children. Two of the boys—Nick and Joe—kept up the work, and Shawn finally learned the skill from his uncles. One big difference—Shawn wanted to make the wine commercially. He found new meaning in the old joke, "We're from the government and we're here to help." He recalls, "I went to get a license to make raisin wine and found out it was against the law to make wine from dried fruit!" Shawn is an actor by training, and he talks as if he's trying to project to the back of the auditorium. He's so animated and emotional that the conversation seems, well, Italian. "I went to the Texas Alcoholic Beverage Commission to find out why we couldn't make wine from dried fruit, and no one knew. It turned out the reason stemmed from Prohibition. The revenuers didn't like dried fruit because it lasted a long time and was easy to hide."

So Shawn lobbied to get the code changed. After about a year of pointing out—in the nicest possible way, of course—that the law was archaic and idiotic, the code was changed. But it turned out the code wasn't the only problem. There was a law regulating the issue, so Shawn would have to get a new law passed.

"I started on the three representatives for the area. The good news was that the 76th Legislature was coming, so I did the lobbying on the locals and did e-mails with legislators all over. When we finally got to the floor, they passed it unanimously. Texas, through my little efforts, was now going to be able to produce and market raisin wine."

Now at least a dozen Texas wineries now offer raisin wine.

But the story's not over. Once Shawn got the legislature to approve raisin wine, he found out the feds wouldn't allow raisin wines over 14 percent alcohol, something to do with the designation Table Wine (under 14 percent alcohol) versus Dessert Wine (over 14 percent).

So Shawn had to start lobbying the federal government to allow him to make wines over 14 percent. He went ballistic looking for a solution. After all he'd been through, he wasn't about to stop. Finally, an Alcohol, Tobacco and Firearms agent in Buffalo helped locate a code offering a designation called Other Than Standard Wines and told him he could sell his wine that way. Shawn still wanted to call his 14.5 percent wine Raisin Wine rather than Dessert Wine, but went ahead and called it OTS for Other Than Standard so he could start producing the wine.

Later his petition to the federal government went through and he got permission to label his wine Raisin Wine. By that time all of his customers knew it as OTS, so he kept the name.

How does it feel to finally be able to make his family's heritage wine? "It's like in *Field of Dreams* when everything clicks and falls into place," he says. He looks up and gives a big smile. "The whole thing is surreal."

The Best Wines

Shawn makes more than raisin wine. He also makes wines from fresh fruits. Of those, **Strawberry Wine** is a winner. But he hangs his hat on the **OTS Raisin Wine.**

I have to admit to some trepidation about tasting this raisin wine. I loved the story and was proud for him for successfully jumping all those hurdles. But making wine from raisins sounded a little, I don't know, cloying. Of course, I lustily pursue wines from Europe made from grapes that differ from raisins by only a drop or two of juice. Amarones, Sauternes, Trockenberenausleses bring 'em on. But raisin wine? Well, here's another example of what you can learn if you prevent your preconceived notions from ruining your enjoyment of something out of the ordinary. I had my first eye-opener at Poteet, and here's another.

One of my favorite styles of wine is what the Australians call Sticky Wine. The best are made from old Muscat fortified with brandy, aged in wood and with a myriad of fascinating flavors—butterscotch, toffee, hazelnuts and caramel, as well as the floral character of the grape. Shawn's **OTS Raisin Wine** reminds me of those Muscat stickies. The OTS hits 16.5 percent alcohol, without any fortification from brandy or anything else. It's got the Australian version's great creamy mouth feel, and, true to its making, you get real aromas of Thompson seedless grape raisins.

Consider my eyes opened. Again.

❧ Frascone Winery

311 Bayside Dr., Anahuac, TX 77514. Fri.–Sun. noon–5 pm or by appointment. (409) 252-4506, www.frasconewinery.com

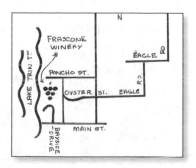

The road to Frascone Winery winds through Gulf Coast wetlands and deepwater harbors. This is not the fancy coastal area. Instead, you'll find a mix of working people who decide to retire here, oil patch workers and people who just plain love the coast.

Flooding is a problem every five years or so. The residents are sanguine about the issue. Jimmy Frascone say they've been through two floods in the ten years they've lived here. Glenda, who is checking inventory for the taxman, shouts from the back room: "We're not leaving! We love it here!"

As for wine, Jimmy grew up in Minnesota, where his family has made wine for generations. His job as a radar construction engineer kept him and Glenda traveling far, but over the years they visited more than two hundred wineries. After thirty-

Jimmy Frascone makes Oak Island Red like his grandfather made in Minnesota.

four years of government work he had had all the fun he could stand, so he retired, having done some thinking: "As I got closer to retirement I thought making wine would be something to do to keep me active." He had to fight the label Nazis—my term, not his; he was much more circumspect, but label approval often takes longer than any other part of winemaking. Eventually, Frascone Winery was a reality.

One of the first wines Jimmy made was a blend called Oak Island Red. "It is just like my grandfather made," he tells me, the pride evident in his eyes.

Would he do anything different? He thinks for a moment, looks up almost nervously, like he's really trying to give me what I'm asking for. So I say maybe there's nothing he'd change.

"No, I would change a couple of things," he says. "I'd make a big effort to purchase all my equipment beforehand. I'd have gotten a pneumatic corker and some other pieces of equipment that would have helped. After three years, we're still not profitable, but if I get there, I'll invest it in equipment." That sounds reasonable from a man who built everything in, around and including the winery.

"Yeah, I built everything with my own hands," he says. "I probably should have hired a contractor."

The Best Wines

Jimmy suffers from a malady common in Texas winemaking. He feels like he should be making fancy wines that critics will "ooh" and "aah" over, and he's a little shy about showing the wines that please a substantial portion of the public. That's a shame, because Jimmy is making some very special fruit wines.

Best of the lot, and worth the drive to acquire, is his **Red Raspberry Wine.** As I've said in the Poteet Winery section, if you slapped a fancy French label—something like Framboise de Amour—and put it next to the Chambord, people would happily pay $40 a bottle. Say it's Texas fruit wine and the wine-snob patrol gets apoplexy. Go figure. You and I can be in on the secret: it's great stuff.

His other fruit wine winner is **Cranberry Wine,** a bright, acidic wine that has grown in popularity to the point Jimmy exports it to twenty states.

If you're a wine connoisseur, you already know there is no sin in drinking sweet wines as long as they are good sweet wines. There's also no sin in drinking fruit wines if they are good fruit wines. What I'm worried about is the beginner who's been forced into the cookie-cutter mentality that all wines should resemble dry Bordeaux. For those of you uttering the words "I only like dry wines," welcome to a whole new world of fun. After you try some of Texas's best, give the Alsacienne wines, the Sauternes and the German and Austrian Eiswines a try.

🍁 Circle S Vineyards

9920 Hwy. 90 A, #B-268, Sugar Land, TX 77478. Tue.–Thu. 11 am–7:30 pm, Fri. and Sat. 11 am–8:30 pm, Sun. noon–5 pm. (281) 265-9463, www.circlesvineyards.com

"I don't care where I get the grapes. I want the best grapes I can get. I hope they are from my vineyards, but every year, 50 to 60 percent of my wine comes from others outside Texas."

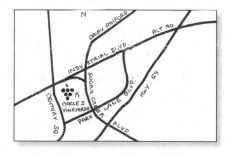

Owner Dave Stacey is in form, expounding on things he holds dear and not afraid to step on a lot of toes, if he has to, to get the best wine possible in his bottles. "Why use an inferior product when you can buy a better one? Half the reason our Texas wines don't get any respect in the national press is that we are using inferior product."

So begins a sojourn with one of the most outspoken Texas winemakers. Given that most of our winemakers are contentious, passionate and frequently given to hyperbole (that's why I like them so much), placing Stacey's frankness that high on the scale means he's up there in the rarified air with winemakers like

Dave Stacey headed a company making racing cars before becoming a full-time winemaker.

Kim McPherson and Ed Auler. Ask a question and you get a direct, if highly opinionated, answer.

So Dave is a proud man. He's a bit tall, with a coiled kind of energy. He's prone to moving around a lot and making declarations loudly. He's worked in the airplane industry and was head of McLaren USA. For those of you who don't follow Formula 1 racing, that's a company that makes race cars as well as extremely fast and expensive road cars. Want to hit 230 miles an hour on the Katy Freeway? McLaren makes a car for you, though its prices are astronomical. Today Dave collects Ferraris while his wife drives a mint 1956 pink T-Bird. Dave also owns the world prize–winning Triumph TR-6.

When I come to his winery, in the middle of a strip shopping center in Sugar Land, Dave is driving an SUV. That's what owning a winery does to you. Suddenly you go from drop-top Ferrari to drop-off delivery truck. But he loves what he does. "I get a lot of personal things out of this business," he says. "I can create. And there's some heritage. I'm the fifth generation of winemakers in my family. I've been making wine since I was five years old."

Most of all, he loves the people in the wine world, and cites one important example: "We didn't realize the impact the people—customers and other winemakers—would have on our lives. My older daughter was in the hospital in New Orleans during Katrina. When I couldn't get any answer at the hospital, I took three friends to go look for her. I had no idea whether my daughter and grandchildren were alive or in trouble, so I just had to go help. I left a note in the window of my tasting room saying 'Daughter and grandchildren missing in Katrina.' When I got back home, there were envelopes with money and letters from customers. It just made me cry." It makes him cry again. It's amazing how loyalty and concern can break through the emotional barriers to elicit tears. I've seen it again and again in my travels.

Dave owns two vineyards, one in Centerville, Texas and one in the Tuscany, area of Italy. Yes, you read correctly, he owns a vineyard in Italy. In fact, his biggest-selling wines start life as Italian grapes; he's intent on making only quality wines, so he'll go anywhere for good grapes. "Look, I have a relationship with about twenty different vineyards," he says. "I buy the best of everything or I buy nothing at all. Mediocrity anywhere in the chain makes mediocre wine."

Dave believes his customers return for more than wine. There's a comfortable, living-room-type area upstairs where people can relax with some wine, have a quiet conversation or just read a book. "If wine is everywhere, and it is, you have to do it better and do something different," Dave says. "One thing we do different is we're in the middle of a city. Second, we make everything by hand. At the cash register you'll either find the winemaker, or his wife or their kids. But the end result is what we're all about. If we can't find good grapes, we don't make it. If you are going to do it, do it right."

Does a character as bodacious as Dave have advice for aspiring winemakers? He doesn't disappoint. "I always ask two questions," he says. "Have you been making wine for ten years? And do you have $500,000? If you answer no to either, then come back when you can answer yes to both."

The Best Wines

Circle S Wines come in two styles, reflecting Dave's view of the wine world. He likes light wines early in the day and heavier wines later in the day, so he makes both. The light wines sport a black cap and usually have low tannins, no oak and a fruit-forward character. For later in the day he makes more traditional wines. These come with a gold cap and are big, oaky, tannic wines. The oak is a costly ingredient. He uses only new, fine grain, medium to medium-plus toast oak that has been drying for three years. He also pays attention to the tasting, using big-bowled hand-blown crystal from Europe capable of holding a whole bottle of wine. Dave does things big.

His best wine is the **Cabernet** under the gold cap. The 2004 vintage was from California, but he'll buy grapes from Washington, or Texas or Italy, too. Wherever he can get the best grapes. This Cabernet is very vanilla from the new oak, but it's also a dense wine with gorgeous aromas and rich flavors.

Magio de Amore is Dave's Super Tuscan blend of 65 percent Sangiovese, 30 percent Cabernet Sauvignon and 5 percent Merlot. True to his statements about quality being first, Dave only makes this wine in the best years. His first vintage was 2000, and he didn't make another until 2004. Tastewise, imagine a Chianti Classico on steroids.

His best Texas wine can stand up on a worldwide table: a **Blanc de Bois** and **French Colombard** cuvee. He does a nice job bringing out the best in both grapes, offering a fragrant wine with nice acids to pair up with Gulf Coast seafood.

Dave is obsessed with the grape selection, which pays benefits, but he won't guarantee to make every wine every year. So if you like a wine when you try it, buy it then. It may not be there the next time you come.

TRIP TWO

🍁 Colony Cellars

35955 Richard Frey Rd., near Waller, TX 77484. Thu.–Sun.
10 am–6 pm. (979) 826-3995.

Don Corley grew up in Del Rio, where he worked for Tommy Qualia's dad cleaning the vineyard floor and picking grapes. All through his career teaching computer science at Del Mar College in Corpus Christi he kept thinking about those days and dreaming of starting his own vineyard and winery.

He had one hundred acres outside Waller. "I wanted to do something after I retired in 1995," he says. "I had been interested in having a winery over the years,

Don Corley checks one of his Colony Cellars wines.

and, by God, I just decided to go ahead and do it."

We're sitting at a table in his comfortable tasting room. Out the back door there's a pond and picnic areas. He intends to build a disc golf course and set up rides through the vineyard. He wants to attract nice families.

His little piece of paradise nearly didn't happen, thanks to our government. "Oh, yeah. Label approval was awful. The stuff they brought up was so petty. There was a while when we were going through the label battle that I just didn't know if I could make it. But I'm glad I did it." He finally jumped through all the hoops and was open on November 9, 2006.

The Best Wines

Don's wines are made from grapes that don't mind the area—Black Spanish, Blanc du Bois and Muscadine. He mixes the three to make three lines of wine: Crisp, Smooth and Rich. Crisp is semidry, Smooth is sweet and Rich is the designation for dessert wines. Each has three colors to choose from: White, Blush and Red. He's targeting Muscadine lovers. He uses carbonic maceration exclusively (that's the system they use in Beaujolais to give it that distinctive taste), so the Muscadine grapes take on more of a "Sweet-Tart meets tropical fruit" flavor.

Which wine you'll like most depends on how you like your Muscadine. My favorite was the **Smooth Blanc** for its mellow and simple flavors.

🍂 Wimberley Valley Winery

206 Main St., Spring, TX 77373. Tue.–Fri. 11 am–5:30 pm, Sat. 10 am–6 pm, Sun. noon–5:30 pm. (281) 350-8801.

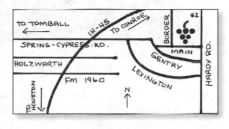

One of the dilemmas facing winemakers is how to deal with the press. Most see greater potential for harm than help. After all, in their view, we are snooty types, interested only in austere, difficult wines. If they don't happen to make austere wines, their fear is that we will ding them in print.

One of the dilemmas facing wine writers is how to get through to winemakers that don't want to deal with us. If I'm doing my job correctly, I should be able to give a fair description of a wine that I wouldn't personally choose. Is it well made? Well priced? Which consumers might like it? I think I do my job correctly.

We had a head-on collision of dilemmas when I set out to see Wimberley Valley Winery. Manager Dean Valentine wasn't interested in talking to me. He had recently faced a writer who gave a perfect description of a Wimberley Valley Wine, then said it was no good. Note that the reviewer did not say he didn't care for it, simply that it was no good. That's a shame, because Dean makes wines with care, using good ingredients and selling at a very fair price. A reviewer should talk about the wine so that a consumer can decide whether they will like it or not; that's my opinion.

The Wimberley Valley success story happened almost simultaneously with the Homestead story. Their wines would go on to have a huge influence on Texas tasting rooms.

Dean Valentine and Howard Pittman started Wimberley Valley Winery in 1983, a time when there weren't many wineries. "We were part of a wave," he says, "but lots of those places are out of business now. In the old days, the more we sold the more we lost. We had really tough financial years up to 1992." That's when they made a discovery.

"We tried making a small barrel of sweet red wine. It sold out at the tasting room in one weekend." Dean feels they'd been trying to sell wine that people didn't want, and it was killing them. "You have to find a niche that makes you more accessible to

The Valentines' Wimberley Valley Winery is on Spring's Main Street.

the public. In the old days, winery owners would plant grapes, make wine and then decide that maybe they should develop a market. That's backwards. What we are doing here is going for the 85 percent of the folks who don't like wine and trying to bring them in the fold. And it's working." It really is. Wimberley Valley Winery is selling 6,000 cases of wine a year through their tasting room in Spring.

By the way, you can't buy wine at the winery. You can't visit the winery. The address is not even marked. When I first went to visit Dean I couldn't find the winery, so I stopped a local lady. She rolled down the window of her SUV and stuck her head out. I asked, "Do you know where Wimberley Valley Winery is?" She leaned over to her daughter who was having a minor tantrum and told her to shush. She scrunched up her face and said, "What?" I asked again. "I'm trying to find Wimberley Valley Winery. Do you know where it is?" She gave me a quizzical look. "There's no winery around here. Are you sure you're in the right place?" Of course, I wasn't. Sure, I mean.

Eventually I found it. Dean had scotch-taped an 8½-by-11 piece of notebook paper on the gate with the street number. The reason for the privacy? Dean lives there. Most of the time he works at the winery. But when he isn't there, he likes to get a little time off. He grows his tomatoes behind the house, works on his old Triumph TR-6 convertible. He doesn't cotton to the idea of visitors on his time off.

Dean grew up in Chicago and started making wine at home. "My grandfather had a farm in Indiana, and every summer we'd all go out there," he recalls. "He had a huge orchard with five different types of American grape vines. He traded grapes for wine from some winery. He got the wine in barrels and kept it the storm cellar." Dean starts to laugh. "My cousin and I used to sneak down there with a rubber hose and siphon all we could get away with."

We went on talking for a couple of hours. We laughed a lot and found out we had some things in common. Tasted the wines. At the end, Dean apologized for not wanting to talk to me. I understood. He is a man who takes what he does seriously and tries to do a good job. And he certainly has come up with some inventive ways to get that 85 percent to try wine.

The Spring location is open to the public. Dean's wife, Jana, runs it. She rescues dogs. Anyone who loves dogs enough to rescue them is A-OK in my book.

The Best Wines

Wimberley Valley Winery aims at consistency from vintage to vintage, so they blend all their wines. Dean has little interest in growing grapes but loves making wine. "We buy everything," he said. "Grapes, bulk wine and concentrate. That way I can change my mix every year to keep it consistent. We buy from all over. New York, California, Texas." Dean is intent on giving the customer a good product and one that appeals to the "other 85 percent." He takes care making his wine and is serious about getting it right.

His best dry wine is the **Sangiovese**. It has all the requisite characteristics of a Chianti: leather and cigar box aromas, medium color, and bright red cherry flavors. He also makes some fruit wines, and I have to admit a fondness for his **New York State Cherry Wine**. It has the pungent nose of cherries and just makes me happy. It's a great wine for a small cold glass after supper.

🍁 Red River Winery

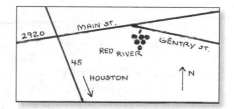

421 Gentry St. #204, Spring, TX 77373.
Tue.–Sat. 10 am–5 pm. (281) 288-9465,
www.redriverwinery.com

Owner Mark Woolington graduated from college in Hawaii in 1986. He hung around, selling everything from sunglasses to subdivisions. Most of his family drifted back to the mainland and, in 1993, so did he. He studied the economic conditions all over the states before settling on the northern side of Houston. He was a property manager, but it didn't work out. The reason? "I've been fired from everything I've ever done. I don't respect authority. So the best person for me to work for is myself." He and his wife and brother formed Red River Winery. But their concept was different from most.

Mark liked the idea of being in the wine business but not the concept of having to grow grapes. His family has a winery—Corry Winery in Enid, Oklahoma—and Mark had put in a few hard summers in the vineyards. So he decided to buy juice from other makers, make his own wine and put it where thousands of people would wander by. The older part of Spring was booming. Folks were coming from all over the metro area for a taste of how life was a hundred years ago, strolling the shady streets, drinking sodas on the veranda and shopping at myriad knick-knackeries. Mark had found his place. What he hadn't counted on was the

Mark Woolington worked in his family's vineyards in Oklahoma.

bureaucratic nightmare that all winemakers have to go through in Texas.

He hadn't done enough research when he opened in 1995. That was when he learned that the public servants of the Texas Alcoholic Beverage Commission and the United States Bureau of Alcohol, Tobacco and Firearms like to move at their own glacial pace. The delays lasted so long that he had to resort to selling wines from other Texas wineries.

When he found out that his location was the number one seller of Messina Hof wines, he felt that his choice of location had paid off big time. By the time Red River Winery finally got the approvals, he couldn't find any juice. Things were looking tough. In 1997, he finally got some help from Pheasant Ridge winery in the way of a good source of juice. That was the year Mark's brother decided to leave.

Red River Winery started selling its own wines but then made a surprising discovery. While they set out to make a living from wine sales, they were actually making more from selling wine accessories. With the housing growth north of Houston, people seemed to have an insatiable desire for wine trinkets. Given the high workload for low profit that accompanies winemaking, Mark is planning on maxing out his wine production at 5,000 gallons per year.

Red River Winery blends, bottles and cellars its wines at the shop. They also provide customized labels for their wines, something that corporate VIP's and celebs like Kenny "the Jet" Smith, Marvin Hamlisch, Ross Perot and Kevin Costner enjoy.

The Best Wines

All winemakers make wine to suit their tastes and business sensibilities. Red River Winery's fit that characterization more than most. The house style is light and aims for broad appeal. And consistency. When I went back three years after my first visit, the original tasting notes were still accurate.

I think their best white wine is the **Semillon**. It has the medium weight and smoky character of the best versions and a longer-than-usual finish. For reds, the **Cabernet Sauvignon** is the best. It's peppery and chocolaty, with light to medium body and a very light amount of oak. Since they are using juice from Pheasant Ridge, it is instructive to taste how two different wineries take the same juice and make different wines.

🍃 Haak Vineyards and Winery

6310 Avenue T, Santa Fe, TX 77510. May–Oct.: Mon.–Fri. 11 am–6 pm, Sat. 11 am–7 pm, Sun. noon–till the music stops; Nov.–Apr: Mon.–Fri. 11 am–7 pm, Sat. 11 am–5 pm, Sun. noon–5 pm. (409) 925-1401.

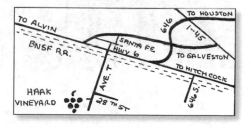

What is a beautiful winery doing hugging the Gulf Coast smack in the middle of hurricane central? That was my first question when I met Raymond Haak. His answer is simple—that's where he lives, and he wanted a winery: "I'm a religious man and I believe the good Lord has brought me to this place in my life. This winery is totally miraculous. I don't know why I am here, but I'm going to find out some day."

How he got there is pretty miraculous itself. Raised right in Santa Fe, he met his wife, Gladys, and they traipsed all over the place in the Air Force. When he returned, he worked days and went to the University of Houston at night. It took him eleven hard years, but he finally got his degree in 1969 in electrical engineering. While working and going to school, he also found time to play in a rock and roll band and to ride bulls.

After graduation he moved into sales. For fifteen years he dealt with the corporate guys in suits. "They remind me of seagulls," he says. "They fly in, eat your food, poop all over your yard and then fly away. I just got tired of it all."

Lots of people were moving to the Houston-Galveston area, so he and his brother decided that some of them might need a place to store stuff. They opened a mini warehouse, and before they knew it the place was full. So they built another, and another, and another. You get the picture. Now they own a lot of mini-warehouses.

But Raymond is a sort of restless fellow and loves a challenge. Around 1975 Gladys gave him two Concord grape vines, which he planted. They took off, so he decided to put in an experimental vineyard and plant thirty vines. He had all those grapes so, though not a wine fanatic, he decided to try his hand at making some

Haak Vineyards has figured out how to make wine from Blanc du Bois grapes.

wine. The first few gallons were so good that he planted 300 vines and made his own wine for the next fifteen years.

Unfortunately, he couldn't sell any of it because he also owned a convenience store, and the archaic and protectionist Texas laws wouldn't allow you to do both. So he made his one hundred gallons a year for personal consumption and dreamed. Finally, he decided to sell the convenience store so he could open a winery. They broke ground in January 2000 and had the winery up the next year. The first month they were open, 5,000 people came through. Raymond Haak felt like he had a tiger by the tail.

Then the traffic just stopped. How did that made him feel? "Look, this is my last hurrah, but I have the time and the passion to make it work and I'm going to." The look of gritty determination lends credence to the statement. His solution was to make the winery a destination for local wine drinkers. By his calculation, folks who live within one hour of his winery consume 500,000 gallons of wine per year. He just wants a small percent of that business.

So Raymond and Gladys have been offering a lot of fun activities aimed at getting families to visit their winery. They put in a beautiful shop with wine-related gear and foods. They are offering free Sunday concerts. But the real draw has become the wine. Over the last six or seven years, Raymond Haak has grown from a pretty good winemaker to a really good winemaker. Walking the winery with his assistant, Vicki Parker, I realize how far the winery has come since my first visit in 2002. Raymond is quick to give some of the credit to Vicki, and I can see why.

But most importantly, Raymond Haak has done the state a big favor. Along with Bob Cottle of Pleasant Hill Winery, he has figured out how to make really good wine from a mediocre grape. The Blanc du Bois grape had only one thing going for it: resistance to Pierce's disease. Now it also has Haak and Cottle going for it. No one believes in the grape like these two, and no one has done so much to make it a winning grape.

When the book is written on twenty-first century Texas wines, these two guys will have their pictures next to the grape. If you've had bad versions elsewhere, don't be deterred. Raymond has figured out the secret.

The grit and determination I saw when I first met Raymond is still there. He's aiming to make Haak Vineyards one of the best anywhere. Given his progress and his personality, I wouldn't bet against him.

The Best Wines

As it has at a lot of other wineries, Pierce's disease decimated Haak's vineyards. Now he just grows Blanc du Bois and Lenoir, two varieties that resist Pierce's. The dirt around Santa Fe is tough to deal with, a thin layer of topsoil on top of a foot of gummy, sticky clay. So Raymond decided long ago to purchase a lot of his grapes. At first he bought from California for the cheap prices and good quality. But he now supports only his fellow Texans. "We no longer buy any wine from California," assistant winemaker Vicki Parker says. "But what we'd really like is to see more hot-weather varietals grown in Texas. We'd like to focus on three things: Mediterranean varietals, Blanc de Bois and Madeira."

That just about hits all my favorite Haak wines. As I mentioned earlier, they've made a stunning **Blanc du Bois.** Raymond's had the courage to do what almost no one else has—make a dry Blanc du Bois. Sugar covers a multitude of winemaking sins and also shades the bitter, stemmy tastes of normal Blanc du Bois. Raymond's version has the seductive aromas and fruity density of an Alsatian Gewurztraminer or Muscat. Other Texas winemakers should be taking lessons from Raymond.

Reddy Vineyard Malbec was a big surprise for me. It has many of the enticing strengths of the Argentine versions from the Mendoza area—lush, soft tannins along with rich, dark plum and cherry aromas. It also has a velvety mouth feel that sets it apart. The grapes came from Vijay Reddy's vineyard in Brownfield. I can't wait to taste what happens as his vines get older and more intense.

The other pick from Haak is what he calls **Madeira**, a spectacular wine that's true to the original. It's made and stored in good barrels sitting in hot rooms—the Portuguese call these estufas—so that evaporation intensifies and oxidizes the wine. Given its young age, Haak's wine is the match of most true Madeiras.

Here's my one small issue: the name. This wine is from Texas, not the island of Madeira. Plus, it's made from the Jacquez grape—better known by its slightly less classy name, Black Spanish—while true Madeira is made largely from the Tinta Negra Mole grape. Here's something I really don't understand. Europeans in hot climates have come up with a number of strategies for making wines that will survive in their heat. The Spaniards created Sherry, named for the town of Jerez de la Frontera; the Portuguese made Port, named for its hometown of Oporto; the islanders of Madeira created the wine named for their island. Texans? Well we have the climate, especially on the Gulf Coast. So what do we call our wines? Sherry, Port and Madeira. We need new names.

That little issue aside, Haak's Madeira has everything going for it. Aimed at the rich and sweet end of the scale, it has all the nutty, caramel aromas and unctuousness you could hope for. They took a chance in making this wine; not everyone knows what to expect, and not many folks will take a chance on a $30 Texas wine. Once you taste it, you'll understand.

Keep your eye on this winery.

¶◎ FOOD

Galveston

Gaido's, 3800 Seawall Blvd. Lunch and dinner daily. Expensive. (409) 762-9625. Seafood is the name of Gaido's game. Ultra-fresh, simply prepared and nearly perfect, just like they've been doing it since 1911. Everything down to their salad dressing is homemade. The fresh flounder is scrumptious and the raw oysters are worth a trip by themselves. The locally caught seafood is always the best choice. Gaido's doesn't take reservations, and the wait at peak times can seem to last forever.

Houston

There will be upstarts that outdo these tried-and-true places, but for that, you have to get fresh information. For in-vogue restaurant evaluations, check the *Houston Press* Website, www.houstonpress.com, home of the best restaurant reviews in the city. There is also an annual *Zagat Guide to Houston*. I'm skeptical about the listings—if you remember "regression towards the mean" from statistics classes you'll know why—but they have loads of fans. This is just a start. These restaurants have been consistently superb and in business a long time, and are always booked in advance. Be sure to make reservations.

Back Street Café, 1103 South Shepherd Dr. Lunch and dinner daily. Moderate. (713) 521-2239. The Back Street Café is good anytime, but beware, it sits off the street and is hard to find. Look for the valet parkers. American comfort food with graceful twists and turns, but they lighten up on their weekend jazz brunch. Delicious and creative fare like their crab cakes and eggs with citrus beurre blanc ($11.95) has me coming back whenever I'm in Houston.

Café Annie, 1728 Post Oak Blvd. Lunch Tue.–Fri., dinner Mon.–Sat. Expensive. (713) 840-1111. Saying a place is "the best" is fraught with danger. Opinions and posteriors, you know. But Café Annie would have to be on anyone's short list of nominees for Best Restaurant in Houston and has been that way since it opened in 1980. More to our purposes, owner Robert Del Grande is and always has been a big supporter of Texas wines. His sommeliers can make spot-on recommendations.

Ruggles Grill, 903 Westheimer Rd., within walking distance of the Lovett Inn. Lunch Tue.–Fri., dinner Tue.–Sun., also a breathtaking Sunday brunch. Moderate. (713) 524-3839. For the last fifteen years chef Bruce Molzan has been knocking out creative American food with the emphasis on fresh local ingredients. Brunch is a mob scene, but once you get to your table everything is relaxed. Settle in and enjoy a crab omelet or their decadent Belgian waffles. Chef Susan Molzan's desserts are remarkable.

Spring

Old Town Spring has several restaurants. I've found that the quality varies dramatically so am hesitant to give specific recommendations. Ask the tasting room folks and shop owners for the best places. Once you get out to the highway you can find virtually any chain restaurant you can think of.

⌂ SHELTER

Galveston

Hotel Galvez, 2024 Seawall Blvd. (877) 999-3223. The grand old lady of Galveston hotels. Sitting atop a hill overlooking the Gulf of Mexico, the Galvez has seen its share of ups and downs over the years. Thankfully, the Wyndham chain has put some money into it, making it as pretty as when it was first opened in 1911.

Houston

Grant's Palm Court Inn, 8200 Main St. (800) 255-8904. The best hotel in Houston at its ultra-low price point. Family owned and operated with a homey feel, pretty pool and a perfect location. It also books early, so make your reservations early. www.palmcourtinn.com.

Lovett Inn, 501 Lovett Blvd. (800) 779-5224. Exactly what you thought you'd never find in Houston—a quiet, civilized and homey respite in the middle of the big city. It's a beautiful old house with thirteen guest rooms, all at decent upper-moderate prices. It's also in the middle of one of Houston's most energetic and artsy neighborhoods. www.lovettinn.com.

FUN

Houston

Fred Hartmann Bridge. If you've seen *Blade Runner* you have an idea of what the nighttime view from here looks like. Smokestacks belching hundred-foot flames, safety lights festooning the oil pipes and processing towers, the city lights of Houston forming the background. It's like being in another world. On Highway 146 between La Porte and Baytown. Go as dusk turns to night for the full effect.

The Houston Museum District is a marvelous aggregation of culture. My favorite stops are **The Menil Collection,** (713) 525-9400, **The Museum of Fine Arts**, (713) 639-7300 and **The Contemporary Arts Museum**, (713) 284-8250. www.houstonmuseumdistrict.org.

The Houston Theater District is the downtown home to the **Houston Symphony,** **Houston Grand Opera** and **Alley Theater.** When you're in town, check what's going on. People come from New York and San Francisco to see the Houston Grand Opera; it's that good. Located all around Jones Plaza. www.houstontheaterdistrict.org.

Space Center Houston, 1601 NASA Rd. (281) 244-2105. If you have any interest in the U. S. space program, this is a must. You get a chance to see genuine Mercury, Gemini and Apollo space capsules, tour the Johnson Space Center and simulate a moonwalk. Open year round except Christmas. www.spacecenter.org.

Spec's Liquor Warehouse, 2410 Smith St. (713) 526-8787. How does a wine store rate being in this category? By having over 8,000 different wines. Go and be amazed.

Galveston

The **Galveston-Port Bolivar Ferry** is a reminder of the old days. It is the link for two segments of State Highway 87 and operated by the Texas Department of Transportation. The 2.7-mile trip takes about eighteen minutes to get across one of the most bustling waterways in the world. The real fun starts when a huge tanker is in the harbor. Free.

The Strand. During the nineteenth century, Galveston was one of the richest cities in the South. Cotton was king. The wealthy lived in the area surrounding the thirty-six-block commercial area known as The Strand. Despite a history of terrible hurricanes, the surrounding mansions and The Strand still stand. Trendy shops and museums now dominate the area. If the weather is good, take a stroll. If you get tired you can always take a horse-drawn carriage and pretend you're in a Dickens novel. www.galveston.com/thestrand.

Spring

SplashTown Waterpark on IH-45, part of the Six Flags empire. (281) 355-3300. Chosen as one of the top ten water parks in the U. S. Fifty acres, forty rides, a gazillion screaming kids.

CHAPTER 6

The Wine Roads of the
Piney Woods

T he Piney Woods area has seen the biggest percentage of winery growth of any area since the last edition of this book—a 400 percent increase. Of course, last time around there was just one winery.

Why so few? I don't really know. Maybe winemakers are afraid of the area. Most of the area is dry, in terms of alcohol, that is. In terms of humidity, it's as bad as New Orleans, which creates nightmare-proportioned mold and mildew problems. But the proof of the pudding is in the eating, and there are some very good wines in the Piney Woods.

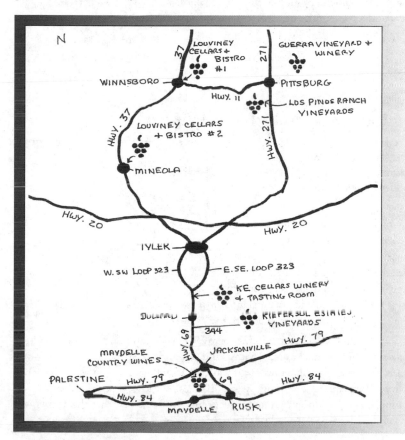

For tasting them, my strategy would be to take a good book and make a weekend of the Kiepersol B&B. It's a relaxing place, and both food and accommodations are first-class. Prices are high but perfectly appropriate for the quality. I've been in several of the rooms, and while all are luxurious, the Paarl Room would be my number one choice because of its beautiful view of the grounds. It includes a patio with hot tub.

The perfect trip would be to book two nights at the Kiepersol B&B. On the first morning, head for Guerra to gauge how you feel about Muscadine wine. From there, head to Los Pinos for lunch. I'd pick a nice bottle of Red Mesa and some tapas.

From there, amble over to either of the Lou Viney locations for more wine and tapas (get the stuffed mushrooms). End the evening at Kiepersol's Tyler location, KE Cellars, where you'll find one of the top three selections of Texas wine in the state. Then, back to your B&B for a great dinner.

The next morning, try to wangle an invitation to the Kiepersol Winery, and taste through their line. Then go down to Maydelle for fruit wines and a little free comic entertainment. Sometime after lunch come back to the Kiepersol B&B, get a book and a good bottle of wine, sit out on the porch and just relax.

TRIP ONE

Guerra Vineyard and Winery

2170 Country Rd. #4110, Pittsburgh, TX 75686. Sat. noon–5 pm and by appointment. (972) 791-3004, www.guerravineyardandwinery.com

Dr. Manuel Guerra and his wife, Rosemary, have spent the past forty years caring for their neighbors in Pittsburgh. When their children expressed an interest in raising large animals, they bought thirty-six acres of farmland just outside town. Rosemary is from a farm family in Iowa, so she also wanted to get her hands dirty and grow some fruit.

We meet one cold winter afternoon so Rosemary can pour her wines and tell me her story. She's a small woman, with a kind face and a farmer's outlook on Mother Nature. She's trying to figure how to thwart the feral hogs that just tore out half of her vines. "I'll plant back to get us up to 800 vines," she says. "I just don't want to do any more than that. In our ground, Muscadine grows so fast that the shoots will touch each other across the trellises within days."

In 1994 she planted 800 Muscadine vines, intending to make southern-style jams, jellies and syrups. While waiting for the vines to start producing, she decided to make some fruit wine from blackberries, blueberries, pears, peaches, strawberries, cranberries and cherries. People liked it, so they made a Muscadine wine, too. Then the vines started producing so much fruit that they had to come up with a use. That was the birth of Guerra Vineyard and Winery.

Rosemary expresses the frustration, the almost love-hate relationship that farmers have with their plot of land. Planting something and watching it

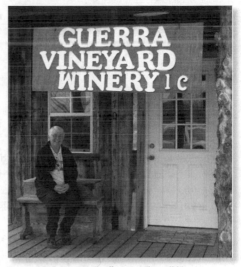

Rosemary Guerra can smile even after wild hogs tore out half her vines.

grow is among life's great treasures. Seeing it ruined by weather or animals is heartbreaking. Either way, you have to get up every day and do your best to make tomorrow a better day.

Rosemary now works the vines while her daughter, Ann, and son-in-law, Mark, make the wines. Dr. Guerra makes it all possible by keeping his practice as a general practitioner in Pittsburgh.

Even after the hogs got the grapes, Rosemary took it philosophically. She's putting up electrical fences as deterrents. When the weather gets a little warmer she'll be back in the fields, planting more Muscadine.

The Best Wines

Guerra Vineyard and Winery produces a lot of different wines. How you react to them depends very much on how you like the Muscadine grape. If you're one of its many fans you'll find a lot here, ranging from dry to dessert wines. Recently, Guerra has been making hybrid wines from fruit and Muscadine, calling them names like Foxy Blueberry. Foxy refers to the nature of the Muscadine grape, which smells, uh, foxy. The combo of fruit and grape creates other interesting flavors, so the **Foxy Blueberry** tastes like blueberries and Welch's grape jelly.

They also make fruit wines, the best of the lot also being their best wine. That's **Cranberry Wine,** a wine that is just slightly drier and gathers some welcome tartness from the cranberry.

Los Pinos Winery

658 County Rd. 1334, Pittsburgh, TX
75686. Fri. and Sat. noon–midnight,
Sun. noon–5 pm. (903) 855-1759,
www.lospinosranchvineyards.com

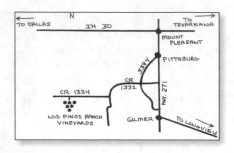

Jeff Sneed was sitting in Southern California looking for a path out of the OC civilization. An architectural engineer, he designed glass and metal skyscrapers all over the world but was tired of having to manage multinational forces. "I would get a phone call at three in the morning from a project where I had Mexican crews building in China for Korean owners," he recalls. "It was just crazy."

So he started fantasizing about a simple life somewhere. Maybe do a little farming, grow a few grapes, make a little wine. He had been home-making wine for thirty years for personal consumption, and it was something he enjoyed. Though originally from Illinois, Jeff focused on Texas. He read ads on the Internet, and whenever he could put together five or ten properties to look at he'd fly over and make the rounds. In December 2000 he selected some acreage south of Pittsburgh. Four months later, he was installing his vineyard.

Making wine commercially intrigues him. "Because I'm an engineer, I have to understand the physics and science behind wine," he says. "I was tasting a California Cabernet and thought it was pretty good. Then I read the label and was intrigued. What would make different Cabernets taste different? They're all the same grape. Then I started thinking, how could I make a better wine?"

That's where Jeff's cultural heritage comes in. "I'm Swedish," he says, "so I'm never satisfied. It's like, Perfection is expected but excellence will be tolerated." He drops those little quips like he's the Henny Youngman of winemakers. Another favorite: "My grandfather said that you learn more from your failures than your successes, so now I'm a borderline genius."

Jeff Sneed, originally an architectural engineer, oversees the Los Pinos wines, and his wife, Dana, makes the tapas at the tasting bar.

Mainly you notice how happy he is. Wearing a brown fedora and sporting wildly anachronistic glasses, he just grins all the time. Jeff has married an East Texas girl, Dana, a chef by trade and now the tapas maker at the winery. His son works behind the bar, and his best friend is on the road marketing Los Pinos wines.

The happy surprise for Jeff has been how much he loves the hospitality side of the business. He wants everyone who walks through the door to feel like they're a part of a great big Italian family. And plenty of people have walked through the doors. Pittsburgh is a dry town, so a Texas winery is the only place to get adult beverages to take home. Jeff was blown away when more than a thousand people showed up on opening day. Since then, they've sold more than 70 percent of their wine right at the tasting room.

When you go, take a look at his wacky labels. Jeff's sense of humor shows through on the names, pictures and descriptions, like the Texas version of Bonny Doon's Randall Grahm. But there is method to his mayhem. "I don't want to compete with the French," he says. "I don't want to compete with the Californians. I want to build a Texas wine industry."

What makes him proud? He sits back and lets a very contented smile spread across his face. "It's the whole winery and the ambience of it. I jump out of bed in the morning. I'm completely contented." He pauses. "I need not one more thing in my life."

The Best Wines

Jeff makes wines for his customer's tastes, and his customers like their wine sweet. **Pinky Tuscandero** is the biggest seller, a sweet pink wine. During fermentation Jeff takes his sweet wines to dry, then adds back sugar. If you like blush wines, this one is well made.

For dry wine lovers, the **Red Mesa** is the best choice. It's a nice dry red wine with soft tannins, good oak, and a long finish. It is made from Ruby Cabernet and Merlot, an uncommon pairing, but one that works nicely here.

🍁 LouViney Vineyard and Winery

111 E. Broadway, Winnsboro, TX 75494. Thu. 4–9 pm, Fri. and Sat. noon–10 pm. (903) 342-0485.

121 East Commerce St., Mineola, TX 75773.
Thu. 4–9 pm, Fri. and Sat. noon–10 pm.
(903) 569-1493, www.louviney.com

Stepping into LouViney on a cold winter afternoon, we were greeted by a softly burning fire in the fireplace, comfortable seats and sofas and a

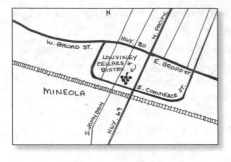

pleasant buzz from a very happy crowd. This is the place where three women make some local magic. Susan Jones is the winemaker, her twin sister, Susann Briggs, is the chef and Nancy Briggs, the marketing maven, is Susann's sister-in-law—although Susan asks that I refer to her as their sister because "we love her like she's been with us forever."

I'm sitting with Susan, talking over the operation in LouViney's original location, a two-story building in Winnsboro that once housed a saloon; a second location opened in 2006 a few miles south, in Mineola. Friendly locals are stopping by to say hi, getting and giving hugs and greetings. The place has a burnished light and a warm, happy feel. Susann (pronounced like Suzanne) and Nancy stop by to see if they need to answer any questions. My first one is, with the stresses of opening and running two winery/restaurants, how on earth do you all get along so well?

"Have you seen that movie, *The Exorcist?*" Susan asks. "When we were getting open, that was Nancy." Nancy says, "Yeah, they said my head was spinning and I was spitting green peas." Susan is quick to add, "But we all still love each other and get along really good."

That getting along really good is demonstrated when a sudden rush of customers come in. All three women jump to and work like a well-honed team, each assuming whatever responsibility is necessary.

When Susan sits back down, I ask about the winery's name. She laughs. "See that older woman sitting in the corner?" she says. I see an attractive, gray-haired woman, sitting and chatting with a friend. "That's LouViney; that's my mom.

Susan Jones (winemaker), Susann Briggs (chef) and Nancy Briggs (marketing maven), from left, run LouViney Cellars and Bistro.

When she was growing up in West Texas, my mother was one of fifteen children. Her grandfather needed a nickname for each of the kids and her nickname was LouViney. She hated it then, but it was the perfect name for the winery. Now she tells everyone that she's LouViney."

The three women got into business in an odd way. Susan and Susann had been making wine for twenty years whenever they could get some Muscadine grapes. Susan didn't even drink wine when they started. "I just love the whole thing about growing grapes, seeing them grow. It's just great." When Susan found fifty-five acres near Winnsboro, Susann said they should try growing some grapes. After a few courses at Grayson, they planted two acres of Blanc du Bois and Black Spanish grapes.

At this point they are financing everything out of their own pockets, so they're taking things slow. Susan still works in property management at Raytheon in Dallas. Susann is an order fulfillment manager at Samsung in Richardson. Nancy is a physical therapist.

Says Susan: "Our places have exceeded our expectations, and people are loving the place. We have very high expectations of our staff and want them to cater to our customer's every needs." She laughs. "Our staff referred to us as the three B's—bitches—but they say its butterflies, bees and bats."

What motivates her to be in such a tough business? She looks at me with a steely gaze, as if I've asked something incredibly stupid, but there's a mischievous grin underneath. "It's our passion! We love it! Failure is not an option."

The Best Wines

Until their vineyard starts producing, the ladies are purchasing a good deal of their wine from other Texas winemakers. **Rouge** is made from Blanc du Bois and Black Spanish. It's an almost dry wine that would be really delightful as an aperitif or with summer food. We tried it with Susann's Hip Hoppin' Stuffed Mushrooms and loved the pairing.

PHAT Cat is a Muscat Canelli from Homestead Winery. When they called it Muscat Canelli no one would buy it. Then they switched to PHAT Cat and sold out immediately. Either way it is a fragrant dessert wine with enough bright acidity to curb the sugar. PHAT, for those of us outside the Hip-Hop culture, stands for Pretty Hot and Tempting. Check the label for confirmation.

TRIP TWO

🍂 Kiepersol Estates Vineyards

3933 FM 344 East (look for the winery
sign), Tyler, TX 75703. By appointment.
(903) 894-8995, www.kiepersol.com

🍂 KE Cellars

4574 Hwy 69 S., Tyler, TX 75703. Mon.–Sat.
11 am–9 pm. (903) 939-9805. On the
south side of Tyler, this has one of the top
two or three Texas wine selections in the
state. If you can't get access to Kiepersol's
main winery, this makes a nice stop.

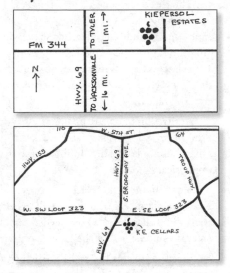

This is the story of a family that
has embodied the Great American
Dream. Spending time with them,
I feel humbled, impressed and
invigorated. Just so I don't put too fine a point on it, I am proud that these people
are Texans.

The story started in 1983 in South Africa. Pierre de Wet's wife had passed
away at an early age. The township revolts were expanding, with guerillas setting
off random bombs and going on killing sprees. With daughters Marnelle and
Velma (pronounced vel-MAY), ages two and four, and not much else, de Wet, a
fifth-generation farmer in South Africa, headed for the United States.

De Wet's oldest daughter, Marnelle, born in 1979, tells the story, raising goose
bumps on my arms. "Our mom passed away from cancer and Dad just wanted to
start a new life. He took us in each arm and came on a visitor's visa. He worked
in rice fields and we lived in a travel trailer. Then he met a South African guy who
said we should come to Tyler. We came in our travel trailer and a brown GMC.
We prayed our way from California. We got this far and our car stopped and died."
Pierre took that as a sign that he belonged in Tyler. He started a rose nursery and
made it work. Then he started consulting with other rose nurserymen. Marnelle
says, "He has an innate feel for agriculture. He can grow anything." In another gift,
President Reagan signed a one-year (1987–88) amnesty for certain immigrants.
Pierre and his children fit the rules, and he was able to gain citizenship for all.

Then Pierre met a man who handled agriculture investments for a group of
retirement funds. He asked Pierre to help fix a few poorly performing investments.
Pierre was quite successful, and suddenly everyone wanted him to help manage or

The tasting room at Kiepersol Winery.

fix their agricultural investments. Before long he was managing more than 14,000 acres of permanent crops, including apples, cherries, pistachios, almonds, oranges, grapefruit and lemons. He was no longer relegated to an old brown GMC; now he flew to consulting jobs.

When Marnelle and Velma expressed an interest in following their father into agriculture, he didn't want them doing anything unfeminine (please don't go PC on me here, he's sincere). "I wanted my daughters to continue the farming lifestyle but to do something feminine, classy and posh," Pierre says. Establishing vineyards and a winery provided the answer. "Their hearts were in wine and they really did all the work. Marnelle planted the vineyards and I gave her a hand whenever I could. But my involvement is less than an hour a week." What he did do was surround the vineyard with a 330-acre housing development with street names like Merlot Lane. To cap it off, he put in one of the prettiest restaurant/B&B's in the Unites States.

The winery's name harkened back to their native South Africa. In 1900, a group of Boers witnessed British soldiers in a field running from a lion toward a tree and shouting what they understood to be "Kiepersol!" The Boers named the tree Kiepersol, only later realizing that the soldiers were actually shouting that they hoped the tree would "keep us all." The de Wets adopted the Kiepersol tree as their symbol, seeing their development as a welcoming place for those seeking refuge in the finer pleasures of life.

Marnelle would be the winemaker. She had no schooling in winemaking but did have the opportunity to apprentice with Peter Luthi at Trefethen Vineyards in Napa. She makes up for any lack in training with dedication. Each of the 35,000 vines gets individual attention. She describes the vines as her "babies." Velma left the wine business to concentrate on her first love: animals. She handles the family's

Pierre de Wet with daughters Velma, left, and Marnelle.

one thousand head of cattle. "She was more interested in the animal husbandry," Marnelle says. "She's Daisy Duke in the flesh."

Marnelle has a message for her fellow Texas winemakers. Though she's young and may not have the experience of some of the others, she feels strongly that when Mother Nature throws a curveball you shouldn't run from it. "We get Pierce's, but when we do, we pull the vine and plant another," she explains. "Because of that, we are always blending wine from new and old vines, which gives us more complexity." A freeze in 2006 may have destroyed many of the West Texas grapes, but "the freeze naturally thinned the crop and the rest made incredible wine." The shortage may have required them to bring in outside grapes and blend them, but "that allows us to show off what we can do and what Texas is capable of. Our 2006 wines are going to be incredible."

The Best Wines

Marnelle de Wet Durrett focuses mostly on red wines. But while we were visiting, she popped a bottle of **Semillon** that hadn't hit the market. It was terrific, full of smoky rich character and with a creamy mouth feel.

I tried her **Kiepersol Estates 2005 Sangiovese** as a barrel sample, and it was also splendid wine. What extraction. And it's filled with dark fruit, menthol, leather and earthy truffle aromas. Marnelle says it's the best wine she has made to date. She's right. Her other best wines are the **Syrah** and **Reserve Merlot**. The Syrah's fragrance features roses, caramel, lavender and a very Rhone-like hit of black pepper. The Reserve Merlot has soft tannins that cradle you with a velvety mouth feel and bright red berry flavors to keep the rest of your senses interested.

Marnelle's wines have gotten better each year she's made them. If she can keep the trend going, she could be one of our best. Now's the time to go taste.

Maydelle Country Wines

Rt. 4, Box 19102, Rusk, TX 75785.
Tue.–Sat. 10 am–6 pm. (903) 795-3915,
www.maydellewines.com

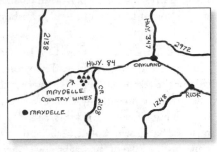

It takes some guts to put a picture of yourself on your Website wearing an acid-casualty styled tie-dye T-shirt. But, then, Steven Harper is a tie-dyed-in-the-wool, wide-eyed optimist, content to follow his interests and casually observe the world ticking by. Just ask him how he decided to be a winemaker.

"Because I could," he says, with an accent that drips deep East Texas. Then he pauses to wait and see if I laugh. I do, so he goes on a roll. "I'd been an amateur winemaker for ten years and had the land, and when the law changed where I could, I did."

Of his entry into the wine world he says, "I always wanted to dabble with it." "Then, somewhere around my birthday in 1985, I said to my wife that I wanted one of them winemaking kits at that store in Tyler. She thought I'd never do anything with it. Well, I put my first medal on the wall the next year. It seemed like maybe I was onto something." He had done everything from trimming trees to working for a paper mill to working at Rusk State Hospital, but when he won that award he thought he saw an opening. He went to work for the folks that owned that supply store in Tyler. After a while he bought the store, then took it out of the high-rent Tyler market and moved it to suburban Maydelle (population 250, last time anyone counted).

Setting up a winery was the next order of business. Since Texas law requires wineries in dry areas to use mostly Texas fruit, Steven decided to focus on what grows best in his neighborhood. That would be Muscadine grapes, peaches and blackberries. Then one day, he made a discovery that changed his life. Accidentally.

One of the great fruits of Texas is the grapefruit. Others had tried to make grapefruit wine, but it was usually too sweet to cover the bitterness inherent in squashing the fruit. When commercial operations make juice, they drop hundreds of grapefruits in a giant squasher and flatten them. The white pulp between the sweet sections and the extracted oils from the skin add up to bitterness. Steven tried a gentler approach.

"For my grapefruit wine, I drive down to the valley and get good grapefruit. Last week I picked up 1,500 pounds of grapefruit, brought them straight home, cut every one of them in half and hand squeezed everything to keep out bad tastes from the pulp and oils." If that sound like a lot of work, imagine this. Steven has decided lemons might make some good wine, too. So the day after he finished pressing his grapefruit juice, he went down to the Valley again, picked up one ton of lemons, brought them home, cut them in half and pressed every last one by hand.

Sounds like work that OSHA would call dangerous for carpal tunnel syndrome and for harmful acid reactions on your skin. Does Steven want to do this for the rest of his life? His answer is characteristically nonchalant. "I wouldn't know what to do with myself if I wasn't making wine. I sure didn't know what to do with myself before I did this, and if I quit, I wouldn't know what to do. But my business has grown exponentially and I love it. It's still an adventure. If the thrill is gone, maybe I'll quit. But right now, I just love what I'm doing."

¶◎ FOOD

Kiepersol Estates B&B Restaurant, 21508 Merlot Lane, 11 miles south of Tyler. Dinner Mon.–Sat. Dress code. Expensive. (903) 894-3300. Specializes in grilled meats. Prices are high, but the quality is there. The house specialty is beef, and steaks are always top grade. Try one with a bottle of Kiepersol Sangiovese for the full Kiepersol experience. Breakfast is for residents only; be sure to try the Kiepersol Eggs Benedict, an unbelievable amalgam of tenderloin steak, eggs and Hollandaise.

Larissa House, 301 W. Larissa St., Jacksonville. Mon.–Sat. 11 am–8 pm. Moderate. (903) 586-5356. Good salads and steaks (check out the delicious rib-eye), plus you can BYOB.

Mansion on the Hill-Restaurant and Club, corner of Hwy. 64 E. and Old Henderson Hwy., Tyler. Mon.–Sat. 5–9:30 pm. Dress code. Moderate prices. (903) 533-1628. A semifancy place for steaks and fresh seafood. The club part signifies you can get a drink.

Sadler's Kitchen, 221 S. Main St., Jacksonville. Tue.–Fri. and Sun. 11 am–2 pm, Fri. and Sat. 5:30–8:30 pm. Inexpensive to moderate. (903) 589-0866. Great home cookin', especially the burgers and pot roast.

⌂ SHELTER

Kiepersol Estates B&B, 21508 Merlot Lane, 11 miles south of Tyler. Closed Sundays. (903) 894-3300. See description above under Food. Though expensive, it's a bargain for what you get. Spend a little time at the bar and meet some of the most interesting folks in East Texas. www.kiepersol.com.

Jefferson has a huge number of B&B's, so many that I recommend using a service. The best one I found was AAA Reservations, (800) 299-1593, www.jeffersonreservations.com.

☼ FUN

People from outside Texas are always amazed that Texas has one of the largest forests in the United States; driving south on Highway 69 gives you a peek at its beauty. During the last two weeks of March and the first week of April, it comes alive as the dogwoods bloom. At the same time, azaleas pop out and nearly every house turns into a showplace. Within sixty miles of Tyler there are so many antiques that even the *Antiques Roadshow* people would go dizzy. Jefferson has the best antiquing, but the shops are literally everywhere.

The Tyler area is synonymous with roses. **The Tyler Municipal Rose Garden**, 420 S. Rose Park Dr., (903) 531-1212, has fourteen acres of lovely roses. They're in bloom from early May to mid-November, but the best time to go is summer.

APPENDIX

How to Taste

I am not going to try to make you into an arrogant wine lover, nose in the air, waxing rhapsodic in the secret codes of the trade while swishing and swirling $200 wine in a $175 glass. There are already too many of us. But I do want to encourage you to taste wine in a disciplined manner. Here's the procedure.

The word *taste* doesn't convey the experience. In the old days, we used to say, "First you taste it with your eyes, then you taste it with your nose. Only then do you taste it with your mouth."

We live in more enlightened times, so we now say, "Look at it, then smell it and then taste it."

Start by looking at the wine. White wines should vary between a straw yellow and golden, red wines between violet and brick. Brown is bad, in either case. In most cases, the wine should be clear and clean. When you swirl it around in your glass, it should be thicker than water, much like apple juice.

Aroma accounts for a lot of wine's pleasure, so take your time. Stick your nose right in the glass and sniff away. Swirl it around and sniff again. Try to describe the smell to someone with you and don't use the word *grape*. Is it powerful or light? Does it smell like flowers, fruits, vegetables, spices? Does it remind you of cedar or coffee or creme brulé? Do you catch a scent like butter, steel or wet wool? Make up your own ideas, but try to figure it out. If you smell five or ten pleasing aromas at one time, you have stumbled on a complex wine. That is a high compliment.

Now you can finally taste the wine. This is where you can get in trouble. The professionals would tell you to put a tiny bit of wine in your mouth, hold it cupped in your tongue, part your lips and inhale air over the wine. One time I was teaching this method to a group of doctors and nurses and accidentally inhaled the wine. As my life was passing in front of me, I put my hands to my throat, choking. I managed to open my eyes long enough to see all the medical professionals howling with laughter. Now I know better. Like President Clinton, I don't inhale.

Instead, sip a little bit of wine and just let it sit in your mouth for a few seconds. How does it feel? Not how does it taste, but how does it feel? Is it rich, does the alcohol burn, do the tannins feel dusty? Then pay attention to the taste. Do you pick up fruit, acid, sweetness or bitterness? Swallow it and quietly count how long the flavor stays in your mouth. Good wines last.

Now the most important part—did you like it? No analysis, just decide whether it's something you'd want a second drink of. If so, enjoy. If not, look for a place to dump the rest. Every tasting room has a dump bucket and you won't insult winemakers by using it. They would rather see you move to the next wine and hopefully find one you want to buy.

That dump bucket has another important use. People who taste a lot of wine usually follow the whole procedure I've outlined, but they spit the wine into the bucket rather than swallow it. I go to several tastings a year where I am served over 100 wines. I had to learn to spit. It will embarrass you the first time or two. Don't worry; everyone in the room will just think you are a wine professional.

Once you've tasted a wine, be thoughtful about how you express your opinion of it. Few things annoy me as much as wine writers who confuse their personal likes and dislikes with the Absolute Truth. "It's bad wine" is almost always an incorrect statement. "I didn't like it, but you might" is usually closer to the truth.

I've tried to choose personal opinion over pronouncement wherever possible, at least when it comes to negative comments. I've found that I am occasionally guilty of being overcome by enthusiasm and declaring a wine good or great. Of course, you may not like it. So how can you or I predict whether we will agree?

To avoid the issue, I've tried using descriptive terms instead of judgments wherever possible. I've also developed more sensitivity to public tastes by quietly observing what goes on in tasting rooms. Texas winemakers call sweet red wine "Chateau Cash-Flow" because the majority of tasting room buyers like sweet wines. But before you start denigrating the bourgeois tastes of these folks, you should be aware that Texas is not unique in this; you'll find the same thing along Route 29 in California's Napa Valley.

Ultimately, though, you need some kind of yardstick for my tastes, so you won't have to ferret them out reading between the lines. Here they are.

I like all sorts of dry wines. If you were to sneak a look in my cellar you'd find mostly Sonoma Zinfandels; Napa Cabs; Pinot Noirs from Oregon, France and California; big-boned Rhones and many Texas red wines. In my cooler you'd find mostly Alsatian whites, especially Pinot Gris and Gewurztraminers; Viogniers from California, Texas and France; and Chardonnays and Sauvignon Blancs from Texas, Chile and California.

When it comes to sweet wines, I love the late-picked wines from Alsace and Bordeaux and Germany. I'm also a sucker for a good Port. And I've come to appreciate the many Texas offerings that are made with care for quality; some aren't. An example: Before I started writing this book, if you'd told me that one day I would develop an affection for a strawberry wine from Poteet, Texas, I would have replied that you couldn't possibly be right. I would have been wrong.

Thus the only way you will ever really find out about Texas wines is to go and try them yourself. Then, if you have the inclination, compare your findings and mine. Perhaps we will agree. If we don't, then hopefully my descriptions have been consistent enough for you to decide for yourself whether the wine appeals to you. In any case, be sure to try things that might not at first appeal to you. You might find your own version of that strawberry wine.

Part of tasting in a disciplined manner is knowing when to stop. If you've heard that Texas DWI laws are lax, that's wrong. Drinking before or while driving is very serious business in Texas. If a law enforcement officer has a reasonable suspicion that you've been drinking, you'll be stopped. If the officer thinks you're drunk (.08 blood alcohol level), you'll be arrested. If he thinks you might be drunk, you'll get tested. Even if you're below .08, the officer may still prove impairment. If you refuse the test, you're basically guilty until proven innocent and your license is suspended for six months.

The first conviction carries a minimum three-day vacation in jail and a ninety-day license suspension—if you get a nice judge. If you get a tough one, you can pay $2,000, spend six months in jail and not be able to drive for a year. Second offense could be a year in jail, two years without your license and a $4,000 fine. Three strikes, and you could be looking at ten years in jail with a $10,000 fine. Just carrying an open container in the passenger area is a Class C misdemeanor that carries a fine of up to $500.

Obviously, the best solution is to take along a designated driver. If you have to drive and want to drink, ask the tasting room people for the spit bucket. If that still doesn't do it for you, remember that an average 160-pound man is legally drunk when he's had three five-ounce glasses in one hour. An average 120-pound woman hits her limit after two five-ounce glasses. These are averages, and you might be legally drunk on a lot less. If you drink more, be prepared to sit somewhere for several hours and stare at the wall. Or take a cab. Don't drive.

Tasting Terms

One of the legitimate knocks against wine lovers is that we speak in code: "The wine was green, tart and dry with a crisp and oaky subtext, but the grassy and herbaceous nose joined with just a tinge of asparagus and hints of cedar boxes to remind me of mangoes and guavas . . ."

I'm ashamed to tell you how easy that was to write.

The conundrum is trying to develop words to describe senses. Here's a little exercise to help you understand the dilemma. Take a pen and paper and try to write about eating an apple without using the word *apple*. You can discuss how it feels, tastes, looks and smells— but you can't use the word *apple*. So how does an apple smell if you can't say "apple-y?" You see the point? That's what we have to face in describing a wine.

Experienced conductors can look at a page of music and hear it in their minds. This isn't a God-given gift. It comes from hard work and lots of experience. Wine lovers who have tasted a broad range of wines learn to use descriptive terms just like a musician uses written music. When someone describes a wine as *tannic*, it tells me as much as the term *allegro* tells a musician.

Here are a few terms to help you talk about wine. Don't get crazy over learning them. Just read them, and, like any new word, try to use them when you can.

By the way, don't limit yourself to these words when you're describing wines. Say what the wine tastes, smells and looks like to you. For instance, some Zinfandels remind me of Dr. Pepper. What's in Dr. Pepper? Cherry and prune juice, I think. I could say that the wine tastes like cherries and prunes, but I love to use the Dr. Pepper description. Especially in a roomful of wine connoisseurs. Half of them puff up and act as though I had brought an electric guitar to an opera. The other half snickers nervously and wonders if I'm being serious. I am totally serious. That's what it reminds me of.

Do try to use these words. But don't limit yourself.

Dry. We might as well get the most confusing word out of the way first. Dry means without sugar, not without sweetness.

During your tasting travels, you will come across wines that are so fruity you would swear they are chock-full of sugar. These wines may have a sweet taste, like jams. But if they have no residual sugar, they are dry.

Many Texas wines are sweet with sugar. The public demands them. But a lot of the winemakers won't drink their own sweet wines. It has nothing to do with snobbiness.

Sugar masks flavors that they want to taste. Plus, it can leave you feeling more hung over than alcohol.

The point is, you don't have to be on one team or another. You can find good and bad examples of dry wine. And you can find good and bad wines with sugar. Don't get hung up on the term. During fermentation, yeast lives on the sugar in the grape juice, converting it to alcohol. The term *dry* simply tells you the winemaker allowed the yeast to consume all of the sugar. Except in some parts of France.

The French have their own way of doing things. Imagine that your legislature enacted a law stating that, in your little part of the world, you would call the color red "yellow."

In the Champagne area of France, *extra dry* means "we added sugar." Go figure.

Acid. Crazy as those French folks are, they truly understand wine. To them it is a food, not an entertainment. Wine enhances the appetite and relaxes the diner. Even more important, the wine's acid cleans your mouth with every drink, making each taste a new experience.

Don't mistake acid for sourness. Think of it this way. A lemon is very acidic, but it is also refreshingly crisp. It makes your mouth tingle and your lips pucker. That is because nature balanced the acidity with fruity sweetness. It is the same with wine. Most wines can carry a lot of acid, yet the main way you experience it is as a cleansing crispness. If a wine is sour, the winemaker probably was working with poor grapes.

Every person has a different appreciation for acid. Unfortunately, many wine drinkers start with cheaper wines that are unbalanced and too acidic, and they decide they don't want acid in their wines. If you fit into that category, tell the winemaker you want to experience a well-balanced, fruity and dry wine with good acid. Then you can decide what level of acid you like.

Malolactic Fermentation. Don't let the term scare you. When winemakers wants to tone down acid, they put the wine through a second fermentation. It converts tart malic acid into smoother lactic acid and adds a buttery character. When a winemaker uses Malo, as it's frequently called, they'll usually tell you.

Tannin. This refers to red wines. The way wines get red is through post-crush contact with the seeds, stems and skins of the grapes. They carry tannin and transmit it to the wine. You don't really taste tannin so much as feel it on your tongue and the inside of your mouth. Good tannins make the wine taste rich and smooth. That's what all winemakers aim for. Too much makes your tongue feel like tanned leather. That's apt; tannin's used to tan leather. Have you ever left a teabag in your tea for an hour or so? Remember how the tea felt in your mouth? That's the tang of too much tannin.

Oak. When Emeril Lagasse asks if we want to kick it up a notch and yells "Bam!" he's tossing in spices. When a winemaker wants to kick it up a notch, he puts the wine in oak. But oak kicks up more than flavor. It boosts the smells, flavors and depth of the wine. It also lends a little vanilla and toast aroma to wine, if done right. If the wine is over-oaked, all you can smell is toast and vanilla. American and French oak taste different. The American is more vibrant, the French more elegant. Some people like one or the other, and some can't stand either. For a great learning experience, ask a winemaker how they decide whether to use American or French oak, or no oak at all. Better yet, ask if you can taste a wine from the barrels.

Terroir. The word is pronounced "tare-WAHR." It is a French term with a number of parts. The easiest definition comes from the following question. If the same winemaker makes a Cabernet Sauvignon from two different vineyards, why don't they taste the same? Terroir. It is a combination of the location, the climate, the dirt and whatever else makes one vineyard different from another. It's really not so hard to understand. If fish lovers were terroir fanatics, they would talk endlessly about the difference between Scottish salmon and Alaskan salmon. If they thought terroir wasn't that important, they would settle for farm-raised salmon.

Other terms:

AVA. This stands for American viticultural areas. The term is an attempt of the Bureau of Alcohol, Tobacco and Firearms to give the public some help. Here is how they define the AVA.

The establishment of viticultural areas and the subsequent use of viticultural area names as appellations of origin in wine labeling and advertising will help consumers better identify the wines they may purchase and will help winemakers distinguish their products from wines made in other areas.

Texas has six AVAs: Texas High Plains, Texas Hill Country, Bell Mountain, Fredericksburg in the Texas Hill Country, Escondido Valley and Texas Davis Mountains. While some of Texas's best wineries are in these AVAs, several of the best aren't. The problem with AVAs is that they really don't tell you anything other than where the grapes came from. You also might see another related term, *appellation of origin*, which is even less helpful. The government regulates use of the term, but an appellation can be an area as large as a country.

Estate Bottled Wine. Another Bureau of Alcohol, Tobacco and Firearms term that is more helpful if only because it goes beyond geography to cover production. To be estate bottled means that the grapes must come from vineyards owned or leased by the winery, that the vineyards and winery are in the same AVA and that the grapes, juice or wine have never left the control of the winery. Trying to uphold these standards is a little like trying to play golf with just a driver and a putter. If you are Tiger Woods, you might be able to do it.

The problem with these designations is that they leave out the role of the winemaker. Some very good wines blend grapes from all over. The bottom line is this: pay attention to the designations, but don't let them color your opinion about what's in your glass.

How to Start Your Own Winery

The most frequently told joke among winery owners goes like this:

Question: Do you know how to make a small fortune in the winery business?

Answer: Start with a large one.

Somehow, no matter how difficult and no matter how many fail, folks are still drawn to the business like teenage boys to Brittany Spears. What we need is a sensitivity training session for the life of a winery owner—an opportunity to walk a mile in their shoes.

Here's what it's like.

You wake up one morning and decide you want to change your career. Wine sounds like fun. Everyone always seems to enjoy themselves while they're drinking good wine. The local agricultural economist agrees, citing the fact that you can generally sell an acre of grapes for $1,500 to $2,500 a year. That's certainly better than corn, cotton or wheat. But where do you put it?

Land in West Texas runs under $1,000 an acre. But you've always liked the Hill Country. Nice people. Relatively decent weather. Austin and San Antonio close by. So you get a real estate agent, thinking a 20-acre vineyard in the Texas Hill Country appellation would be nice. You find a pretty little chunk of land outside Fredericksburg for $15,000 an acre. For a 20-acre vineyard, plus room for your home and the 150-foot Pierce's disease buffer zone around the vineyard, you'll probably need about 30 acres.

First you have to get soil samples to make sure it's a good place for grapes. You have to have neutral pH or you'll face either root rot or having to add a lot of lime. Also, to make sure it drains well, have someone come out and dig a six-foot deep hole and see how quickly water empties from the hole. Does the land have a well? You'll need one that can put out 40 acre feet of water just for your vineyard, more if you are going to live there. By the way, you can't use city water, if it's available—too much chlorine. If you need a well, plan to spend $10,000 to $50,000.

Everything checks out. You love the land and decide to buy it. Write a check for $450,000.

Spend the next two years on site prep and ordering your vines. You'll probably want to put deer fencing around the vineyard: $35,000. Then it will be time to clear the land and rip the soil to a depth of six feet.

Next up, you have to decide which grapes to grow. That's easy. You love first growth Bordeauxs and Mondavi's Opus One. So you pick Cabernet Sauvignon and Merlot. All your friends drink Chardonnay, so you choose to plant that also. You join TWGGA (Texas Wine and Grape Growers Association) and go to a local meeting. You meet all the other vineyard owners and tell them your plans. Most of them tell you that they sell more sweet pink wine than anything else. But you have courage in your convictions and forge ahead with your plans.

Planting your vineyard costs $25,000 an acre, if you do the work yourself. We're talking bone-breaking stoop labor. You'll want to hire it out; plan on $35,000 an acre. Once you've experienced some of the sunburn, calluses and back pain, you decide to buy some equipment to automate the process. That little Kubota M9540 Tractor looks nice. With the implements you'll need, think $60,000.

Now you've got the field planted. Look out and enjoy it. It will be three to five years before you can harvest a grape and ten years before the vines have enough age to produce really stellar wine. In the meantime, Texas weather, Pierce's disease, fungus and varmints will all try destroy your vineyard. By the fourth year, you are getting 35 to 50 percent of your potential crop. If you can get good juice, that means you might be able to sell wine next year.

Next you buy your winery equipment. Between the stemmer/crusher, the fermentation tanks, the bottler, the lab equipment and the building to house the winery and tasting room, you're looking at $500,000, minimum. If you want good stuff, expect to pay more.

From the morning you woke up and thought about changing your career, seven years have passed. No money has come in. $1,810,000 has gone out.

I won't even go into the psychological expense of dealing with the Bureau of Alcohol, Tobacco and Firearms or the Texas Alcoholic Beverage Commission. Friends already accuse me of being a rabid Libertarian, and I don't want to give them any more fuel.

Now it's time to sell your wine. Your Cabernet and Merlot will generate about three tons per acre of good juice. The Chardonnay, about two tons. In a good year (and there are not many of them), with no loss from weather or pests, you'll get about 50 tons of grapes. That translates into roughly 3,000 cases or 36,000 bottles.

Your annual costs for everything from replanting to tractor repair will be about $150,000 or $4.17 per bottle. You have to buy bottles, labels, corks and boxes. That's about $1.50 per bottle. Unfortunately, fashions have changed since you started planning. Now Cabernet and Chardonnay are out, Syrah and Viognier are in.

But your wine is good. Your friends love it. You think it should easily fetch $18 a bottle in the stores. Except you can't sell to the stores. Texas has a three-tier system, which pretty much locks down shelf space, so you really have to sell to a distributor, and they get a substantial chunk of change from each sale.

In order to have it on the shelf at the local mega-mart at $18, the store will pay the distributor about $10.80. To get the distributor to sell it to the store for $10.80, you have to sell it to the distributor for $6.48. That leaves you with a profit of 81 cents per bottle. If you can sell your entire production (a big if), you'll take in $24,300 before taxes. But wait. Don't forget the debt repayment, which for an 80 percent loan at 7 percent over 30 years would be $115,603 per year.

On second thought, forget about the taxes.

Next time you uncork a Texas wine, think about the amount of time, money and psychic energy required to create it. I don't know about you, but knowing the details makes me respect the winemakers of Texas even more. They are a group of obsessive pioneers and iconoclasts that clearly care more about the romance than the commerce. That's one of the reasons I devote so much of this book to a look at the characters in the business. They all deserve our respect for simply sticking to their dreams.

RESOURCES

Texas Monthly (www.texasmonthly.com) has great travel and food writers like Joe Nick Patoski, Suzy Banks and Patricia Sharp. Besides making the monthly updates on restaurants, a search through the back pages for travel tips is filled with gold. A perfect example— Joe Nick Patoski's *Big Bend Guide* (www.texasmonthly.com/ranch/bigbend), which has up-to-date and accurate information; besides that, his prose is a joy to read. The magazine also breaks up the state the way this book does, so a search through the archives will match up geographically with *The Wine Roads of Texas*.

Texas Highways (www.texashighways.com). You'll be amazed that a magazine published by a state government could be this good. Beautiful photography, good writing and lots of news you can use.

Texas Department of Agriculture (www.agr.state.tx.us). The Ag Department offers a lot of help for wine lovers and would-be winemakers. Judy Evans (www.gotexanwine.org)

is a font of information, and always willing to help push the cause of Texas wine. For future winemakers, their booklet called *Texas Wine Grape Guide* is required reading.

Texas A&M University (www.winegrapes.tamu.edu). For future farmers, A&M's Agricultural Extension Service is a big help. For other services offered, check the Website. Then, for a little instructive comparison, check what the Californians have (wineserver. ucdavis.edu/). Let's hope A&M moves forward or relinquishes control to a university that wants to do this.

Texas Tech University (www.hs.ttu.edu/TexasWine/default.asp). Tim Dodd is accessible and cares. Call him with questions and not only will you get an answer, but it will be enlightened and friendly.

TWGGA (www.twgga.org). Many vineyard owners and winemakers belong to the Texas Wine and Grape Growers Association, a good route for folks interested in the business side.

Grayson County College (www.grayson.edu). Since no one else is doing it, this little college in Denison stepped up and offered an enology program. Many Texas winemakers have attended.

Texas Travel Bureau (www.traveltx.com). Tons of up-to-date info provided by the state, broken up in the same way this book is.

ACKNOWLEDGEMENTS

You wouldn't be holding this book in your hands were it not for the following people.

Emily, my sweet loving wife, center of my life for over thirty years. She read, analyzed and offered opinions about the book, and then cajoled and hounded me until I finished it. God bless her.

My mother and father, neither of whom drank wine. They didn't like it. They did like me, however, and filled me with the confidence to try anything.

Emmet and Lisa Fox, who told Virginia Wood that they thought I would make a good wine writer. They've offered endless friendship and professional support ever since.

Virginia Wood, food editor for the *Austin Chronicle*. She gave me my first job writing about wine, which led to the opportunity to write this book. And two other newspaper editors—Cathy Barber and Linda Murphy—who gave me state and national platforms.

Ed Bailey, who had the idea to make my book into a PBS series; Tom Spencer, who artfully made the concept real; Michael Vilim and Larry Peel, who provided the first underwriting for the film; and Susan Auler, who pushed the TV show through and carried the concept forward until money was in hand.

Susan Combs, former commissioner of the Texas Department of Agriculture, who changed the course of Texas wine. If one person restored my faith that good deeds can be done and politicians can remain altruistic, Susan Combs is that poster child. In most of the winemaking community there is a secret wish that Susan might someday be crowned empress. Enlightened despotism, indeed.

Finally, thanks to my family. It always helps to know you've got people who love you no matter what. It's a wealth you can't count with Quicken, and in this I am rich.

INDEX

MORE TEXAS BOOKS
from Maverick Publishing

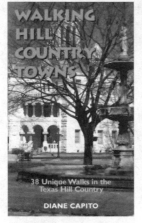
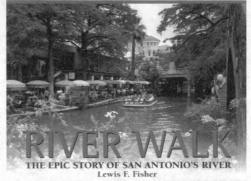
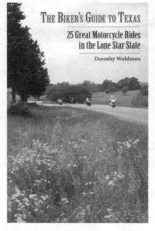
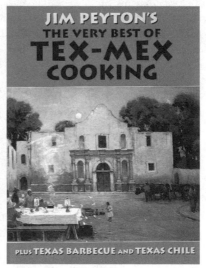